THE
PERVERSE
ECONOMY

THE PERVERSE ECONOMY

THE IMPACT OF MARKETS ON PEOPLE AND THE ENVIRONMENT

Michael Perelman

First published 2003 by
PALGRAVE MACMILLAN™
175 Fifth Avenue, New York, N.Y. 10010 and
Houndmills, Basingstoke, Hampshire, England RG21 6XS.
Companies and representatives throughout the world.

PALGRAVE MACMILLAN is the global academic imprint of the Palgrave Macmillan division of St. Martin's Press, LLC and of Palgrave Macmillan Ltd. Macmillan® is a registered trademark in the United States, United Kingdom and other countries. Palgrave is a registered trademark in the European Union and other countries.

ISBN 1–4039–6271–5 hardback

Library of Congress Cataloging-in-Publication Data

Perelman, Michael.
    The perverse economy : the impact of markets on people and the environment / Michael Perelman.
        p. cm.
    Includes bibliographical references.
    ISBN 1–4039–6271–5
    1. Economics. 2. Economics—Sociological aspects. 3. Economic development—Environmental aspects. 4. Income distribution. 5. Labor productivity. 6. Labor economics. 7. Smith, Adam 1723–1790—Views on labor economics. 8. Scarcity. 9. Value. I. Title.

HB71.P467 2003
330—dc21   2003046735

A catalogue record for this book is available from the British Library.

Design by Newgen Imaging Systems (P) Ltd., Chennai, India.

First edition: November, 2003
10 9 8 7 6 5 4 3 2 1

Printed in the United States of America.

Contents

Introduction   1

One
Adam Smith and the Farm Worker Paradox   7

Two
Resources   21

Three
Value   79

Four
Patience   119

Five
Environmental Efficiency   133

Six
Back to the Farm Worker Paradox   145

Seven
A New Direction   175

References   185

Index   207

Introduction

Walking along a city street, I look up at a gleaming office building filled with busy people. Hundreds, perhaps thousands of them are manning computers, telephones, fax machines, or copiers or maybe just shuffling paper—work that is coming to occupy the majority of employees in advanced market economies. Many seem to be working at a frantic pace. For many of these people, prosperity must seem almost like a birthright. Others, working long hours trying to get ahead, also expect at the very least a middle-class lifestyle.

Great wealth flows to some of the people who occupy these offices, and even more to those who employ them from afar. But what exactly do they do? How do their activities contribute to society?

In what seems to be a world apart, in the countryside, a number of immigrant laborers are working hard amidst a toxic soup of agricultural chemicals. Yet, without these people or others like them, the economy would grind to a halt. What would people eat without such workers sacrificing their own health in the fields? Despite their undeniable contribution, these people earn pitiably little. So little that one small study of North Carolina farm workers found that 47 percent of them were food insecure, including 9.8 percent with moderate hunger and 4.9 percent with severe hunger (Quandt et al. 2003).

During the 1990s, the median income of individual farm workers remained less than $7,500 per year while that of farm worker families has remained less than $10,000 (United States Department of Labor 2000)—a mere pittance compared to the privileged workers who occupy the spacious offices. Certainly nothing compared to those who give the orders to the crews in the offices. At one point, during a series of lectures to young women, the young Alfred Marshall, who would become the dominant figure in economics during the late nineteenth and early twentieth centuries, raised the question, "how is it then that men consent to remain agricultural labourers?" (Marshall 1873, p. 103). Marshall let the question drop; so too did the economics profession as a whole.

What explains this disparity between the office workers and the field workers? You can look for an explanation in the books that supposedly explain the workings of the labor market. There you can read that everything follows from the inexorable laws of the market. Supposedly everyone earns a reward commensurate with his or her productivity. Economists can tell you with assurance that the farm workers live in poverty only because their productivity lags far behind the average level for the economy as a whole.

In contrast, many of the people who work in the more spacious offices enjoy enough rewards to lead a life of comfort, or even luxury. Economic theory proposes that they earn their elevated station in life because of their high productivity, even though you may have a hard time identifying exactly what they produce.

Press the economists further and they may explain that the people in the offices who market and distribute the goods and services must be productive—no, highly productive—since their wages are so high. People who get these jobs often have some higher education, which supposedly augments their productivity, even though their educational training probably has little or nothing to do with their actual responsibilities on the job.

How does this productivity manifest itself? These office workers figure out ways to wrap products in layer after layer of packaging. They devise advertising that makes people feel a necessity to buy goods. They may even calculate the extra profits that will accrue to their employer by cutting corners on their products.

The economists' circular logic concludes that high wages are evidence of superior productivity and that superior productivity necessarily earns high wages. In effect, then, whatever exists is necessarily rational, unless something somehow interferes with the natural workings of the market. Even the excess education is rational because it serves as a signal of a workers' commitment to work productively.

Within this framework, the employees in the offices who shunt money around—sometimes in stocks, sometimes in bonds, and sometimes for directly productive investments—must be even more productive. Indeed, these people must be extraordinarily productive. After all, they appropriate the lion's share of the wealth.

In contrast to the successful members of the economy, the lowly farm workers have little education. Economic theory teaches that their skills are widely available. Many more people living in poor countries would willingly take their jobs. How could a person like that possibly be worth as much as a successful worker occupying a lavish office?

Besides, the food that the farm workers grow is not worth very much, giving further proof of their meager productivity. Of course, this conventional image could possibly have a different interpretation. What if their low salary partially explains why the food they grow is inexpensive? What if the high salaries that some professional workers earn merely reflect the fact that they happen to represent sectors of society that enjoy special privileges? After all, circular logic can work in both directions.

Finally, what if the much-vaunted productivity of these highly compensated workers depends, in large part, on the continuing ability to draw down scarce resources? Or even worse, what if economic productivity, in general, would actually be negative if proper account were taken of the resource costs of production?

Plan of the Book

The purpose of this book is to call for a wholesale rethinking of the way that markets treat both labor and the resource base upon which we all depend. Many excellent books already exist that make the case that workers should be treated with justice and resources handled with care. I concur with that view, but this book has a different objective.

The unique contribution of this book is, I believe, in analyzing the relationship between the environmental crisis and the social crisis within the context of modern economic thinking. Economists see the global economy moving ahead at breakneck speed. Each year, millions of people enjoy the opportunity to move up into the ranks of the middle and upper classes.

Even so, all is not well in this world. The comfortable lives of the fortunate minority rest upon a precarious foundation. The environment cannot sustain the increasing demands that modern technology places on it. In addition, appalling inequality strains the social fabric.

I am concerned that formal economic analysis justifies self-defeating policies. The wanton use of the environment and callous abuse of the least advantaged will undermine the very objectives that economists see themselves as furthering. This claim will probably not make sense to most trained economists, who tend to believe that market forces will inevitably lead to desirable outcomes.

Of course, economists are not inhuman brutes who welcome the mistreatment of human beings or nature. Most see themselves as furthering a scientific analysis of human activity. Many of those mainstream economists who have an interest in policy sincerely believe that a greater reliance on markets can correct both social and environmental problems. Unfortunately, the method that they use to understand the world is rigged in such a way that market solutions either give the best of all possible outcomes or that with a little jiggering markets will produce comparable results. Within the economics community critical assessment is most unwelcome, and for good reason. Economic theory rests upon a foundation of embarrassingly unrealistic assumptions.

This book will explore how economics narrowed its scope so radically that it was left with tunnel vision; how it separated its view of the world so radically that it is at odds with the prevailing view of the natural sciences; and how continuing to accept market discipline threatens to undermine both human capacities and nature—the very forces upon which our future depends.

Chapter 1 sets the stage by showing how Adam Smith tried to grapple with the wretched conditions of farm workers. Smith's discussion is still relevant today. Those who supply the most essential products for human life still receive the least reward—what I will call the farm worker paradox. Although Smith's treatment of the subject was unsatisfactory, to his credit, at least he stumbled upon it, where virtually all later economists have successfully avoided any discussion of the farm worker paradox. Unfortunately, he let the matter drop quickly.

Chapter 2 discusses how economics treats scarcity. Just as most economists have avoided the farm worker paradox, they have steered clear of the subject of scarcity. This approach is surprising since many economists regard their discipline as the theory of the allocation of scarce resources.

Chapter 3 looks at the nature of economic theory rather than the economic theory of nature. It analyzes how the core of economic theory works to eliminate any concern with either scarcity or the conditions of the least favored workers.

Chapter 4 extends the discussion of economic theory, concentrating on the way that economic theory discounts the future, ensuring that concern about future scarcity would be outside the ambit of conventional economics.

The subject of chapter 5 is environmental efficiency. The purpose of this chapter is to illustrate the complexity of environmental processes and to show how ill-equipped economics is to analyze such processes.

Chapter 6 returns to the farm worker paradox. It shows how economists have intentionally forged their theory to undercut any calls for social justice.

Chapter 7 discusses how all market societies abandon conventional economic thinking in the face of severe crises, such as during an all-out war. Faced with such a threat, modern economies turn to planning rather than markets. I conclude with an exploration about how a similar strategy could help to resolve the environmental crisis as well as the farm worker paradox.

1

Adam Smith and the Farm Worker Paradox

An Excursion into the Past: Professor Adam Smith's Curious Lecture

My question—why those whose work is most necessary typically earn the least—has a noble pedigree. Almost two and a half centuries ago, Adam Smith, often considered to be the patron saint of economics, also puzzled over the unfortunate fate of farm workers. In fact, this very question seems to have provoked him to formulate the centerpiece of his economic theory—the division of labor.

Before I discuss the case of Adam Smith, I want to assure you that I am not doing so merely as an exercise in stale antiquarian nostalgia. Because Smith wrote before economics became formalized, he was able to see things that we modern economists leave unnoticed. Admittedly, in many, if not most cases, modern economists are absolutely correct in forgetting what Adam Smith had to say. In some exceptional cases, however, Smith still offers a fresh approach that is in many ways superior to the contemporary fashions of modern economics.

In the 1762–1763 academic year, more than a decade before he published his famous, *Wealth of Nations* (1776), in the course of delivering a lecture to his students, Smith let himself stray from his narrow course. Although he was intent on teaching his students that the emerging market would promise a better life for all, Smith's legendary absentmindedness might have been at work. In any case, Smith uncharacteristically remarked, "The labour and time of the poor is in civilized countries sacrificed to the maintaining of the rich in ease and luxury" (Smith 1978, pp. 340 and 338).

In general, Smith did not have much patience with such uncomfortable intrusions of reality. His objectives were far more ideological. He wanted to show how markets lead to the best of all possible worlds (see Perelman 2000a).

Seemingly catching himself off-guard, Smith swiftly fled from his subject. I doubt that he wanted to leave his students with the thought that the impoverished agricultural laborers, who represented the majority of the workers in his society, found themselves unjustifiably compelled to work long hours in difficult conditions for a meager existence.

Smith immediately tried to neutralize what he had just said by claiming that the most disadvantaged members of society enjoy a far greater degree of "plenty and opulence" than they would in a "savage state" (Smith 1978, pp. 340 and 338). He went even further, preposterously proposing, "an ordinary day labourer...has more of the conveniences and luxuries than an Indian [presumably Native American] prince at the head of 1,000 naked savages" (Smith 1978, p. 339).

But then the very next day while giving his lecture, the situation of the impoverished farm worker intruded into his thoughts again. Smith observed:

> The labour and time of the poor is in civilized countries sacrificed to the maintaining of the rich in ease and luxury. The landlord is maintained in idleness and luxury by the labour of his tenants. The moneyed man is supported by his exactions from the industrious merchant and the needy who are obliged to support him in ease by a return for the use of his money. But every savage has the full enjoyment of the fruits of his own labours; there are no landlords, no usurers, no tax gatherers.... [T]he poor labourer...has all the inconveniences of the soil and season to struggle with, is continually exposed to the inclemency of the weather and the most severe labour at the same time. Thus he who as it were supports the whole frame of society and furnishes the means of the convenience and ease of all the rest is himself possessed of a very small share and is buried in obscurity. He bears on his shoulders the whole of mankind, and unable to sustain the weight of it is thrust down into the lowest parts of the earth from whence he supports the rest. In what manner then shall we account for the great share he and the lowest persons have of the conveniences of life? (Smith 1978, pp. 340–41)

The entire passage is extraordinary. Smith began with an eloquent portrayal of the hardships of the farm workers, whom he correctly credited with supporting the entire society. But how could he square that evaluation with his lecture from the previous day? Then, Smith had asserted that the poor laborer was better fed, clothed, and housed than a savage prince. To add to the confusion, just as his students were hearing about the unsustainable weight borne by the unfortunate farm worker, Smith suddenly changed directions again and asked them to account for the "great share he [has]...in the conveniences of life."

In short, Smith's lecture was running off in two contradictory directions. On the one hand, the farm workers live in poverty. On the other hand, they have a "great share...in the conveniences of life."

At that point, Smith retreated from addressing the farm workers' real world conditions. In this regard, he found comfort in an earlier theory of the division of labor. His next words to his students were: "The division of labour amongst different hands can alone account for this"—meaning what he had referred to as "the great share" that these workers enjoyed (Smith 1978, p. 341). To make his point, Smith turned the attention of his class to what he himself called an admittedly "frivolous" example, the pin factory.

By the time that he published his famous, *Wealth of Nations*, Smith tried to explain away the farm worker paradox—that those who supply the most essential products for human life receive the least reward. At this stage in his work, we hear no more about the "most severe labour" of the farm workers. Instead, Smith paints an unflattering portrait of their work ethic:

> The habit of sauntering and of indolent careless application, which is naturally, or rather necessarily acquired by every country workman who is obliged to change his work and his tools every half hour... renders him always slothful and lazy, and incapable of any vigorous application even on the most pressing occasions. (Ibid., I.i.7, p. 19)

To be fair, Smith liberally sprinkled the first part of the *Wealth of Nations* with references to masters combining and conspiring to hold down wages. Smith, however, was far from being a friend of labor (Perelman 2002, chapter 8). Besides, this aspect of his work does not form a significant part of his legacy. Economists today read Smith infrequently. According to their superficial mythology, Smith was the genius who first discovered how markets function justly and efficiently.

Despite the masters' conspiratorial violations of market principles, Smith still mistakenly saw most workers as enjoying considerable prosperity. Moreover, Smith went out of his way to deny the obvious ways in which powerful forces undermined the conditions of the people who worked the land (Perelman 2002). Nonetheless, Smith deserves considerable credit for identifying the farm worker paradox—that the people who do the most essential work earned the least.

Adam Smith on Social Relations and Productivity

Adam Smith, in effect, pinned his hopes on a new type of social arrangement. He suggested that the transformation of the role of the traditional artisanal worker would generate a burst of productivity that would allow a better life for everyone.

Smith certainly underplayed the role of technology in his analysis, but in doing so, he implicitly reminded his readers that productivity changes also necessitate human adaptations. For Smith, these human adaptations involved changing the way people related to one another in the marketplace—something we can call social relations.

Let me explain. Although 100 independent artisan pin makers could theoretically arrange to subdivide their work by separating into several groups, each of which would specialize in a particular part of the process of pin making. One group could make the wire that would become pins; another could hammer the heads, and still another could make the points. This voluntary reorganization would merely involve a change in the physical work that each pin maker would do.

Smith did not even raise the possibility that workers could accomplish this voluntary reorganization of the production process. Instead, he presumed that a single factory owner would hire a number of individual workers and assign them their specific tasks. The pin makers would no longer be independent artisans. They would no longer work as they thought best. They would be wageworkers, taking orders from an employer. This changing status of the artisan represented a dramatic revolution in their social relations within the productive system.

Even so, Smith missed the mark. He assumed that merely reorganizing traditional work without any accompanying technical change would allow for improved conditions for all. While an enterprising employer certainly could wring some additional productivity out of a rearrangement of the division of labor, such productivity gains were definitely limited. Even if new arrangements could create an increase in productivity, such changes would be unlikely to allow for continual improvements.

The key to the massive transformation in technology that followed Smith was a similarly massive substitution of inanimate for human energy rather than an increasingly fine division of labor. Smith's silence about the role of fossil fuels is remarkable because James Watt, who perfected the steam engine, was a friend of his who even worked at the same university.

Yet Smith does deserve considerable credit for attempting—even half-heartedly—to account for the divergent fates of those people who worked in the fields and the people, such as Smith, myself, and those who enjoy privileged positions in the gleaming office buildings. In addition, Smith was right on target with his concern about social relations being integral to the operation of the economy. His identification of changing social relations as an essential component of increasing productivity was a lesson that modern economists would do well to relearn.

Social relations affect how work is organized—who does what. Social relations also affect the division of what society produces—who gets what. Whether Smith was or was not an economist—after all he was a professor of moral philosophy—his ruminations about the poor farm workers and the division of labor illustrated how his admittedly partial understanding of social relations touched on these questions.

Social relations were central to Smith, but not in the sense that I mentioned in the last paragraph. Smith was less interested in economic progress than in seeing a fundamental change in people's behavior. He cheered the rise of the market because he believed that economic forces would cause people to acclimate themselves to market values. In this way, the traditional behavior of aristocrats, peasants, and workers would give way to a style of life that Smith preferred. In Smith's utopia, everybody would have the mindset of hardworking artisans and shopkeepers.

In this sense, Adam Smith certainly was not an economist. In fact, we would be justified in saying that he was not even particularly interested in economics as such, except in so far as the development of the market will create the sort of behavioral change that Smith found desirable (see Perelman 2000a, chapter 9).

Smith's interest in changing human behavior is not very relevant to our story, except that it offers a likely explanation for the absence of James Watt and fossil fuel in Smith's story. He probably did not want social relations in a market economy to be contingent upon natural conditions. While he used natural conditions to explain how societies evolved toward market societies, for Smith, natural forces seem to play no role once a society established a market economy. In that sense, Smith's economics set a strong precedent for modern economics.

Markets and the Farm Worker Paradox

Today, every student of introductory economics hears the famous story of Smith's pin factory: a single pin worker could only make pitifully few pins, but when an intelligent employer hires a number of workers and assigns a specialized task to each of them, then the number of pins per worker increases dramatically. This improved productivity provides the economy with the wherewithal to supply everyone with more than before.

Unfortunately, Smith never offered any solid evidence that workers actually enjoyed such benefits. In fact, living standards for most people probably decreased during the Industrial Revolution, although some economic historians do believe that living standards did increase at the time.

Whether the standard of living increased or decreased, I am absolutely certain that the masses huddled in great cities would have difficulty in accepting Smith's assertion that they had "more of the conveniences and luxuries" than an Indian prince. Neither would the group of Ojibwas that visited London in the 1840s. Unlike Smith, they had firsthand experience with both Indian princes and members of the English working class. They reportedly told all the English people who attempted to engage them in conversation:

> [We are] willing to talk with you if it can do any good for the hundreds and thousands of poor and hungry children we see in your streets every day.... We see hundreds of little children with their naked feet in the snow, and we pity them, for we know they are hungry.... [W]e have no such poor children among us. (Cited in Tobias 1967, p. 86)

Smith could have salvaged the vision of the justice of market relations, by writing off agriculture as an anomaly, except that agricultural workers were anything but an insignificant segment of the British economy at the time of his lecture. If agricultural workers did not represent the majority of the labor force, not many years had passed since they were.

Smith could argue that agriculture was a residual of a premarket way of life, but markets had penetrated agriculture for a considerable time. In fact, many modern economic historians see evidence of considerable agrarian market relations in medieval times, and even in ancient societies.

Still, the farm worker paradox persists. Even in the United States, however, where corporate farming is commonplace, the farm worker paradox remains perhaps stronger than ever. Certainly, farmers in the United States are attuned to market conditions, possibly more so than most businesspeople. Unfortunately, the increasing market orientation of modern agriculture has done little to improve the conditions of contemporary farm workers. True, modern farm workers have more material goods than those whom Adam Smith described, but the gap between the standard of living of a farm worker and that of the rest of society is probably greater than ever. In addition, they work amidst a lethal chemical stew (see Mills and Kwong 2001).

Market Rationality and the Farm Worker Paradox

Adam Smith, for all his shortcomings, at least understood how social relations affect economic outcomes. In particular, he acknowledged that a person's position in life is a greater determinant of their professional status than his or her inherent abilities. In one of his more memorable statements, he declared:

> The difference of natural talents in different men is, in reality, much less than we are aware of; and the very different genius which appears to distinguish men of different professions, when grown up to maturity, is not upon many occasions so much the cause as the effect of the division of labour. The difference between the most dissimilar characters, between a philosopher and a common street porter, for example, seems to arise not so much from nature as from habit, custom, and education. When they came into the world, and for the first six or eight years of their existence, they were perhaps very much alike, and neither their parents nor playfellows could perceive any remarkable difference. (Smith 1776, I.ii.4, pp. 28–29)

Moreover, Smith's lecture pointed to what I call the farm worker paradox—that the people whose work is most essential to supporting life generally earn the least income. Of course, this paradox is not limited to farm workers; it seems to be a more general principle. For example, within a large urban area, the people who haul garbage away probably prevent more diseases than the local doctors. For example, a two-month strike of the garbage haulers would probably create a greater health risk to a large urban area than a two-month strike of doctors.

Most economists would reply that the farm worker paradox is not a paradox at all. According to their theory, the market ensures that workers earn wages that reflect their productivity. Unfortunately, this theory rests on a curious circular logic. For economists, if people earn high wages, they must be productive; and if they are productive, they must earn high wages. In short, whatever is must be rational, except for policies or institutions that interfere with the free working of markets.

To his credit, Adam Smith's analysis was more advanced than the approach of modern economics. At least, unlike contemporary economists, he was willing to acknowledge the existence of inequities in the determination of wages. He accused incompetent aristocratic landlords, conniving businessmen, and wasteful government of putting workers in a disadvantageous position. His diagnosis was relatively superficial, but at least he recognized that something was awry.

The Complexity of Productivity

A larger problem makes the conventional theory of wages even less persuasive. In a modern, complex economy, an objective measurement of productivity presents all but insurmountable difficulties. For example, economists have never been able to agree about how they could estimate productivity. Such agreement is impossible because productivity is unmeasurable. How then are markets able to measure the unmeasurable in such a way as to make rewards commensurate with productivity?

Contemporary economics does not recognize inequities. Instead, it aggressively attempts to explain them away. In its seemingly objective dismissal of the farm paradox, it points out that low productivity explains low wages. But wait! Just what is productivity? If you could measure productivity in physical terms, such as speed or weight, productivity would be unambiguous, but in a complex economy a precise definition of productivity is elusive.

Very often, people confidently speak of productivity in a way that sounds as if productivity actually were measured in physical terms. For example, when I studied agricultural economics many years ago, I used to hear farm interests repeatedly say that one farmer feeds 30 people. What they did was simply to take the total population, divide by the number of farmers, and voila, they calculated that one farmer fed 30 people.

By the same token, you could just as well say that a young man who operates the checkout stand at a supermarket feeds 1000 people. Of course, this young man could do very little without the existence of a complex supply chain that brought the food to the supermarket. Similarly, farmers rely on a whole range of people in order for them to harvest their products and bring them to the market.

A single break in the supply chain could prove disastrous. I recall some decades ago that a temporary difficulty in the production of bailing wire impeded the delivery of alfalfa to dairy farmers, wreaking havoc with the entire dairy industry. Yet, the cost of bailing wire amounts to an inconsequential part of the entire dairy industry. I suspect if you asked an expert to list the important inputs for the dairy industry bailing wire would go unmentioned.

So, the work of the farmer and the grocery clerk depends on the indirect work of thousands if not millions of people. In his curious lecture, Adam Smith made the same point, but in the process, it led him into confusion, confounding the number of people who worked in producing a product with the value of the product:

> We see accordingly that an ordinary day-labourer, whom we false account to live in a most simple manner, has more of the conveniencies and luxuries of life than an Indian prince at the head of 1000 naked savages. His coarse blue woolen coat has been the labour of perhaps 100 artificers, the shearer, the picker, the sorter, the comber, the spinner, etc. as well as the weaver and fuller whose loom and mill alone have more of art in them than all the things employed about the court of a savage prince; besides the ship which brought the dies and other materials together from distant regions, and all the workmen, wrights, carpenters, coopers, smiths, etc. which have been employed to fit her out to sea and the hands which have navigated her. The iron tool with which he works, how many hands has it gone thro.—The miner, the quarrier, the breaker, the smelter, the forger, the maker of the charcoal to smelt it, the smith, etc. have had a hand in the forming it. How many have been required to furnish out the coarse linen shirt [which] he wears; the tanned and dressed-leather shoes; his bed which he rest(s) in; the grate at which he dresses his victuals; the coals he burns, which have been brought by a long land sea carriage; and other workmen who have been necessary to prepare his bread, his beer, and other food; besides the glass of which his windows are composed, production (of) which required vast labour to bring it to it present perfection, which at the same time excludes the wind and rain and admits the light, a commodity without which this country would scarcely be habitable, at least by the present effeminate and puny set of mortals. So that to supply this poor labourer about 1000 have given their joint assistance. He enjoys far greater convenience than an Indian prince. (Smith 1978, pp. 338–39)

Of course, the quantity of workers whose joint products create Smith's coarse blue woolen coat or a farmer's bailing wire—even if they number in the millions—does not directly translate into the value of a product. The equivalent of a nanosecond of bailing wire work might be all one could find in a quart of milk. This confusion on Smith's part led him to make his absurd claim about the elevated standard of living of the typical worker.

Nonetheless, Smith's description of the complexity of the production system serves as a stark reminder about the difficulty, if not impossibility, of measuring productivity. Modern economists get around this complexity by assuming that market prices provide an accurate representation of the underlying reality.

Unfortunately, prices obscure as much as they reveal. I will elaborate on this subject in chapter 3 on value.

Adam Smith's Two Specializations

Adam Smith associated progress with increasing specialization, both in the case of the famous pin and the complex supply chain that lay behind his woolen coat. This specialization had two dimensions. In the case of the pin factory, a manager assigned each worker a specific task rather than having every worker perform all the tasks involved in making a pin. People have paid less attention to the second dimension of Smith's specialization, which is more indirect than the pin factory. In his example of the woolen coat, different businesses specialize in providing a specific part of the entire production process, whether it be dye, buttons, or wool. Taken together, these businesses produce the coat, but without a manager to direct or coordinate the entire process. Instead, the managers of each business try to insert their firm into the production process based on their understanding of market conditions.

Serious dangers lurk alongside the undeniable efficiencies of specialization for both workers and firms. With regard to the first form of specialization, Adam Smith himself realized that narrowing a workers' responsibilities to the mindless performance of repetitive tasks would do serious damage to the workers' potential development. While I do not for a moment consider this effect to be inconsequential—I have even written a book in which the harm inflected by this arrangement is a major theme (Perelman 2000b)—I wish to concentrate on the second danger, which is associated with the specialization by firms.

Adam Smith did not recognize the dangers associated with specialization by firms because he ignored a major aspect of modern technologies, as well as a fundamental characteristic of markets. Let me begin with the technological dimension. For the most part, technical change tends to increase the scale of production. For example, in Smith's pin factory using the technology of the day, a handful of workers could presumably put out as many pins per worker as a much larger factory. Using modern equipment, the output per worker in a contemporary pin factory would be thousands, if not millions, as many pins as Adam Smith observed.

However, to be efficient a firm using the more modern technology must produce a larger output than firms using the earlier technology. Typically, the efficient scale of production increases far more rapidly than the demand for the product. Consequently, technological change means that fewer factories tend to exist within a particular specialized industry.

Ultimately, this tendency would lead to an industry in which a single business holds a dominant position for each particular part of the production process. While the arrangement might be technologically efficient under certain conditions, such need not be the case. For example, when a firm can exercise monopoly powers it can wield its powers in ways that inflict damage on the rest of society by gouging consumers or suppliers, as well as by wielding its political powers. In addition, a monopolistic firm is likely to become lazy and be less inclined to keep up with potential technological improvements.

I will ignore these two problems and turn to another. When an entire industry depends (to a large extent) upon a single producer, it becomes vulnerable to anything that might disrupt that producer. Let me give a simple example.

The basic product for a computer chip is a silicon wafer, which is useless without the capacity to send and receive signals from a board. A plastic package allows the chip to make the connection with the board. The industry uses specialized epoxy glue for making these packages. In the early 1990s, a single Sumitomo Corporation plant manufactured the majority of the world's supply of the epoxy resin. About 60 percent of all memory modules depended upon the product of this particular factory.

In July 1993, a fire destroyed this factory. Dealers had been paying about $33 for a megabyte of memory before the fire. By the end of the month, the same memory commanded $95. The industry feared that prices would go even higher. So here we have what must normally be a trivial cost within the complex supply chain causing prices to almost triple.

Concentrating production in the Sumitomo plant may have offered an almost imperceptible saving in the total cost of producing a memory chip. Yet it also created a degree of vulnerability. Even though the price spike resulting from the fire lasted for only a few months, it probably created losses equivalent to many decades of the cost savings for any special efficiencies in the Sumitomo plant.

How did the chip industry decide to put all of its eggs in one basket? Imagine a world in which a number of glue manufacturers competed with one another. Suppose that the Sumitomo plant had a slight cost advantage. Each chipmaker facing intense competitive pressure will want to get its materials as cheaply as possible. As the industry shifts more and more of its orders to Sumitomo, that factory improves its efficiency, giving it an even greater competitive edge. As a result, still more chipmakers turn to Sumitomo, until it has a virtual monopoly in the manufacture of the glue. The resulting concentration of the production of glue in a single factory, rather than relying on a large number of small units scattered around the world, may well have increased efficiency of the global semiconductor industry—so long as some accident does not occur.

I should also mention that specialization does not proceed uniformly. Sometimes, when an industry achieves a large enough scale, it could produce most of its inputs. Although separate factories might be specializing in producing the separate parts of the production process, vertical integration might allow a single firm to embrace nearly all of the production required for the final good.

For example, the giant automobile companies of the mid-twentieth century tended to produce most of their own components—including most of their parts, as well as raw materials, such as glass and rubber. This tendency eventually reversed itself, causing the production process to fragment to the point where the automobile companies tended to operate more as mere assemblers of purchased inputs, rather than producers of parts and other inputs.

Questions to Answer Later

Modern mainstream economics does not do a very good job of giving answers to the basic questions that Smith implicitly raised: who does what? who gets what? Smith alerted his readers that he was either unwilling to or incapable of giving answers to such questions. For example, in *Wealth of Nations*, he began with a description of how a classless economy of self-employed people might trade with one another. Suddenly, without any warning, he changed the entire context of his discussion to a class society in which some people worked for wages, while others earned profits: "As soon as a stock has accumulated in the hands of particular persons, some of them will naturally employ it in setting to work industrious people" (Smith 1776, I.v.5, p. 65).

We might well ask, what has changed so that these "industrious persons" now depend upon those "particular persons" to set them to work? Smith's answer was, "the greater part of the workmen stand in need of a master to advance them the materials of their work, and their wages and maintenance" (Smith 1776, I.viii.8, p. 83).

Now let us look more closely at that unexplained event that left masses of people without stock. Before that unexplained event to which Smith referred, most workers owned their own tools at the time (see Ashton 1972, p. 217). Instead, Smith's stock seemed to represent the intermediate goods upon which people worked and the means of providing for their subsistence. At the time, people largely grew their own food and produced most of their own needs, but at the time Smith was writing matters were rapidly changing. Landed interests were forcing many people off their land. Employers generally applauded this practice, since it supplied them with enough "industrious people" to guarantee that wages remained low, reinforcing the powers of the "particular persons" (see Perelman 2000a). Smith went on to explain, "The profits of stock...are [not] regulated by the quantity, the hardship, or the ingenuity" of the work of the employers, but merely by the magnitude of the value of their investment (Smith 1776, I.v.6, p. 66). As the employers reinvest their profits over time, the value of their investments will expand and thus their "productivity" will increase relative to those of the workers.

The ownership of landed property complicates the picture. Although landlords could conceivably earn some profit by their active engagement in the productive process, in Smith's day most of them—or at least most of the more substantial landowners—were absentee landlords who took no active part in organizing production.

The income from this type of ownership was absolutely unrelated to any productive activity on the part of the landlords. In fact, in England many of the aristocratic landlords were so out of touch with their land that Parliament considered it necessary to allow them to enjoy special hunting privileges to provide them an incentive to visit their properties from time to time (Perelman 2000a, chapter 3).

So even if we grant that an outside observer could attribute the meager income of the farm workers to their lack of productive skills, the farm workers at least are engaged in production. We would be justified in posing the question: what then is the contribution of the absentee owners? how is their income justified?

These questions of class and ownership are fundamental to resolving the farm worker paradox, but they are not sufficient for doing so. To get a handle on the farm worker paradox, we will need to consider the nature of productivity within the context of the interaction of the economy with the natural resource base. Toward that end, we will first have to pay some attention to the natural resource base itself.

2

Resources

Extraction vs. Production

Interesting questions typically unleash a chain reaction of further questions. So it is with the questions associated with the farm worker paradox. The typical attempt at resolving this paradox falls back on explanations of the relative productivity of various groups of workers, but this approach begs deeper questions about productivity.

On the most superficial level, how is productivity measured? Is productivity high merely because sellers in more concentrated markets have the ability to mark up their goods more than sellers in more competitive markets?

In other words, does the measurement of productivity suffer from the circular logic to which I referred earlier? Over and above the questions regarding the measurement of productivity, deeper questions remain. In what sense is economic activity productive?

The question of whether the economy is extractive or productive leads to an additional question: is the economy part of the environment or is the environment part of the economy? Within the economic perspective, natural resources as such are not a primary concern; they are merely a factor of production, along with labor and capital goods.

Adam Smith realized that markets provide a peculiar perspective on natural resources in proposing what became known as his diamonds and water paradox. He observed:

> Nothing is more useful than water: but it will purchase scarce any thing; scarce any thing can be had in exchange for it. A diamond, on the contrary, has scarce any value in use; but a very great quantity of other goods may frequently be had in exchange for it. (Smith 1776, I.v.13, p. 52)

In effect, the market reduces nature to little more than a storehouse of exploitable materials (and perhaps to some extent a provider of recreation comparable to the theme park or a movie theater). Nonmarket values disappear. Why worry about water so long as it remains cheap. The extinction of other species are regrettable, mostly because of the loss of their potential as a template for the production of some new product, such as a pharmaceutical commodity.

Resources sometimes take on great values, even though they contribute little to the quality of life. Diamonds, as Smith once noted, have a high value, only because of the demand of the extremely rich (Smith 1978, vi.71, p. 358). The value of the resources destroyed in the quest for such valuable commodities count for little. For example, people desire gold for its decorative properties, but its extraction is environmentally destructive. Previously, mining operations used mercury, which still pollutes California although it is more than 150 years after the Gold Rush. Now miners use cyanide instead, creating still other environmental disruptions.

Economics provides strong justification for the ongoing extraction of resources for relatively trivial purposes. The philosopher, Alfred North Whitehead, once wrote: "all societies require interplay with their environment; and in the case of living societies this interplay takes the form of robbery.... The robber requires justification" (Whitehead 1929, p. 105).

The ecological perspective offers a different interpretation of the world. Within that context, economic activity represents the condition of only one species—albeit the dominant species in terms of its effect—impacting upon the overall environment.

Let me put these questions in a physical context. One of the most fundamental concepts in science is the Second Law of Thermodynamics, which holds that energy spontaneously tends to become diffused. Production, and even life itself, depends upon access to concentrated basins of energy, whether they be in the form of food or fossil fuel. In the words of Ludwig Boltzmann, one of the pioneers in this field:

> The general struggle for existence of animate beings is therefore not a struggle for raw materials... nor for energy which exists in plenty in any body in the form of heat (albeit unfortunately not transformable), but a struggle for entropy, which becomes available through the transmission of energy from the hot sun to the cold earth. (Mirowski 2002, pp. 47–48; citing Boltzmann 1974, p. 24)

The entropy, which Boltzmann mentioned, refers to the degradation of matter and energy, upon which all life depends. For example, the use of energy causes it to dissipate in the form of heat. All energy sources, including even the sun, tend to run down over time, in the sense that the energy becomes increasingly less available as it becomes less concentrated. You can replenish some energy sources, but only by using up even greater energy sources. In this sense, the Second Law of Thermodynamics seems to rule out the possibility of productivity.

However, economists mean something else when they speak of productivity. An economic system is productive for economists in the sense that it manages to combine labor and resources to create something more desirable than the sum total of the time and resources that go into the production process. Obviously, the production process can turn out something more directly useful than the natural resources that it converts into finished consumption goods. For example, the agricultural system can, in effect, convert petroleum, which is inedible, into nutritious food.

Alternatively, the economy may be merely extractive; that is, the economic system may be just drawing down an irreplaceable reservoir of natural resources. In contrast, although some traditional agricultural systems operated destructively, many had the potential to rely for the most part on renewable resources. For example, the supply of petroleum is fixed. Eventually, the time will come when the modern agricultural system, dependent as it is on petroleum, will have difficulty finding an adequate supply of fuel. Kenneth Deffeyes, a petroleum geologist, put the dichotomy between extractive and productive systems into stark contrast, pointing out:

> Economists and geologists start from completely different viewpoints. Economists state that oil discoveries depend on the level of investment put into the search. Geologists claim that showing up at the cashier's cage with dollar bills does not increase the amount of oil in the ground. As usual, both are partly correct. (Deffeyes 2001, p. 70)

This tension between physical laws, which ultimately render productive systems virtually impossible, and economic analysis, which presumes that productive systems are the norm, represents an important theme in this book.

The Economic Implications of the Debate

This question about whether the economy is productive or extractive feeds back into the earlier discussion of the farm worker paradox.

Here again, Adam Smith comes into play. Prior to Smith and a group of slightly earlier French writers known as the Physiocrats, economists assumed that the economy as a whole was not productive. Instead, they viewed the economy as a zero-sum game.

Unlike Smith and the Physiocrats, these early economists maintained that economies must depend upon foreign trade to prosper. In the view of most pre-Smithian economists, the profit that one entity earns necessarily comes at the expense of someone else. Since profits are merely a transfer of wealth from one party to another, a national economy can only prosper at the expense of the rest of the world.

These French writers insisted that only agriculture was productive, linking productivity to biological processes. Smith broke that link, suggesting that all those who produce for the market could be productive. This approach might be Smith's most original contribution, implying that value can soar irrespective of the underlying ecological system.

Now, if the economy is purely extractive, then profits are merely the result of shunting costs elsewhere. Modern economists accept that some shunting exists. They refer to that phenomenon as externalities, which they presume to be a relatively minor part of the overall economic process. Instead, they follow Smith in attributing profit to human creativity.

If the economy is indeed productive, as Adam Smith suggested, then those who are the most privileged might have some legitimate grounds for counseling the most disadvantaged that calls for redistribution of wealth and income would not be in their best interest. Instead, future economic growth resulting from the reinvestment of profits will be the most likely or even most efficient strategy for bettering the condition of the poor. The privileged might also have a legitimate case in suggesting that their special expertise is crucial in increasing productivity. For that reason, the farm workers could possibly be well advised to accept their situation in the hope of future benefits.

If, however, the economy is purely extractive, then such advice has no grounds whatsoever. In an extractive world, impoverished workers may have little to show for their labors in the future—only a diminished world facing crushing shortages of natural resources.

Nicholas Georgescu-Roegen, an economist who had more ecological awareness than any of his generation, pointed out that economics had difficulty coming to grips with the concept of extraction because of a serious flaw in economic theory. In particular, economic theory faces a nearly impossible task of comparing stocks of resources with flows of resources. The quantity of petroleum in the ground is a stock, while the amount of petroleum used each year is a flow (Georgescu-Roegen 1971). Economists use a technique called discounting that allows for comparisons between stocks and flows, but as I will explain later, this procedure leaves much to be desired.

The productive/extractive dichotomy defies easy resolution. Neither perspective is satisfactory. The dichotomy itself arises because of the tendency to view human activity apart from the natural environment. How can we bridge the intellectual gap between what people do and the environment in which they live without falling into hopeless romanticism?

I do not pretend to have the answer to the dichotomy. I do offer a critique of the purely economic perspective to prepare the way for the next step.

The Importance of Resources

The cumulative effects of resource extraction are incalculable, especially because the economy continues to grow making ever-more demands on the environment. Even though growth may not be particularly rapid, the cumulative effect is huge. John Robert McNeill provided some perspective for this process. He observed:

> 500 years ago the world's annual GDP (converted into 1990 dollars) amounted to about $240 billion, slightly more than Poland's or Pakistan's today, slightly smaller than Taiwan's or Turkey's.... By 1820, the world's GDP had reached $695 billion (more than Canada's or Spain's, less than Brazil's in 1990s terms). (McNeill 2000, p. 3)

While the world economy took more than three centuries to almost triple during that period, recent growth has been explosive in comparison, in large part because of a more intensive exploitation of resources. For example, one study estimated that humanity was using 70 percent of the total capacity of the global biosphere in 1961, but then grew to 120 percent by 1999 (Wackernagel et al. 2002).

Even if this estimate is too pessimistic, eventually, a time will come when the possibility of continued economic growth will be virtually exhausted. After that, negative growth becomes inevitable.

A comparison of Western Europe and China is useful in contemplating the relationship between resources and growth. By all accounts before the Industrial Revolution, early Chinese science and technology was well in advance of its Western European counterparts. As late as 1750, indicators of economic success for Western Europe and China were relatively similar. Suddenly, with the Industrial Revolution Europe pulled far ahead, while the Chinese economy stagnated. Kenneth Pomeranz makes a powerful case that the Europeans were able to draw upon the resources of much of the rest of the world, especially those regions that fell under colonial rule (Pomeranz 2000).

While China did a magnificent job of finding creative uses for virtually every possible resource, the handicap of relying on its own domestic resources put the Chinese at a serious disadvantage. Even so, the Chinese managed to accommodate a growing population. As Adam Smith observed:

> In rice countries, which generally yield two, sometimes three crops in the year, each of them more plentiful than any common crop of corn, the abundance of food must be much greater than in any corn country of equal extent. (Smith 1776, I.xi.b.37, p. 176)

One form of foreign trade was also crucial in allowing China to support her population. China introduced crops from the New World: sweet potatoes, peanuts, and corn (Bray 1984, pp. 427–28). These crops, however, were not particularly important in the densely populated lowlands where rice already produced enormous quantities of food per acre. Instead, these crops temporarily loosened the environmental restraints in the highlands (Pomeranz 2000, p. 58).

Although the Chinese did not rely on foreign trade for much else, they did maintain extensive trade relations with the West. In return for their exports, the Chinese mostly imported silver, which served as their monetary base, rather than resources that would be used in direct production (Flynn and Giraldez 2002). Somewhere between one-third and one-half of the silver produced in the Americas found its way to China (Braudel 1982, p. 198). By the 1840s, the British military had succeeded in coercing the Chinese to accept the import of opium, which curtailed the flow of silver into their land.

Theodore Schultz, a Nobel Prize–winning economist, found that even the poor peasants were exceedingly efficient in applying the technology that they used. They remained poor, nonetheless, because they were caught in a cycle of poverty that did not allow them to accumulate. Without access to the resources that made modern technology possible, they could not break out of the circle of poverty by adopting more efficient methods of production (Schultz 1964).

In short, the Chinese, lacking an external empire and having to make do largely with the resources that the nation had on hand could not keep pace with the dynamic European pace of economic growth. In Europe, breaking free of the social relations of feudalism allowed for revolutionary technological progress, but in China, lacking the resources to fuel modern technologies, the technological benefits of transforming social relations would have been far more limited. True, China could have eliminated some of the wasteful consumption of the elites. Over time, improved education would have made for certain benefits, but the Second Law of Thermodynamics represented a more profound barrier for China than for Europe, which could call upon the resources of its empires.

Economists' Perspective on the Future

Despite the obvious importance of natural resources, economists have typically paid little attention to the subject. For example in JSTOR, an electronic collection that includes 13 of the most important economic journals from the time of their inception, except for the last four or five years, the term scarcity appears in a title only 27 times, as of July 2002, or an average of little more than two articles per journal. At least two of these journals have been publishing for more than a century.

More often than not, the message of these few papers about scarcity is that concern over conservation is unwarranted because markets are effective in managing resources. Consider the opening sentences of the most influential article on the economics of resources:

> Contemplation of the world's disappearing supplies of minerals, forests, and other exhaustible assets had led to demands for regulation of their exploitation. The feeling that these products are now too cheap for the good of future generations, that they are being selfishly exploited at a too rapid rate, and that in consequence of their excessive cheapness they are being produced and consumed wastefully has given rise to the conservation movement. (Hotelling 1931, p. 137)

Perhaps, in an effort to show the distance between economics and the environmental perspective, the author went so far as to suggest that the existence of monopoly could perhaps make the economy deplete resources at an excessively slow rate (Hotelling 1931, p. 138).

Taking a broader perspective, Harold J. Barnett and Chandler Morse, authors of what for many economists is the bible of resource economics, declared: "Nature imposes particular scarcities, but not an inescapable general scarcity" (Barnett and Morse 1963, p. 11). In other words, we may experience a shortage of some particular resource, but such shortages do not present an obstacle to further growth. New technology will allow us to create plenty of substitute technologies. Barnett and Morse based their optimistic conclusion on economic indicators rather than material conditions. For example, if looming petroleum scarcity were a real problem, then prices should be trending upward. However, just as was the case with the passenger pigeon, new technology facilitated the capture of petroleum. Richard Norgaard, a resource economist from the University of California, Berkeley, estimated that in the absence of such new technology, extraction costs would have risen 70 percent between 1939 and 1968 (Norgaard 1975).

Ironically, although economists display a nonchalance regarding future natural resource scarcity, they often display a touching sensitivity concerning the future when analyzing the public sector. They have developed a whole new subdiscipline named intergenerational accounting, which emphasizes that the present population supposedly is paying insufficient attention to the burdens that it is bequeathing future generations. They spread the alarm that Social Security is facing bankruptcy and that current policies threaten to saddle future generations with excessive taxes.

Holland: Prosperity Without Resources

How is it that scarcity played such a minor role in the development of economic thought? The answer has to do with the sort of matters that concern economists. Economists tend to overlook those parts of the economy that function smoothly, and concentrate on what appear to be more pressing problems.

Economists initially equated scarcity with a shortage of gold. A little background might make this assertion seem less ridiculous to a modern reader. Seventeenth-century Holland was the first successful, modern market economy. As such, Holland was a source of amazement for the British economists, who wondered how a country so bereft of natural resources could obtain such prosperity. One English author marveled:

> The abundance of Corne groweth in the East Kingdoms: but the great Storehouses for Grain, to serve Christendome, and the Heathen Countries (in times of Dearth) is in the Low-Countries... [T]he great Vintage, and Staple

of Salt, is in the Low-Countries... The exceeding Groves of Wood are in the
East-Kingdomes: But the huge Piles of Wainscot, Clapboards, Fir-deale,
Masts, and Timber are in the Low-Countries. (Keymer 1650, p. 8)

John Evelyn, an important intellectual of the day, picked up this same
theme in his *Navigation and Commerce: Their Original and Progress*
(1674). Evelyn, who by then was a member of the Council for Foreign
Plantations, agreed that a paucity of natural resources posed no significant barrier to affluence. He reported that although the Dutch had no
indigenous grain, wine, oil, timber, metal, stone, wool, hemp, or pitch, yet
by commerce they have obtained them all so that "the whole world seems
but a Farm to them" (cited in Bowle 1981, p. 160).

Many modern economic historians believe that the major advantage
that the Dutch enjoyed was specialized knowledge that it had accumulated regarding the Baltic markets where it was dominant. Such informational monopolies are very difficult to maintain over a long period of
time. As this knowledge became more widespread, much of the Dutch
advantage dissipated.

England had already begun to emulate the Dutch by the time Evelyn
was writing. According to his account: "Asia refreshes us with Spices,
Recreates us with Perfumes, Cures us with Drougs and adorns us with
Jewells." From Africa come ivory and gold; from America silver, sugar,
and cotton; from France, Spain, and Italy "wine, oyl and silk"; Russia
"warms us with furrs," Sweden supplies copper, Denmark masts. All this
wealth comes by the sea, which "makes the world's inhabitants one
Family" (cited in Bowle 1981, p. 161).

While Holland was able to monopolize much of the world's trade for
a brief period of time through its superior knowledge of markets, that sort
of control no longer seemed viable by the time that England replaced
Holland. Lacking faith in market relations, England and the other
European countries that later emulated her strategy—including
Holland—sought to dominate crucial resource bases. At first, they relied
on direct colonization and then on a more efficient means by installing
and maintaining compliant governments to administer these peripheral
economies on behalf of the European interests.

Scarcity: The Dog that Didn't Bark

Holland produced no important advances in economics, even after the
economy settled into a comfortable, but modest prosperity. In the words

of one Dutch economic historian:

> The only writers of Dutch origin who figure in the general histories of
> economic thought in the eighteenth century—Bernard Mandeville, Jacob
> Vanderlint, Matthew Decker and Isaac de Pinto—all lived abroad when
> they published the works which now are acknowledged as significant con-
> tributions to economic analysis (Davids 2001, p. 258)

British political economists, in contrast, were continually worried about
one problem or another, but the thought of scarcity rarely troubled them,
except for an almost obsessive concern about the inadequacy of precious
metals. More often than not, those authors writing before the nineteenth
century whom we now regard as economists were actually self-interested
individuals. They wrote books and pamphlets with an eye to convincing
influential people to support their preferred policies. Until the nineteenth
century, the courses closest to the discipline of economics in the universities were taught as part of moral philosophy, which was a wide-ranging
subject that also included questions about marriage and the law. Adam
Smith, for example, was a professor of moral philosophy.

In an effort to maintain, and even increase, the strength of the
kingdom, British laws prohibited the export of precious metals during
the seventeenth century. Although few people might have recognized it at
the time, the inflow of gold and silver promoted the development of markets by speeding the rate at which people left the subsistence economy to
work for wages.

Even more generally, gold could potentially purchase virtually anything. In the words of one of the three Dutch writers mentioned before,
"Money Answers All Things" (Vanderlint 1734). So, common sense suggested that because the accumulation of gold was important, the export
of precious metals would be detrimental to this accumulation.

Many of these early political economists were business people who
needed to export precious metals to obtain commodities, such as spices,
which they intended to resell at a substantial profit. They argued that if they
were permitted to work without interference, their export of precious metals would ultimately lead to the accumulation of even more gold and silver.

These early pamphleteers were especially aware that international trade
was the essential element in the early accumulation of wealth, in effect correctly identifying one of the conditions that initially allowed Great Britain to
distance itself from traditional economies, such as China. Thomas Mun, a
trader whose work stands up much better than that of his contemporaries,
used the example of pepper, to show how trade brought riches into Britain:

> Also wee ought to esteem and cherish those trades which we have in
> remote or far Countreys, for besides the encrease of Shipping and

Mariners thereby, the wares also sent thither and receiv'd from thence are far more profitable unto the kingdom than by our trades neer at hand: As for example; suppose Pepper to be worth here two Shillings the pound constantly, if then it be brought from the Dutch at Amsterdam, the Merchant may give there twenty pence the pound, and gain well by the bargain; but if he fetch this Pepper from the East-indies, he must not give above three pence the pound at the most, which is a mighty advantage, not only in that part which serveth for our own use, but also for that great quantity which (from hence) we transport yearly unto divers other Nations to be sold at a higher price. (Mun 1664, pp. 130–31)

Mun described how Duke Ferdinando of Tuscany had the foresight to lend him 40,000 crowns interest free to buy goods from Turkey to trade in Tuscany to enrich both Mun and the duke (Mun 1664, pp. 138–39).

Money Answers all Things

The absence of a serious discussion of natural resources alongside an almost excessive concern with gold was not an accident. In effect, money collapsed the complex system of environmental dependencies into a single monetary dimension. Money truly seemed to answer all things, thereby allowing a neglect of all consideration of resources.

Getting money to answer all things was an attractive idea, but it was not a certainty. People at the top of society realized that the monetary route to prosperity required a certain degree of control over the real world.

Mun was far from alone in contending that trade was crucial to increasing prosperity. Evelyn's friend, William Petty, an often uncanny yet somewhat erratic economist, attempted to quantify the contribution of international commerce to England's prosperity by proposing that "every Seaman of industry and ingenuity, is not only a Navigator, but a Merchant, and also a Soldier." In other words, one sailor is the equivalent of three domestic workers. He concluded, "The Labour of Seamen, and Freight of Ships, is always of the nature of an Exported Commodity, the overplus whereof above what is Imported, brings home money, etc." (Petty 1690, p. 259).

Keying in on the military dimension of trade was no accident on Petty's part. He was well aware of the role of force in international affairs, having served with Cromwell in the conquest of Ireland. In fact, Petty was in charge of the survey of Ireland, which was used to divide up the fruits of conquest among the invading soldiers.

The early economists were quite aware of the importance of precious metals for national defense. To begin with, the influx of gold and silver enriched the treasury, either directly or by facilitating the collection of taxes. For example, some modern authors believe that England owed its victories over France during the eighteenth and early nineteenth centuries to its superior ability in raising the taxes to finance its wars (Ferguson 2001). Indeed, centuries earlier, a counselor to Louis XII of France once said a king needs three things to win wars: "First, money; second, money; and third, money" (Jones 1994, p. 130).

Although England's immediate defense rested on its navy, England did much of its fighting abroad—often relying on paid mercenary armies. Gold was also useful in creating military alliances with other nations. For example, between 1757 and 1760, Britain subsidized Frederick the Great to the tune of about £670,000 a year (Ferguson 2001, p. 267).

At the time, states vied with each other to capture exclusive control of the most lucrative trade routes. The merchants required state power to ensure that their trading activities could function unimpeded by rival states. (The merchants were not beyond calling upon the state to prevent competition from rival domestic traders.) So in the eyes of these political economists, gold, together with the military power that gold could procure, almost seemed sufficient to acquire whatever natural resources were needed.

The Problem of Insufficient Scarcity

One even more pressing obstacle stood in the way of getting money to answer all things. The merchant-economists were painfully aware that the goods that they marketed depended upon the exhausting labors of those who had little more than their capacity to work. These merchants used state power to force the domestic population to work harder for longer hours to provide more wealth for the wealthy (Perelman 2000a). Corralling reticent workers to make these commodities seemed to be a far more pressing concern than the seemingly remote possibility of future resource scarcity.

Consider the case of Thomas Robert Malthus. Despite his supposed concern about population, Malthus, unlike the later Malthusians, actually opposed effective population controls. As early as the first edition of the *Essay*, he expressed implicit opposition to contraception in his comments on Condorcet. By the fifth edition, he had become much more straightforward. He clearly condemned "artificial and unnatural modes of checking population," not only on the grounds of their "immorality," but also on "their tendency to remove a necessary stimulus to industry" (Malthus 1817a, iii, p. 393). By the sixth edition, the good parson was so emphatic on this point that he even seemed to prefer prostitution to birth control (Malthus 1826, ii, pp. 158 and 175; see also Winch 1965, p. 59).

Later, in his *Principles of Political Economy*, Malthus dropped any pretense of concern about overpopulation. There, he was quite clear about the likely impact of population control if workers were to take his earlier warnings about overpopulation seriously: "prudential habits, among the labouring classes of a country mainly depending upon manufactures and commerce, might ruin it" (Malthus 1820, p. 236). What sort of ruin did Malthus fear? He worried that fewer children might lighten workers' expenses. Relieved of the burden of caring for as large a family, workers would not feel as much compulsion to work as hard as before.

In addition, Malthus feared an even greater danger: the possibility of a limited supply of workers. Without a teeming population of workers in need of jobs, rising wages could cut into profits. Hearkening back to the literature following the Great Fire of London a century and a half before, Malthus proposed that the ultimate threat to the economy was a deficiency in demand.

An excess of food rather than a shortage was a far more frequent concern of the early economists. Too much food would lower prices, meaning that workers would not have to work as hard to avoid starvation. As a result, continual shortages of food—but not so extreme as to cause widespread famine—seemed to be the ideal situation (Perelman 2000a). Even Adam Smith, often portrayed as a friend of the working class, advocated a similar view, proposing that merchants who raise the price of grain perform a positive function by teaching the poor the importance of thrift. In his words:

> By raising the price he [the corn merchant] discourages the consumption, and puts every body more or less, but particularly the inferior ranks of people, upon thrift and good management.... When he foresees that provisions are likely to run short, he puts them upon short allowance. Though from excess of caution he should sometimes do this without any real necessity, yet all the inconveniences which his crew can thereby suffer are inconsiderable in comparison of the danger, misery, and ruin, to which they might sometimes be exposed by a less provident conduct. (Smith 1776, IV.v.a.3, p. 524)

Both Malthus and Ricardo looked to Ireland, supposedly burdened by overpopulation according to popular accounts, as a society with insufficient population. According to Ricardo:

> The facility with which the wants of the Irish are supplied, permits that people to pass a great part of their time in idleness: if the population were diminished, this evil would increase, because wages would rise, and therefore the labourer would be enabled in exchange for a still less portion of his labour, to obtain all that his moderate wants require. (Ricardo 1817, p. 100)

Malthus was less extreme, observing:

> the predominant evil of Ireland, namely a population greatly in excess above the demand for labour, though in general not much in excess above the means of subsistence on account of the rapidity with which potatoes have increased under a system of cultivating them on very small properties rather with a view to support than sale. The Land in Ireland is infinitely more peopled than in England; and to give full effect to the natural resources of the country, a great part of the population should be swept from the soil into large manufacturing and commercial Towns. (Malthus 1817b, p. 175)

Both Ricardo and Malthus would have been pleased if Ireland's population had grown so large that the Irish masses would have been unable to feed themselves; so that, in Smith's earlier cited words, they would "stand in need of a master to advance them the materials of their work, and their wages and maintenance" (Smith 1776, I.viii.8, p. 83).

A Brief Encounter with Scarcity

At the same time that the early economists were concentrating on the scarcity of precious metals and the strategies for accumulating even more of them, people close to the seat of power, especially the British Admiralty, worried about a shortage of timber. At the time, a single, third-rate, 74-gun, ship of the line could take up to 3,800 trees, or about 75 acres of woodland (de la Bédoyère 1995, p. 173). While much of that wood would go to waste, the ship makers required wood with relatively precise shapes.

This concern about timber became even more pressing during the Second Dutch War in 1652, when the Dutch, with the help of the Danish government, succeeded in cutting off British supplies of timber (Albion

1926, p. 206). The resulting shortage of masts was particularly threatening to the British—a nation dependent on ships for trade and maintenance of its Empire. The mast shortage continued until the end of the Dutch wars in April 1654 (Albion 1926, p. 210).

In 1662 the Commissioners of the Navy, fearing an impending scarcity of timber supplies, addressed a series of inquiries about the management of the woodlands to the Royal Society. The problem was all the more urgent because the necessary trees took the best part of a century to replace, while the lifetime of a ship was far less.

John Evelyn, who was also the secretary of the Royal Society, took up the question, writing his masterpiece, *Sylva*, the first book that the society ever published. His intention was to appeal to the landed nobility and gentry to plant oaks. In the very first paragraph of his introduction, Evelyn alerted his readers to the urgency of preserving the forests, leading, of course, with national defense:

> Since there is nothing which seems more fatally to threaten a Weakening, if not a Dissolution of the strength and of the famous and flourishing Nation, then the sensible and notorious decay of her Wooden-walls [meaning, Britain's ships], when users through time, negligence, or other accident, the present Navy shall be worn out and impair'd; it has been a very worthy and seasonable Advertisement in the Honourable the princi-pal Officers and Commissioners, what they have lately suggested to this Illustrious Society, for the timely prevention and redress of this intollera-ble defect. For it has not been the late increase of Shipping alone, the mul-tiplication of Glass-works, Iron-Furnaces, and the like, from whence this impolitick diminution of our Timber has proceeded; but from the dispro-portionate spreading of Tillage, caused through that prodigious havock made by such as lately professing themselves against Root and Branch (either to be reimbours'd of their holy purchases, or for some other sor-did respect) were tempted, not only to fell and cut down, but utterly to grub up, demolish, and raze, as it were, all those many goodly Woods, and Forests, which our more prudent Ancestors left standing, for the Ornament, and service of their Country. And this devastation is now become so Epidemical, that unless some favourable expedient offer it self, and a way be seriously, and speedily resolv'd upon, for the future repair of this important defect, one of the most glorious, and considerable Bulwarks of this Nation, will, within a short time be totally wanting to it. (Evelyn 1664, p. 197)

Robert Albion, in his exhaustive study of timber and British naval power, reflected on Evelyn's influence:

> Evelyn boasted in the preface of the 1679 edition that several million timber trees were planted as a result of his book alone. Shortly after the

> Napoleonic Wars, the elder Disraeli wrote, "Inquire at the Admiralty how
> the fleets of Nelson have been constructed, and they can tell you that it
> was with the oaks which the genius of Evelyn planted." [Later opinion
> suggests that Evelyn was merely recording a practice that was already
> underway.] Whether or not the Sylva actually caused the planting of
> "millions of timber trees," it is certain that the Restoration plantings
> matured in time to carry the Navy through the wars of the later
> eighteenth century. (Albion 1926, p. 131)

Interestingly, three years before Evelyn wrote his masterpiece, he
published a short work, entitled *Fumifugium*, a powerful indictment of
London's horrible air pollution. He seems to have sensed that the intensive burning of coal, the major cause of the foul air, was related to deforestation. Evelyn could do no more than to propose that Britain relocate
its coal-intensive industries elsewhere, although he admitted that planting
more trees might relieve the situation a bit (Evelyn 1661).

This brief encounter with the threat of a scarcity of timber illustrates
a recurring theme in the way society regards resources. From time to time,
society, or at least opinion makers, suddenly reverts to a crisis mode in
response to the threat of some short-term resource shortage. Just as suddenly, the crisis evaporates—in this case because of the availability of a
relatively secure source of timber from the North American colonies and
the power of the British navy to maintain access to markets for timber
outside the Empire. Once the crisis passes, we hear no more about the
resource. For example, during the 1970s with the disruption of supplies
of oil from the Middle East, worries about the scarcity of oil were common. A couple of decades later, people in the United States were driving
their SUVs without a thought about oil supplies. Virtually nobody pays
attention to long-term threats to the resource base.

Economists, who should be attuned to scarcity, with few honorable
exceptions, seem to exhibit a trained incapacity to recognize problems of
resources. The timber episode was no exception. Although Evelyn was a
close friend of William Petty, the most important economist of his time,
no economists to my knowledge ever followed up the Naval concern with
scarcity. I might also note that while a utilitarian concern motivated
Evelyn's publication, ironically, in the end, he probably had a larger influence on the ornamental use of trees than on the protection of the natural
resource base. In the words of George Perkins Marsh, possibly the most
important environmentalist of the mid-nineteenth century United States:
"There is no doubt that the ornamental plantations in which England far
surpasses all other countries, are, in some measure, the fruit of Evelyn's
enthusiasm" (Marsh 1864, p. 194).

Evelyn himself seemed to have let go of his own previous concern with resource scarcity. Indeed, we have already quoted Evelyn's own views from only a decade later about how the Dutch were able to prosper with only the barest resource base. What could have changed his perspective? I suspect that the 1666 Great Fire of London only two years after the publication of Evelyn's masterpiece changed the mood of the time regarding scarcity. That fire raged incessantly for five days, consuming 373 acres within the city walls and 63 acres outside (Saunders 1970, p. 86). What took centuries to build and days to burn was quickly rebuilt to the amazement of all. In this sense, the fire seemed to negate altogether the problem of scarcity.

The powerful incentives created by economic demand seemed to be responsible for rapid economic growth following the fire. Access to gold or timber no longer seemed to be a limiting factor. Nicolas Barbon, one of the more active builders in the wake of the fire, some years later wrote a pamphlet reflecting the spirit of a new economic perspective that emphasized the demand-driven nature of economic growth. He proclaimed:

> The Wants of the Mind are infinite, Man naturally Aspires, and as his Mind is elevated, his Senses grow more refined, and more capable of Delight; his Desires are inlarged, and his Wants increase with his Wishes, which is for every thing that is rare, can gratifie his Senses, adorn his Body, and promote the Ease, Pleasure, and Pomp of Life. (Barbon 1690, p. 14)

Fears of resource scarcity fell from popular view so completely that many otherwise intelligent people, including Barbon, took up the idea at the time that the resources of the world were infinite. Even respectable scientists of the time proposed that minerals had the capacity to regenerate themselves when exposed to air (Finkelstein 2000, pp. 92 ff.).

Imperialism and Extraction

As the industrial revolution picked up steam, some prescient British intellectuals realized that the fate of the economy was tied up with a continuing access to adequate supplies of coal (see Rashid 1981). By the middle of the nineteenth century, William Stanley Jevons, revered by economists as one of the most important figures in developing their formal theory of value, confronted the challenge of trying to maintain a growing standard of living within the constraints of a sustainable world. In his book entitled, *The Coal Question*, he wrote:

> The plains of North America and Russia are our corn fields; Chicago and Odessa our granaries; Canada and the Baltic our timber forests; Australia contains our sheep farms, and in Argentina and on the Western prairies of North America are our herds of oxen; Peru sends her silver, and the gold of South Africa and Australia flows to London; the Hindus and the Chinese grow our tea for us, and our coffee, sugar and spice plantations are all in the Indies. Spain and France are our vineyards and the Mediterranean our fruit garden; and our cotton grounds, which for long have occupied the Southern United States are being extended everywhere in the warm regions of the earth. (Jevons 1906, pp. 306–07)

This theme that the English could draw upon the world economy echoes the British description of the Dutch in the seventeenth century. Jevons, however, went on to warn that the British were depending on an unsustainable form of production:

> While other countries mostly subsist upon the annual and ceaseless income of the harvest, we are drawing more and more upon a capital which yields no annual interest, but once turned to light and heat and motive power, is gone for ever in space. (Jevons 1906, p. 307)

Jevons concluded his book with a stark acknowledgment of the environmental limits to economic growth:

> If we lavishly and boldly push forward in the creation of our riches, both material and intellectual, it is hard to over-estimate the pitch of beneficial influence to which we may attain in the present. But the maintenance of such a position is physically impossible. We have to make the momentous choice between brief but true greatness and longer continued mediocrity. (Jevons 1906, pp. 459–60)

Jevons's book created a substantial stir, impressing even the prime minister, William Gladstone. In response to the book, the government formed a royal commission to study the subject (Peart 2001, pp. 263–64).

In one important respect, Jevons was misleading. He was convinced that finding a substitute for coal would be difficult (Jevons 1906, pp. 3, 321, and chapter 8). Of course, coal is not the only possible energy source. It is not even the only fossil fuel. Nicholas Georgescu-Roegen, mentioned earlier, stands out among economists as a lonely voice warning about the necessity of taking the Second Law of Thermodynamics seriously. According to Georgescu-Roegen, "Had Jevons referred to the reserves of low entropy in the Earth's crust instead of coal...he would have presented us with a clear picture of one side of man's struggle with the limited dowry of mankind's existence on earth" (Georgescu-Roegen 1971, p. 296). But, as Georgescu-Roegen observed, Jevons probably did not know about the Second Law. Clausius had only formulated it in the same year that Jevons first published his book (Georgescu-Roegen 1971, p. 296). A few decades after Jevons published *The Coal Question*, ecology evolved as a separate branch of science. In 1913, some of the leading British ecologists founded the British Ecological Society. These ecologists saw their mission as serving the interest of the British Empire.

These imperial ecologists did not go as far as Jevons in recognizing the overriding importance of taking the inevitable depletion of resources into consideration. Although these scientists were very much aware of the importance of colonial commodities in maintaining the British lifestyle, the tone of their work suggested that better ecological management by the colonial authorities would suffice to provide adequate resources.

In their eyes, the indigenous people of the colonies had badly abused their environment. The science of ecology would allow the modern British authorities to radically transform the habitat, rectifying the damage that those "primitive" people had done.

These ecologists convinced themselves that commercially oriented ecology was more "natural" than the degraded state of nature that the indigenous people had created. Just as Darwinians at the time believed that human beings were the high point of evolution, the imperial ecologists thought that they would be raising the environment to a higher level by creating an ecological arrangement that maximized the output of commercial commodities (Anker 2001).

These ecologists developed a new vocabulary for their science, in keeping with their colonial political vision. In the words of Peder Anker, who wrote a marvelous study of the ecologists of the British Empire:

> The terminology that describes plants and vegetation resembles colonial language. Plants "establish themselves on soil 'prepared' for them," higher forms of plants "kill out the lowly pioneers," and establish new plant "associations," "kingdoms," "societies," "clans," and "colonies," and certain species "dominate" these "communities." This terminology was appealing to the colonial administration. (Anker 2001, p. 36)

The importance of colonial resources was not lost on people in power. In 1912, Churchill himself had made a fateful decision that oil, rather than coal, would thereafter fuel the ships of the Royal Navy. This decision had far-reaching consequences because it meant a dependence on foreign oil supplies rather than Welsh coal (Churchill 1917, p. 589). Once he had made that momentous commitment to oil, the future prime minister, Winston Churchill, was brutally frank about England's dependence upon imported resources. Writing in a January 1914 cabinet note, the year after the founding of the British Ecological Society, he warned:

> We are not a young people with an innocent record and a scanty inheritance. We have engrossed to ourselves an altogether disproportionate share of the wealth and traffic of the world. We have got all we want in territory, and our claim to be left in the unmolested enjoyment of vast and splendid possessions, mainly acquired by violence, largely maintained by force, often seems less reasonable to others than to us. (Cited in Ponting 1994, p. 132)

Other countries have also fought wars over resources. For example, Jonathan Marshall has made a strong case that "[t]he United States' war with Japan from 1941 to 1945 was primarily a battle for control of Southeast Asia's immense mineral and vegetable wealth" (Marshall 1995, p. xi). In the future, scarce water supplies may spark even more wars than oil.

Denying Scarcity

Although those who had the responsibility for maintaining the Empire displayed a keen awareness of the threat of scarcity, economists tended to deride those who would dare to raise the question—even an economist of Jevons's stature.

While almost unanimously praised for his efforts in pioneering the "scientific" value theory that most economists still accept today, the legacy of *The Coal Question* subjected Jevons to more than a century of ridicule by the same mainstream economists. Ordinary intellectuals uninformed by rigorous training in economics could safely warn about the dangers posed by looming scarcity, but that a leading economist could do so was unthinkable. I never took a class that mentioned Jevons without some snide remark about his "foolish" book on scarcity.

John Maynard Keynes, probably the most influential economist of the twentieth century as well as an accomplished controversialist, launched the most famous attack on Jevons's *Coal Question*. While praising much of his economic work, Keynes mocked Jevons's concern about resource scarcity. Keynes attributed Jevons's book to personal eccentricities, which exhibited themselves in compulsive behavior, such as hoarding paper. Keynes mocked Jevons's mistaken belief in "the approaching scarcity of paper as a result of the vastness of the demand in relation to the supplies of suitable material (and here again he omitted to make adequate allowance for the progress of technical methods." He concluded that for this and other reasons, "there is not much in Jevons's scare which can survive cool criticism" (Keynes 1936a, p. 117).

But, of course, scarcity was the farthest thing from Keynes's mind. Writing in the midst of the Great Depression, he was concerned that the wealth-creating capacity of the economy was bound to outstrip the capacity to consume in a purely market-driven economy. He expected that in the near future modern market economies would "have built all the houses, roads and town halls and electric grids and water supplies and so forth which the stationary population of the future can be expected to require" (Keynes 1936b, p. 106).

Of course, Jevons was far more realistic than Keynes, at least in so far as the question of resources was concerned. Both wanted to see the build-up of productive capacity, but Jevons realized that to do so would eventually lead to serious problems, incapable of ultimate resolution.

Jevons, however, was swimming against a current that he himself was instrumental in creating. While *The Coal Question* was written for popular consumption, Jevons's theoretical works were highly influential in turning economics away from a concern about scarcity. His pioneering approach to economics shifted its perspective away from a dynamic analysis of the forces that determine the cost of production. Instead of beginning with production, Jevons called upon economics to concentrate on a theory of consumption (Jevons 1871). In effect, this new style of economics focused on how consumers' choices rather than production drive the economy.

Economists do not deny that individuals face conditions of scarcity. More than a half century after Jevons pioneered this new economics, now known as neoclassical economics, most economists still downplay the importance of scarcity. After all, poverty still weighs upon a large portion of society. Even the affluent would like to consume more.

Economists readily accept that scarcity, in general, represents an obstacle to be overcome. In fact, economists typically define their discipline as the science of allocating scarce resources (see Robbins 1969, p. 16). However, the overarching scarcity that economists study is the general scarcity of capital; that is, complex conditions artificially collapsed down to a single monetary measure.

This sort of scarcity does not represent an ultimate barrier to the economy. With the appropriate degree of saving and investment, economists envision a process of capital accumulation that can always promise to continue to build up enough stock of plant and equipment to continually produce more and more goods and services.

But, as I will discuss in chapter 3, when pressed, economists cannot give a satisfactory definition of capital. They cannot even measure it. For example, plant and equipment depreciate over time, but economists have no satisfactory method of measuring this depreciation—only a few rough rules of thumb with no basis in theory.

Each school of thought has its own interpretation of capital. None are consistent with each other. Besides, economists continually widen their concept of capital. For example, economists include the aggregate accumulation of education and experience, what they call human capital, as part of the capital stock. I will expand on the subject of human capital later.

Keynes's Vision of a Post-Scarcity World

Keynes never devoted much attention to the problem of scarcity. His world seemed to be one of plenty. He famously wrote about the delightful life that international trade brought to the affluent Londoner before World War I:

> The inhabitant of London could order by telephone, sipping his morning tea in bed, the various products of the whole earth, in such quantity as he might see fit, and reasonably expect their early delivery upon his doorstep; he could at the same moment and by the same means adventure his wealth in the natural resources and new enterprises of any quarter of the world, and share, without exertion or even trouble, in their prospective fruits and advantages. (Keynes 1919, p. 6)

Keynes neglected to mention that he was reminiscing about a time when England was "climbing towards its peak of plutocratic splendor" (Dangerfield 1961, p. 259). But then again Keynes rarely took the problem of scarcity seriously, during less prosperous times. Even during the Great Depression, Keynes wrote as if the world were on the verge of an "economic Eldorado where all our reasonable economic needs would be satisfied" (Keynes 1931, pp. 347–48; see also 1930a, p. 328). After all, scarcity did not cause the Great Depression; the economy only lacked sufficient demand at the time.

Only during World War II, when the problem shifted to meeting the high demands of wartime did he temporarily concede: "In war we move back from the Age of Plenty to the Age of Scarcity" (Keynes 1940, p. 384). With the passing of war, he returned to his vision of an economic Eldorado, in which nobody would have to worry about scarcity ever again. From where did all this wealth come? Could Keynes have believed that it flowed voluntarily from the rest of the world to England by free trade alone? Why then did Britain, along with a few select Western countries prosper, while most of their trading partners languished in poverty? Keynes could not be totally oblivious to this anomaly. After all, he began his career helping to administer India, albeit from a comfortable distance.

Strangely, throughout his life, Keynes was largely silent about the Empire's contribution to British prosperity. The major exception was an essay entitled, "National Self-Sufficiency" (Keynes 1933). There, he reported on his own intellectual development:

> I was brought up, like most Englishmen, to respect free trade not only as an economic doctrine which a rational and instructed person could not doubt but almost as a part of the moral law. I regarded departures from it as being at the same time an imbecility and an outrage.
>
> Looking again today at the statements of these fundamental truths which I then gave, I do not find myself disputing them. Yet the orientation of my mind is changed; and I share this change of mind with many others. (Keynes 1933, pp. 233–34)

Keynes went on to say:

> The protection of a country's existing foreign interests, the capture of new markets, the progress of economic imperialism—these are a scarcely avoidable part of a scheme of things which aims at the maximum of international specialization and at the maximum geographical diffusion of capital wherever its seat of ownership. (Keynes 1933, p. 236)

Most modern readers of this essay probably recall Keynes's elegant description of the modern economic predicament as a "parody of an accountant's nightmare" (Keynes 1933, p. 241). Keynes continued: "We have to remain poor because it does not 'pay' to be rich. We have to live in hovels, not because we cannot build palaces, but because we cannot 'afford' them" (Keynes 1933, p. 242).

For Keynes, the waste of unemployed human resources prevented the economy from creating the Promised Land. He seemed to take for granted the role of the natural resource base in providing the material comforts associated with a successful economy, apparently, far more concerned with the aesthetic aspect of nature.

Even so, Keynes must have known about the economic importance of the colonies in the construction of his Eldorado. I assume that this silence had more to do with discretion than ignorance.

The Partial Arrival of Eldorado

In one sense, Keynes was absolutely correct about Eldorado. Yes, he ignored the roles of both resources and the colonies. However, in terms of labor, the developed market economies have indeed transcended the traditional limitations that scarcity supposedly imposes. This condition represents a dramatic break with traditional economic relations.

In the early years of capitalism, the key to economic development was mobilizing as many workers as possible. For example in eighteenth-century British political economy, most of the major figures were obsessively searching for new ways to increase the supply of available labor. For example, Joseph Townsend, the self-declared "Well-Wisher to Mankind," proposed that when farm workers return from threshing or from ploughing in the evenings, "they might card, they might spin, or they might knit" (Townsend 1786, p. 442).

Others went even further. For example, William Temple called for the addition of poor, four-year-old children to the labor force (Temple 1770, p. 266; see also Furniss 1965, pp. 114–15). Anticipating modern Skinnerian psychology, Temple speculated, "for by these means, we hope that the rising generation will be so habituated to constant employment that it would at length prove agreeable and entertaining to them." Not to be outdone, John Locke, often seen as a philosopher of liberty, called for the commencement of work at the ripe age of three (Cranston 1957, p. 425).

By the time that Keynes was coming into his own as an economist in the 1920s, technology was advancing so rapidly that the production of goods was expanding at the same time that total labor requirements were shrinking rapidly (see the insightful analysis in Sklar 1992). Employers no longer had to worry about how to find enough workers. The problem at hand was to find new sources of demand to keep unemployment from soaring.

Prior to this modern state of affairs, the traditional rationale for keeping wages in check was to free up productive capacity. In other words, with fewer productive resources going to meet the demands of the working class, more efforts could be directed toward the creation of the capital goods that would pave the way for future growth. Once the economy reached this partial Eldorado, this logic made no sense whatsoever. Resources still posed potential limits to production. For example, between 1920 and 1969, energy inputs increased more than three times as rapidly as the number of man-hours employed (Schurr 1982). In addition, in a few select instances, workers with particular occupational skills might be in short supply, but labor in general surely is not particularly scarce.

The major impact of keeping wages in check is to increase potential profits. However, to actually realize these potential profits, business had to find alternative sources of demand. I have never seen a justification for this state of affairs other than reverting back to the traditional theory that pervasive scarcity requires marketplace rationing.

Keynes correctly set out to refute this archaic mindset, but he never did so in a systematic way. As a result, his successors managed to neutralize the most challenging aspects of his work and then integrate Keynes into conventional economics.

Marshalling the Troops

Jevons's confusing message about resources—that scarcity of coal loomed as a serious danger and that scarcities do not exist within the theory of economics—was not entirely unique at the time. Keynes's mentor, Alfred Marshall, also gave contradictory signals regarding resources. Throughout his works, he would refer to biology, often suggesting a reasonable awareness of resource problems. For example, in the opening pages of *Industry and Trade*, he wrote:

> But nature's opportunity cannot long retain their present large generosity; for the world is small. Science may indeed enable a fairly vigorous life to be maintained in tropical regions, which have hitherto proved fatal to high energies: but ere very many generations have passed, the limitation of agricultural and mineral resources must press heavily on the population of the world, even though its rate of increase should receive a considerable check. (Marshall 1919, p. 2)

In many ways, Marshall's words display a deeper sensitivity to environmental limitations than Jevons's book, yet Marshall escaped unscathed because he had the good sense to bury his insights within what were otherwise thoroughly conventional books. Moreover, Marshall occupied what was probably as distinguished an academic position as anybody in the world.

Like Jevons, Marshall was highly influential in changing the vision of economic theory. Marshall's contribution, however, was not in laying pathbreaking theoretical advances. In the words of Philip Mirowski, Marshall was "first and foremost, a textbook writer, a populariser and synthesizer of contradictory doctrines," better compared to authors of stories that illustrated economic morals, such as "Jane Marcet, Henry Fawcett and Harriet Martineau rather than Walras, Jevons and Edgeworth" (Mirowski 1990, p. 83).

This comparison certainly would have galled Marshall. Prior to Marshall, economics was known as political economy. He renamed political economy as economics—a previously obscure term. The new name appealed to him because it made the subject sound more like physics. In the same spirit, he did everything humanly possible to make economics seem like it was comparable to the sciences (Maloney 1985). In this spirit, he proudly announced: "Never again will a Mrs. Trimmer. a Mrs. Marcet. or a Miss Martineau earn a goodly reputation by throwing [the principles of economics] into the form of a catechism or of simple tales" (Marshall 1897, p. 296).

Although Marshall's efforts increased the prestige of the discipline, they also made economics lose touch with the material world that it purported to explain. Ultimately, this maneuver turned economics into an abstract and all-too-often barren theorizing. Certainly, the complexities of dealing with the natural environment were far too difficult to force into simple mathematical forms. Economists had an easier time when they could work with simple numbers that were supposed to measure concepts, such as Gross Domestic Product or capital.

Over time, economics became increasingly formal and increasingly arid. Within a few decades after Marshall wrote, the discipline required that economists present their ideas in formal mathematical models if their colleagues were to take them seriously. As a result, the sort of discussion of scarcity that Marshall and Jevons offered had no place in the economic literature.

In conclusion, within the conventional economic perspective, with enough investment, the economy can presumably overcome any specific scarcities through a combination of substitution and technical change. So, while economists accept that economies can face a generalized scarcity of capital, they deny the sort of specific scarcity that Jevons discussed in *The Coal Question*.

The nineteenth-century warnings about the looming shortages of whale oil are a favorite example for economists to bring up when they want to dismiss such concerns with scarcity.

Walter Wriston, former chief executive officer of Citicorp, provided a typical description:

> The tragedy of our Civil War disrupted whale oil production, and its price shot up to $2.55 a gallon, almost double what it had been in 1859. Naturally, there were cries of profiteering and demands for Congress to "do something about it".... Meanwhile, men with vision and capital began to develop kerosene, other petroleum substitutes, and innovations based on technology. (Wriston 1986, pp. 142–43)

The moral of this story is that nobody has to worry about scarcity. The market will take care of everything.

Overcoming Scarcity

No one can doubt that a society can learn to exploit its resources more intensively. Consider the case of the United States. In part, the ready availability of abundant resources reflected the material conditions of North America. A relatively small number of people arrived on a thinly populated land that had not had to withstand centuries of intensive resource use, such as was common in Northern Europe.

Over time, however, society took strong measures to augment the known-resource base. The U.S. government took pains to dispatch people first to chart the land and then to discover what extractable resources were available (Wright 1990; and David and Wright 1997). As a result, between 1870 and 1910 the United States either led or nearly led the world in the production of copper, iron ore, antimony, manganese, mercury, nickel, silver, and zinc (Schmitz 1979, pp. 9–16).

By the time that Marshall and Jevons were writing, both Western Europe and the United States were rapidly increasing their imperial reach, bringing more and more resources within their economic ambit. This success in developing the resource base could have easily appeared as confirmation of the economists' vision of interpreting the world in terms of an accumulation of capital—at least everything seemed to be working more or less the way the theory implied.

Marshall clearly reflected the increasing reach of the imperial economies, as well as the technological achievements of the time. At the very beginning of *Industry and Trade*, immediately after explaining the plan of the book, Marshall wrote:

> No previous age has had such large opportunities as the present for applying material resources in the elevation of human life. The forces of Nature are being turned back upon her to compel her to render ever larger returns to man's efforts in every branch of industry; any resistance that she may offer to the agriculturist and the miner being quickly reduced by the incessant development of fresh sources of rich supply, and by easy and rapid communication between distant places. New countries are quickly falling into line with old. (Marshall 1919, p. 1)

Despite Marshall's enthusiasm, those efforts to develop the resource base could not eradicate the fact that eventually society will have to confront the reality of a significant resource barrier. In fact, intensifying the resource discovery process will probably just hasten the onset of significant shortages capable of undermining the standard of living. In short, the sort of problem that troubled Jevons is real, even if Jevons had erred in the specifics.

Of course, Jevons's prediction about future scarcity was not wholly accurate. In all likelihood, the decisive crunch will not be a scarcity of coal. Water seems a more likely candidate to me, but nobody can be certain. Ultimately, the combination of new technology and accumulated capital, which is supposed to allow the economy to transcend any particular scarcity, still depends on the availability of natural resources. In short, economists have not yet managed to repeal the Second Law of Thermodynamics.

Undoubtedly, a combination of new technology and substitution can help to relieve any perceived scarcity, although such efforts will generally create pressure elsewhere on the resource base. Sooner or later, the continued economic demands will overwhelm the resource base.

Although economists generally have had a tendency to downplay resource dependence, practical people, especially those close to the seats of power, are more inclined to understand resource dependence, especially within a political context. Those clear-sighted people recognize that the rest of the world is not inclined to voluntarily cede advantageous access to the world's resources to rich countries, such as Britain. Just recall the words of Winston Churchill.

Even people without any particular expertise in the field recognize the importance of oil imports for the health of the U.S. economy—so much so that people in the United States used to ask, perhaps half seriously, "what is our oil doing under their desert." So, what does modern economics contribute to our understanding of resource dependence?

The Curse of Oil

Although economists were intrigued that nations without a rich domestic resource base could still prosper through trade, until recently, they were less inclined to understand the opposite phenomenon: nations blessed with valuable resource endowments frequently fail to benefit from them, especially when such wealth is concentrated in a small number of valuable resources held by a tiny minority. Indeed, the real beneficiaries of resource abundance are often found far away from where the resources are located. True, economists over the centuries observed that resources did not necessarily bring wealth. In general, they tended to fault the deficiencies of the impoverished suppliers of resources rather than recognize the role of power in causing the outcome.

As a general rule for relatively poor nations, an abundant natural resource base is associated with a lower rate of economic growth (Gylfason 2001; and Sachs and Warner 2001). This association of poverty and a rich natural resource base has a long history. For example, had the Spanish not found gold in Latin America, the suffering of that part of the world would have been immensely lessened.

Nor did the massive flows of gold and silver from the mines of Latin America do much to help the Spanish develop a modern economy. Instead, the wealth from Latin America changed the nature of Spanish society. This new environment put a premium on behaviors that ultimately stunted Spain's nascent industry. At the same time, a good deal of the precious metals from Latin America eventually flowed toward Britain.

Many early political economists argued that a sparse endowment of natural resources is actually advantageous, because it requires people—meaning poor people—to work very hard to survive (Perelman 2000a, chapter 5). Even today, a rich natural resource endowment does not necessarily provide people with an adequate standard of living. For example, the sad fate of many countries that heavily rely on oil deposits for their income has led observers to talk of the curse of oil.

The production of oil is typically associated with a grossly unequal distribution of wealth in which a few people enjoy fabulous riches, while the majority of people either gain little or fall further behind. Certainly, the common people of countries as far apart as Nigeria, Iran, and Venezuela have little to show for their rich oil deposits. Despite the national wealth, the poor people in many oil producing countries suffer from high rates of child malnutrition; low spending levels on health care; low enrollment rates in primary and secondary schools; low rates of adult literacy; and exceptionally high rates of child mortality (Ross 2001). Oil is not unique in this respect. Outside of Botswana and possibly South Africa, diamonds have also been associated with misery.

The origins of the curse of oil do not lie in the physical properties of petroleum, but rather in the social structure of the world. The conditions associated with a rich oil deposit makes a dictatorial form of government particularly attractive to those with access to power. The source of wealth is concentrated in relatively few sites, which require a small number of workers, leaving much of the population superfluous to the interests of a ruler. Dictatorial government is well suited to maintaining severe inequities. More often than not, these countries lack democratic traditions, further facilitating the dictatorship.

A rich natural resource base can also be socially divisive, especially if the benefits are not widely shared across a nation. This problem will be even more intense if, as is often the case, the regions with the resource suffer massive environmental disasters from the extraction process, while the profits flow elsewhere. I can state almost as a categorical law that in a market society the damage from environmental disruption will fall most heavily on the poor and vulnerable.

In addition, a rich natural resource base makes a poor country, especially a relatively powerless one, an inviting target—both politically and militarily—for dominant nations. In the case of oil, the powerful nations will not risk letting such a valuable resource fall under the control of an independent government, especially one that might pursue policies that do not coincide with the economic interests of the great transnational corporations. So, governments that display excessive independence soon find themselves overthrown, even if their successors will foster an environment of corruption and political instability.

After all, dictatorial governments make convenient clients for the rich nations of the world. Paying off a dictator along with a small retinue of cronies is far less expensive than providing a good standard of living for the entire population.

In return, rich countries expect that the dictator will successfully maintain the compliance of the general population. Yet, despite the dictatorial powers of the leaders, the central government is often weak. Rather than developing its infrastructure, it often concentrates on funneling more wealth to its commanders. The grotesque maldistribution of wealth breeds discontent to which challengers to the government can appeal. Groups from both inside and outside the nation who want to control this wealth for themselves frequently try to overthrow the government, making revolution, civil war, or military interventions from abroad relatively common, without protection from the Great Powers.

This dysfunctional environment disrupts efforts to create other forms of productive activity. Over and above the problems of corruption, a massive windfall of natural resource wealth is not conducive to rational investment programs. Instead, grandiose schemes sprout like mushrooms, leaving almost inevitable disappointment in their wake.

Natural resource prices are notoriously unstable. During boom times, the oil-rich governments finance great projects with debt, predicated on the great wealth that the resources promise in the future. Once prices fall, these governments have trouble servicing the debt (Manzano and Rigobon 2001). More often than not, the ultimate victims are those who can least afford it. As the governor in Bertold Brecht's play, *The Caucasian Chalk Circle*, proclaimed: "Those who have had no share in the good fortunes of the mighty often have a share in their misfortunes" (Brecht 1961, p. 114).

The great wealth that these resources produce attracts a number of other destructive forces. Local business tends to focus on get-rich-quick ventures. In addition, the unequal distribution of wealth breeds pervasive corruption. Alongside the grand scale of corruption practiced by the leaders, minor functionaries whose salaries barely provide for their subsistence feel that they must live by taking bribes.

Oil has still other perverse associations. For example, one characteristic of successful economic development is the existence of a strong set of linkages between the major industries and a wide range of other businesses that either support or draw upon them. In the case of oil, few such linkages exist. Instead, a major multinational corporation typically brings in a set of preexisting technologies, employing skilled foreign experts, while imparting few skills to the indigenous people. To make matters worse, the extraction of oil frequently destroys the environmental conditions that allowed people to survive prior to the arrival of the oil companies.

In short, in the modern world oil is not likely to bring benefits to the mass of the population. The curse of oil seems to be a reflection of the farm worker paradox raised to a global scale: those who sacrifice the most (in terms of quality of life or demands placed upon them) enjoy the fewest benefits.

This general rule is not without exceptions. For example, the recent North Sea discoveries brought newfound wealth to already developed nations. Ironically, although Holland had been a classic case of development despite a poverty of resources, in recent years Holland became synonymous with some of the problems associated with abundant resources. The expanding petrochemical sector's foreign earnings drove up the currency at the same time that it drew resources away from the rest of the economy, making it less competitive in world markets. This condition has come to be known as the Dutch Disease. Holland, of course, remained prosperous and the Dutch Disease metastasized into the curse of oil.

Norway offers an example of a country using its resources relatively wisely. But, then again, oil is not the dominant resource in the Norwegian economy. Even so, Norway suggests the way that oil could ideally be used. Rather than allow its oil revenues to enrich a few property owners, Norway has managed the wealth flowing from its North Sea oil deposits for social purposes rather than let private interests predominate in the disposition of oil revenues. Today, the United Nations ranks Norway as the best country in the world according to its Human Development Index (United Nations Development Programme 2001, p. 155).

Norway, however, is, for obvious reasons, unique. Then again, Norway has done nothing to my knowledge to upset the major transnational petrochemical corporations. Moreover, Norway is relatively safe from military intervention. Even the best spin doctors would have a hard time demonizing Norway and whipping up other European nations to join in an attack on that country.

A Digression on Gold

The reference to the Spanish experience in the last section recalls the discussion about the early economists' recurring worries about a shortage of gold. Certainly, the unraveling of the Spanish economy bore some similarities with contemporary countries suffering under the curse of oil.

The scarcity of gold is significantly different from what we usually mean by scarcity. Typically, scarcity indicates a restriction on the ability to take advantage of the physical qualities of some material—for example, food or fuel. The scarcity of gold does not square with that kind of scarcity, since the usefulness of gold as a monetary object depends upon its scarcity rather than its physical attributes.

Food or fuel may be more expensive when they are scarce, but their material qualities remain unaltered, regardless of whether they are scarce or abundant. But, in the case of gold, an excessive supply can destroy its usefulness. Imagine that an asteroid deposits mountains of gold around the earth at the time when gold was the primary monetary base for Europe. The value of gold would shrink, but so would its usefulness as a monetary base. The result would be an inflation that would probably disrupt the economy. So while any individual or group can benefit from controlling more gold, if everybody were to have access to more gold the world would be no better off, except for the industrial uses of gold.

True, under the gold standard a more modest increase in the supply of gold could spur economic growth without undermining the value of gold too much. For example, the nineteenth-century gold discoveries, first in California and then in Alaska and South Africa, initiated an acceleration of economic growth (see Friedman and Schwartz 1963).

Of course, other forces besides the quantity of the money supply determine economic conditions. Other factors can explain the pattern of economic growth just as well, if not better. Monetary conditions, however, reflect only one of a multitude of factors that affect the state of the economy.

Many early political economists were mindful of how little Spain benefited from Latin American gold. In fact, Spain became a watchword for the folly of making a fetish of gold. Keynes famously ridiculed gold as a "barbarous relic" (Keynes 1923, p. 138). Nonetheless, he did not rule out gold altogether. For example, he speculated that Spanish gold contributed to British development:

> The booty brought back by Drake in the Golden Hinde may fairly be considered the fountain and origin of British foreign investment. Elizabeth paid off out of the proceeds the whole of her foreign debt and invested a part of the balance (about £42,000) in the Levant Company; largely out of the profits of the Levant Company there was formed the East India Company, the profits of which during the seventeenth and eighteenth centuries were the main foundation of England's foreign connections; and so on. (Keynes 1930b, vi, p. 139)

Keynes was obviously exaggerating. England, unlike China, which sacrificed much of its potential to the acquisition of precious metals, simply stole immense quantities of gold from Spain. Of course, the gold that flowed to Britain did not only arrive in the ships of the privateers. Trade channels also brought considerable gold to Britain. That other gold, together with foreign conquests, the harnessing of the labor force to wage labor, and new technology all contributed to the massive development of the British economy, over and above the fruits of the Golden Hinde.

Economists' Neglect of Scarcity

Almost a century after John Evelyn attempted to bring the looming shortage of timber to the attention of the British public, highly respected political economists were intent on downplaying the problem of scarcity. For example, Josiah Tucker, who was probably more highly regarded at the time than his contemporary, Adam Smith, proposed:

> Only let it be always remembered that the more populous any country is, the more manure and soil will be made by the inhabitants. So that the large towns and populous villages do not only furnish a market for the produce of the country round about, and thereby pay for the labour, and excite the emulation of the husbandman, but also supply him with dung, rags, horn-shavings, ashes, soot, etc., etc., to load his carriages back in order to fructify his grounds for fresh crops. So little cause is there to fear, that a country can be too populous! (Tucker 1758, p. 24)

To his credit, Tucker was arguing against the need to make war to gain land. He was trying to convince rulers who were committed to conquering lands to extend their power that they could more easily improve their agricultural practices. In that way, they could have all the advantages of more land without the inconvenience of carrying on lethal military campaigns.

Later, some economists vaguely addressed scarcity once again by worrying about a future shortage of food. For example, in 1776, Smith saw China as an example of what economists later called a stationary state—an economy that had so many people that the effort to provide them with sufficient food exhausted its entire productive potential, leaving no surplus to provide for future economic growth (Smith 1776, I.viii.14, p. 89).

This concern, however, was peripheral to the major thrust of Smith's work. He did, however, help to shape attitudes toward nature by applauding the growing preference for more natural-looking habitats instead of the ornate landscapes that were popular in France. His *Lectures on Rhetoric and Belles Lettres* appear indirectly to have initiated the craze for deer parks, which were closely managed game reserves (Smith 1762–63; Olwig and Olwig 1979, p. 19; Whitney 1924). In a posthumously published essay, he observed:

> It was some years ago the fashion to ornament a garden with yew and holly trees, clipped to the artificial shapes of pyramids, and columns, and vases, and obelisks. It is now the fashion to ridicule this task as unnatural. The figure of a pyramid or obelisk, however, is not more unnatural to a yew-tree than to a block of porphyry or marble. (Smith 1790, p. 183; see also Comito 1971)

More famously, Thomas Robert Malthus, whose name became synonymous with scarcity, wrote his *Essay on Population*, which became a rallying cry for later concerns about overpopulation. In fact, the purpose of Malthus's essay, as I suggested earlier, had little to do with fears of overpopulation. Instead, he was attempting to refute those who proposed a more equitable society. Malthus responded that any efforts to ameliorate the conditions of the poor would be futile because population growth would soon overwhelm any short-term benefits.

Malthus was not concerned with some absolute limit that scarcity imposed; instead, he merely contended that food production would not increase as fast as population. Within Malthus's framework, given enough time, food production could increase sufficiently to feed virtually any level of population. But again, Malthus was not particularly concerned with population growth as such; he was only using population as an argument against social reforms.

Malthus's contemporary, David Ricardo, was clearly the most sophisticated economist of the early nineteenth century. Many modern economists associate Ricardo with scarcity, but Ricardo's scarcity was an artificial scarcity, created by the English protectionist policy of charging tariffs on imported food (Ricardo 1817).

Ricardo did not believe that scarcity would affect the welfare of the poor. He presumed that the poor would continue to earn a subsistence wage no matter how high food prices rose. Instead, Ricardo warned that rising population would increase rents. Because of the elevated rents, food prices would also rise, forcing employers to pay more in wages, thereby cutting into profits.

In any case, the barrier to increasing the supply of food was political rather than environmental. Repeal of this protectionism would eliminate scarcity, just as trade had relieved the timber shortage more than a century earlier. Although imports of food seemed to be the obvious solution to the threatened reduction in profits, the landlords who controlled Parliament resisted this policy, which would diminish their rents.

The Destruction of Forests

Besides destroying soil fertility, early farming practices devastated forests on the North American continent. I recall reading somewhere that when the Europeans first arrived in the United States people claimed that a squirrel could pass from the Atlantic seaboard to the Ohio Valley without once having to touch the ground. Despite the obvious exaggeration, such sentiments reflect the rich forest heritage of that part of the world.

Virtually no American voices registered dissent regarding the devastation of the forests, with the exception of George Perkins Marsh, mentioned earlier as the most perceptive environmental observer of the mid-nineteenth-century United States. Unlike John Evelyn, Marsh's warnings had little influence, probably because he did not connect environmental deterioration with national military strength.

Instead, trees were, in the eyes of most farmers, a nuisance that they first had to clear from their land before planting their fields. Commenting on agricultural conditions in North America, Adam Smith observed, "the expense of clearing the ground is the principle obstacle to improvement" (Smith 1776, IV.vii.b.28, p. 577). English travelers reported about what they interpreted as the Americans' aversion to trees (Weld 1799, pp. 23–24, 29; cited in Gates 1960, p. 3).

Trees in this context had no economic value whatsoever. Instead, the destruction of trees actually constituted an "investment," and a substantial investment at that. As late as the 1850s, clearing an acre of land took 33 man days (Primack 1962, p. 491).

In fact, the economic value created by the removal of trees vastly exceeded the underlying economic value of the land itself. Stanley Lebergott cites a contemporary report from the early nineteenth century of a 70-acre lot that sold for a jackknife, a paper of pins, two quarts of molasses, and a dozen needles (Lebergott 1984, p. 87; citing Backus 1961, pp. 3 and 8). In the 1830s, raw land in western New York sold for only 29 to 49 cents per acre. After the land was cleared of trees and bush, it became worth $10 an acre (Lebergott 1984, p. 87).

Of course, some forest clearing was necessary if the world were to support the present population, but in leveling the forests, a rational society would have been taking account of the ecological losses involved in that action. At one point, Karl Marx, in considering the situation in the advanced capitalist economies of his day, even went so far as to speculate that the destruction of the forests by mindless profit-seeking created conditions that Marx called "another hidden socialist tendency" (Marx to Engels, March 25, 1868; in Marx and Engels 1942, p. 237).

The modern environmental movement justifiably decries the destructive clearing of the tropical rainforests without going as far as Marx. Environmentalists warn that clearing the forests exposes the soil to erosion, destroys the habitat for indigenous people, as well as other creatures, and even affects the climate. Taking only a few of the environmental costs of forest clearing into account is suggestive of the magnitude of the problem. For example, Robert Repetto, senior fellow and former vice president of the World Resources Institute, estimated that in the Philippines, a very restrictive interpretation of the annual losses from deforestation still averaged 3.7 percent of the Gross Domestic Product between 1970 and 1987 (Repetto 1992, p. 98).

Repetto's estimates account for only a few of the grossest forms of environmental deterioration. George Perkins Marsh observed:

> Besides the larger creatures of the land and the sea, the quadrupeds, the reptiles, the birds, the amphibia, the crustacea, the fish, the insects, and the worms, there are other countless forms of vital being. Earth, water, the ducts and fluids of vegetation and of animal life, the very air we breathe, are peopled by minute organisms which perform most important functions in both the living and the inanimate kingdoms of nature. It is evident that the chemical, and in many cases mechanical character of a great number of objects important in the material economy of human life, must be affected by the presence of so large an organic element in their substance, and it is equally obvious that all agricultural and all industrial operations lend to disturb the natural arrangements of this element. (Marsh 1864, p. 108)

All too often, the environmentalists who express sincere concern about the manner in which developing countries devastate their forests neglect to acknowledge—or are unaware—that a comparable policy in their own nation's history helped to create the comfortable existence that many of these same environmentalists enjoy today.

In conclusion, while agricultural production should be counted as a positive value, the loss of the forest environment—as well as other forms of environmental disruption—should also be counted as a cost.

Abusing the Land

By the middle of the nineteenth century, British agriculture was facing a severe crisis in soil fertility. To replenish its soils, the country turned to the importation of organic materials from abroad. "During 1830–70 the depletion of soil fertility through the loss of soil nutrients was the overriding environmental concern of capitalist society in both Europe and North America" (Foster 1999, p. 375).

The growth in the demand for fertilizer was phenomenal. The value of bone imports to Britain increased from a mere £14,400 in 1823 to £254,600 in 1837. The first boat carrying Peruvian guano unloaded its cargo in Liverpool in 1835; by 1841, 1,700 tons were imported, and by 1847, 220,000. European farmers were so desperate for new sources of nutrients for their soil in this period that they raided the Napoleonic battlefields (Waterloo, Austerlitz) for bones to spread over their fields (Foster 1999, p. 375).

In the United States, just as in England, agricultural yields fell dramatically in the early nineteenth century. For example:

> in the once fantastically fertile Genesee valley of New York, corn yields averaged about eight bushels per acre in 1845, down from thirty bushels in 1775. In middle and southern states such as Maryland and Virginia, farmers (growing crops such as tobacco and cotton, both of which are especially hard on the land) faced bleak futures as soil exhaustion became increasingly pronounced. (Skaggs 1994, p. 2)

Although foreign observers of colonial agriculture regarded the wasteful treatment of the land with dismay, economic pressures seemed to demand that farmers deplete the soil fertility. Writing in the early twentieth century, Harvard economist, Thomas Nixon Carver, observed:

> Where land is cheap and labor dear, there will always be wasteful and extensive farming, and it is useless to preach against it.
>
> In spite of the marvelous growth of American agriculture and its apparent prosperity it is doubtful if it has ever been self-supporting in any strict sense before the present period. The average farmer had never counted the partial exhaustion of the soil as part of a crop. Taking the country over it is probable that if the farmers had been compelled to buy fertilizers to maintain the fertility of their soil without depletion, the whole industry would have become bankrupt. (Carver n.d., pp. 90 and 95)

The agricultural sector avoided such a bankruptcy by moving on to new lands after it exhausted the fertility of the older lands. In the words of Lewis Gray in his classic study of agriculture in the southern United States, "Planters bought land as they might buy a wagon—with the expectation of wearing it out" (Gray 1933, p. 446). For example, James F. W. Johnston, a noted English agronomist explained to his readers:

> there is as yet in New England and New York scarcely any such thing as local attachment—the love of place, because it is a man's own—because he has hewed it out of the wilderness, and made it what it is; or because

his father did so, and he and his family have been born and brought up, and spent their happy youthful days upon it. Speaking generally, every farm from Eastport in Maine, to Buffalo on Lake Erie, is for sale. The owner has already fixed a price in his mind for which he would be willing, and even hopes to sell, believing that, with the same money, he could do better for himself and his family by going still further west. (Johnston 1851, i, p. 162; cited in Gates 1960, p. 400)

Adding our earlier discussion of the destruction of forests to the losses of soil fertility makes Carver's case even stronger.

Economic Apologetics of Environmental Destruction

Despite the enormous environmental damage done by early agriculture, some economists still applaud those questionable farming practices. For example, writing a half century after Carver, an economist, Warren Scoville, attempted to refute the widely accepted environmental complaints about the destruction of the soil in early North America:

> The generally held opinion that the so-called "land butchery" practices by the American farmer during colonial and pre-Civil War days was "wasteful" of our land and timber resources falls, I believe, into this category of misconceptions. It seems a sounder view that "land butchery" was not necessarily wasteful either from the viewpoint of contemporaries or from the viewpoint of citizens living today. (Scoville 1953, p. 178)

In a follow-up article, Scoville defended the primacy of economic logic:

> I, for one, would be most loath to defer to the judgment of agronomists and statisticians as to whether our natural resources (or any capital goods, for that matter) should be conserved or in some degree used up. If they can supply economists with the essential data on all possible production and cost functions, this would be highly desirable. But let us hope that our most competent economists would be charged with the responsibility of interpreting the data and of recommending desirable public policy regarding conservation. (Scoville 1954, p. 93)

In other words, the future economic costs of the environmental damage were small relative to the immediate benefits. Scoville never explained how to calculate such costs; that task supposedly was the responsibility of the critics. Lacking such evidence, the land butchery must have been rational because market forces made such practices profitable.

This rationality depended upon two different possibilities that the land offered to the farmers of the United States. First, farmers could move to new land after they exhausted the fertility of their farms. For example, recall the observation of the British agronomist, Johnston, about the absence of local attachment among farmers.

In addition to the possibility of moving to new lands, some of the farmers of North America followed the example of their English counterparts, by replenishing the fertility of their land by importing guano. In the 1830s, guano's price was approximately $30 a ton, according to *American Farmer*, "making it, as may be perceived, a very profitable business" for both purveyors and users (Skaggs 1994, p. 3; citing Skinner 1824).

Alas, supplies of guano were also limited. As John Bellamy Foster tells the tale:

> So desperate was the condition of capitalist agriculture in this period that the mid-nineteenth century saw a frantic search for guano throughout the world and in the rise of a period of guano imperialism. The first great overseas colonial expansion of the United States was a direct outgrowth of this crisis of the conditions of production in agriculture. Under the authority of the Guano Island Act, passed by Congress in 1856, U.S. capitalists seized 94 islands, rocks, and keys around the globe between 1856 and 1903, 66 of which were officially recognized by the U.S. Department of State as U.S. appurtenances. Nine of these guano islands remain U.S. possessions today. (J. Foster 1997, p. 286)

After the guano deposits gave out, farmers turned to another substitute for soil fertility: commercial nitrogen fertilizer. Nitrogen, the most important component of commercial fertilizers, seemed to defy industrialization because, unlike other nutrients, it volatilizes. Capturing nitrogen from the air seemed virtually impossible until German chemists discovered how they could harness free nitrogen into a form that farmers could apply to the land. This process was not magic. It required large quantities of fossil fuel. One student of the subject declared that this synthesis of ammonia was the most important invention of the twentieth century because, he claimed, without it, millions of people would starve (Smil 2001, p. xiii).

So, in practical terms, Scoville's perspective prevailed over that of the more skeptical, Thomas Nixon Carver. After all, massive soil erosion continues to this day. In 1989, for example, the United States Department of Agriculture reported that 2.7 billion tons of eroded sediments are transported to small streams each year (Pimentel et al. 1999, p. 1477). To put this quantity into perspective, about ten tons of soil erodes each year for every person in the United States.

To put this magnitude of soil erosion into context, compare it with food consumption. If the average person were to consume five pounds of food per day, over the course of a year that weight would represent less than a ton. Considering that soil is relatively dry and food contains considerable water, soil losses are even greater compared to the agricultural output.

Of course, agriculture is not responsible for all soil erosion, but certainly a great deal of the erosion occurs on farms. Although soil can erode relatively quickly, a single inch of topsoil can literally require centuries to accumulate.

The Industrial Conquest of Scarcity

A disparate group of people, most notably the great German chemist, Justus von Liebig, Henry Carey—the most creative economist in nineteenth-century United States—and Karl Marx, were all agreed that the deterioration of the soil represented a fundamental threat to the very existence of the market economies of the advanced Atlantic nations. For them, the underlying problem was an environmental imbalance rather than erosion, which was not particularly noted at the time.

Nutrients from the soil moved in the form of food from the farm to the city, where they were discarded or excreted as waste products. The result was a double problem of soil depletion in the countryside and pollution in the city. By closing the loop and recycling the nutrients back to the farms, these writers proposed that society could hope to restore environmental balance (see Perelman 1999a).

The idea of closing the loop of nutrients was not new. Recall that Josiah Tucker suggested the same possibility, but Tucker did so only in the course of theoretical speculations about the possibility of supporting an unrealistically large population. This more modern group was addressing a real problem that was staring them in the face. In Marx's words:

> Capitalist production collects the population together in great centres, and causes the urban population to achieve an ever-growing preponderance. This has two results. On the one hand it concentrates the historical motive power of society; on the other hand, it disturbs the metabolic interaction between man and the earth, i.e. it prevents the return to the soil of its constituent elements by man in the form of food and clothing; hence it hinders the operation of the eternal conditions for the lasting fertility of the soil. (Marx 1977, p. 637)

Henry Carey identified a different cause of the imbalance. Despite his intellectual accomplishments, Carey obsessively attributed all the ills of the world to the nefarious influence of Britain. By ceasing to trade with Britain, the United States could develop a spatial arrangement that would make a rational process of recycling nutrients a natural outcome. According to his market-based analysis:

> The nearer the consumer and the producer can be brought to each other, the more perfectly will be the adjustment of production and-consumption, the more steady will be the currency, and the higher will be the value of land and labour. The object of protection is to accomplish all these objects, by bringing the loom and the anvil to take their natural places by the side of the plough and the harrow, thus making a market on the land for the products of the land. (Carey 1851, p. 190)

Recently, modern corporate leaders have revived Carey's dream of market-driven ecological efficiency (Desimone and Popoff 1997). This vision has taken on the high-sounding term, industrial ecology. At the same time, the U.S. government cynically permits companies to mix toxic waste with fertilizer as a means of reducing the corporations' cost of disposing of these poisons. The steel industry alone produces 650,000 tons of such hazardous waste each year (Wilson 2001, p. 153).

Liebig's path led in a different direction. Among his leading disciples were the same scientists who discovered the industrial technique for manufacturing nitrogen-based fertilizers while the farmers were depleting the known guano deposits. Unfortunately, in the process of creating synthetic products, the chemical industry also created new problems that made recycling more difficult.

For example, Liebig and his disciples were better known for their revolutionary work in organic chemistry than their techniques for manufacturing fertilizer. Their initial success seemed to further the possibility of a closed-loop economy. They transformed coal tar, a hideous waste product from processing coal for the steel and the illuminating gas industries, into a slew of useful compounds. While the recycling of coal tar appeared to be a step in the direction of more intensive recycling, the production of the organic chemicals that the chemists discovered produced huge quantities of toxic waste that made recycling extraordinarily difficult, if not, at least in many cases, virtually impossible (see Garfield 2001, pp. 101 ff.).

Substitutability

The substitution of one resource for another was the key to the economists' optimism that scarcity could be overcome. Earlier I discussed how economists still find great comfort in the substitution of kerosene for whale blubber. They take particular delight in this story because it supposedly exposes the naïveté of the environmentalists who presumably would have predicted the end to indoor lighting because of shortages of whales. By the same token, if the soil eroded, farmers could happily find the necessary nutrients in guano. Once the guano deposits became exhausted, farmers could conveniently turn to manufactured fertilizers. This procedure contributes to another form of scarcity since it requires a heavy consumption of fossil fuels.

This industry created another danger. Chemists soon learned that the same process for producing nitrogen fertilizers could also yield powerful explosives, which could then be used by military forces to fight over access to oil and other resources. Similarly, as fossil fuels become scarcer, many observers expect that atomic energy will become more acceptable, probably leading to a further proliferation of nuclear weapons.

For economists, scarcity ultimately becomes impossible because everything always has a substitute. Just as money can purchase any type of commodity, industry can always find some replacement for any seeming scarcity. Economists believe that before some potential scarcity might cripple a vital technological process, some new technology—in economics jargon, a "backstop technology"—will successfully replace the supposedly endangered one. Not only will the backstop technology substitute for the older one, it will also prove to be a superior technology.

This faith in the possibility of successful substitution suggests an interconnectedness in the economic environment, comparable in some ways to the interconnectedness that environmentalists see. This interconnectedness extends to technology as well. Frequently scientific discoveries intended for a relatively narrow purpose in one industry unexpectedly spill over into other industries, often with extraordinary results.

Economists, however, obscure another sort of interconnectedness when addressing the detrimental effects of the sort of pollution that individual industries spew out upon one another, as well as upon society as a whole. Rather than acknowledge such interconnectedness as commonplace, economists classify it as an externality since the price system does not reflect these effects.

Substitutability, of course, is indeed real in many cases. For example, metal, plastic, and glass can all serve as construction materials. Nonetheless, substitutability has limits. For example, new technology can minimize water requirements, suggesting a degree of substitutability, but ultimately water remains a necessity for life for which no substitute is possible. In addition, converting to substitute materials can require time. Recall the British fear of a shortage of timber for making ships. Today, steel is the primary material for constructing vessels, but the British could not suddenly turn to metal ships. The creation of the technical infrastructure required for the conversion to metal would have required considerable time, even if the British had already possessed the requisite technical knowledge.

In an even larger sense, substitutability is ultimately impossible. Yes, just as with water, we can conserve energy, but literally everything we do creates entropy.

Of course, if nuclear power could be safe and economical, producers could tap a huge reservoir of potential energy, pushing back the boundaries imposed by the Second Law of Thermodynamics. Even so, the boundaries still exist. Fortunately or unfortunately, depending upon one's point of view, nuclear power is still uneconomic. To make matters worse, nobody has yet discovered a way to decommission a plant economically or to safely store nuclear waste products. Even where commercial nuclear power plants exist, they do so only because of the benefit of enormous subsidies. For example, nobody in their right mind would ever dream of building a nuclear power plant if they had to face full exposure from the liability of major accidents. In the United States, the Price–Anderson Act protects the nuclear industry from all but a small portion of the potential liability of a major accident.

The underlying conception behind the faith in substitutability comes from what economists take to be a certainty that the price system will somehow provide the appropriate signals to induce entrepreneurs to take the correct action. In particular, Harold Hotelling's classic article, "The Economics of Exhaustible Resources," attempted to prove that under ideal conditions nonrenewable resource prices should or would rise at a rate equal to the real rate of interest (Hotelling 1931). These rising prices will supposedly warn of the need for conservation, leading people to adopt technologies and consumption patterns that increasingly economize on resources as they become scarcer. Consequently, according to the conventional economic perspective markets have the capacity to ration scarce goods efficiently.

Let me mention two problems with the theory of substitutability. While substitutability sounds wonderful in theory, in practice, people in authority rarely display much confidence in the concept. Recall the words of Winston Churchill regarding the importance of maintaining access to strategic resources. Consider how often the United States has intervened in the affairs of countries upon which it relies for oil. If substitutability seemed practical such activities would have little purpose.

In addition, efforts to devise more efficient use of a resource can be self-defeating. As Jevons had already observed in his *Coal Question*, efficiencies, which might be expected to conserve a resource, can actually make even more intensive use of those resources attractive (Jevons 1906, pp. 152 ff.; see also Binswanger 2001).

Resources and the Farm Worker Paradox

Long-distance trade dates back to prehistoric times. Much of the early trade consisted of luxury goods, but some necessities, such as salt and obsidian (used for arrow heads), were also objects of trade. The economic advantages of trade have been at the heart of economic orthodoxy for more than 200 years. For example, John Maynard Keynes once recalled:

> I was brought up, like most Englishmen, to respect free trade not only as an economic doctrine which a rational and instructed person could not doubt but almost as a part of the moral law. I regarded departures from it as being at the same time an imbecility and an outrage. (Keynes 1933, p. 233)

In the same article, Keynes dared to express some doubt about this doctrine:

> over an increasingly wide range of industrial products, and perhaps of agricultural products also, I become doubtful whether the economic cost of national self-sufficiency is great enough to outweigh the other advantages of gradually bringing the producer and the consumer within the ambit of the same national, economic and financial organisation. Experience accumulates to prove that the most modern mass-production processes can be performed in most countries and climates with almost equal efficiency. (Keynes 1933, p. 238)

Two points are worth mentioning here. First, Keynes never seems to have followed up these thoughts about national self-sufficiency, or what economists call autarky. Second, Keynes implicitly seems to recognize that trade in many raw materials would still be a necessity even if countries were to decide to minimize their international economic engagement. As the world becomes increasingly complex, the dream of autarky slips even further beyond reach for two reasons. First, other things being equal, the larger the country, the less is the dependence on international trade. One could hardly expect a tiny nation, such as Monaco, to have domestic access to every kind of resource, much less to be able to produce the full spectrum of products associated with life in a modern economy. With the fragmentation of states, such as the USSR and Yugoslavia, reliance on trade becomes more necessary.

More important, new technology multiplies the number of essential materials. Just think about the difficulties created by the fire at the Sumitomo glue factory. In this context, no modern economy can be absolutely self-sufficient.

In any case, trade allows a nation relatively bereft of resources, such as Holland—especially before the discovery of the North Sea energy supplies—to still enjoy the prosperity that the early British economists so much admired. Theoretically, such trade should make all parties better off. To the extent that international trade allows economies to exchange as equals, as John Evelyn had suggested earlier in this chapter, trade "makes the world's inhabitants one Family." Theoretically, Saudi Arabia with little water can exchange oil for imported crops that require considerable moisture to the advantage of both sides of the trade. This sort of mutually beneficial exchange framed the comfortable vision behind Keynes's earlier cited description of the London businessman enjoying the benefits of commodities produced around the globe.

In much trade, Evelyn's imagined family is thoroughly dysfunctional, in the sense that one party captures the majority of the benefits, often even impoverishing the other side in the process. For example, the great European powers were shameless in their rush to loot their colonies, leaving a legacy that still haunts many parts of the world. Besides the materials they took and the lives that they destroyed, the colonial powers left an institutional structure that still makes life difficult.

The modern economic system consigns those parts of the world that lack the wherewithal to provide a decent life for their people to the role of specializing in the least rewarding, most dangerous, and most ecologically destructive activities known to mankind. In fact, Lawrence Summers, then vice president of the World Bank and later secretary of the Treasury of the United States, suggested that Africa was actually under-polluted. He meant that an obvious economic activity for that part of the world was to earn revenue by accepting the toxic waste from the more affluent societies. In his words:

> I've always thought that under-populated countries in Africa are vastly under-polluted; their air quality is probably vastly inefficiently low [sic] compared to Los Angeles or Mexico City. Only the lamentable facts that so much pollution is generated by non-tradable industries (transport, electrical generation) and that the unit transport costs of solid waste are so high prevent world—welfare-enhancing trade in air pollution and waste. (Anon. 1992)

Indeed, toxic waste dumping in Africa can run as low as 1 percent of the cost of disposal in the United States (Clapp 2001, p. 23). The tensions created by such imperialistic trade can produce vulnerabilities that can eventually come back to haunt those that abuse their power.

Ignoring abusive trade relations for the moment, international trade can obscure problems, desensitizing the market to impending disasters. In a world in which each region is relatively self-sufficient, shortages might be more frequent, but they would affect relatively small numbers of people. As a result, people are more likely to be alert to such dangers.

Obviously, trade can often relieve local shortages, as was the case with British timber. Gradually, the widespread relief of many local shortages may set the stage for massive global shortages. People would be likely to rely on the price system to register oncoming shortages. Unfortunately, these potential global shortages may not register in the price system, especially so long as trade allows for substitute supplies. The tragic fate of the passenger pigeons discussed in the next section demonstrates the inadequacy of the price system.

Consider the example of water, an essential element of life. In the United States, most people use water with abandon. In addition, business carelessly degrades fragile water supplies by allowing dangerous pollutants to make valuable water resources undrinkable. Moreover, development prevents the recharge of groundwater by covering an increasing area of the land with cement.

In many other parts of the world, water is already truly scarce. Raising the price may encourage rationing, but at a horrendous human cost. For example, in one notorious case, Bolivia privatized the Cochabamba water company. The new owners, controlled by Bechtel a highly influential U.S. corporation, raised the price of water. Once the people began to revolt, journalists from the United States discovered that the company was expecting people earning the pitiful monthly minimum wage of about $67 to pay approximately $20 for their water. Only after the military used excessive violence against protesters, leaving a young boy dead and hundreds wounded, did the government reluctantly rescind the contract with Bechtel (Rothfeder 2001, p. 109; Finnegan 2002). Bechtel is currently suing Bolivia for restitution.

In South Africa, many people responded to excessive water prices following privatization more passively by turning to polluted water sources, resulting in a cholera epidemic with more than 100,000 cases in a single year. According to an editorial in the British medical journal, *The Lancet*:

> Ebrahim Asmal of the South African Human Rights' Commission noted that about 60% of households in affected areas had inadequate sanitation and, in one province studied, up to 90% of new water connections were not fully functional. He also alluded to last year's assertion that the epidemic started after water supplies were cut because users could not pay newly introduced water fees. Community cost-recovery programmes, promoted by the International Monetary Fund, are a key component of the government's much-criticised macroeconomic policy. Yet, Asmal notes that the country spends approximately R4 billion (US$500 million) treating diarrhoea and dysentery a year, whereas only about R750 million was spent on water in the past financial year. (Morris 2001)

Unlike whale oil, no substitutes for water are on the horizon. Yes, technology can help to conserve water, but water itself remains a necessity. Corporate leaders are currently pressuring countries to allow them to collect their fresh water reserves for a pittance so that they can export it to more arid parts of the earth. That strategy is sure to speed up the inevitable crisis in water.

The Perverse Incentives of Markets

Although the depletion of stocks of the inanimate resources might seem to be a necessary consequence of economic activity, market forces place demands on renewable sources faster than natural processes can replenish them. One of the first hints that market forces are inimical to environmental sustainability came from a British surveyor named John Richards in 1730. Richards estimated the annual yield from allowing a 50-year-old oak tree to survive an additional 50 years to maturity. Comparing the timber yield from the 50-year-old and 100-year-old tree, Richards calculated an increase equivalent to a little more than 3 percent per year. Since the prevailing interest rate at the time was almost double that, economic logic suggested that harvesting the tree at 50 years was preferable to allowing it to survive to maturity (see Scorgie 1996, p. 245). So, while good forestry practices call for a longer harvest period, market incentives impose a conflicting requirement.

Colin Clark addressed an even more intractable problem: the harvesting of whales. He estimated that blue whales had a maximum per annum reproductive potential of perhaps 4–5 percent (Clark 1973, pp. 631–32). Given a much higher expected return on capital, protecting the whale from extinction made no economic sense. He concluded:

> The standard economic argument for the overexploitation of resources (based on the logic of the Tragedy of the Commons [which I will discuss later]) neatly lay[s] the blame on open competition, particularly among the impoverished and powerless. Yet the most spectacular and threatening developments of today, such as the reduction of the whale stocks and the demersal fisheries on the Grand Banks, can by no means be attributed to impoverished and local fishermen. On the contrary, it is large, high-powered ships and the factory fleets of the wealthiest nation's that are now the real danger. (Clark 1973, p. 631)

In other words, profit maximization demands that the most profitable strategy for harvesting whales is to hunt them quickly. Specific whale populations have already disappeared. For example, by 1828, whale hunters had already almost extinguished the bowhead whales remaining in the waters off Greenland's east coast. Today there are none whatsoever (Allen and Keay 2001).

In strictly economic terms, preservation of the species makes no sense because even the stingiest savings account produces interest income faster than whales reproduce themselves (Pimm 1997). Reviewing the standard economic theory of the rational exploitation of fisheries in a market economy, Vernon Smith, in his classic article on the subject, concluded: "This theory...is not able to handle the situation in which a species may be depleted to the point of extinction.... This is perhaps one of the more serious deficiencies of the received doctrine" (Smith 1969, p. 196).

Rather than admit that the decline of the whale stocks confirms the fact that markets are inimical to sustainability, economists commonly trumpet the substitution of oil for whales as evidence of the triumph of the market. By the same logic, concern about looming shortages of fossil fuel must be ill founded since some new technology will once again provide an economical alternative.

Passenger Pigeons

No case better illustrates how markets conflict with sustainability than the fate of the passenger pigeon. In this vein, Gardner Brown, an economist from the University of Washington, once wrote: "The passenger pigeon is a marvelous case study for the economist" (Brown 1990, p. 212). How right he was! Certainly, the fate of the now-extinct creature stands as a stark warning about the inadequacy of the price system. Jennifer Price offered a glimpse into the world of the passenger pigeon before its demise:

> They say that when a flock of passenger pigeons flew across the countryside, the sky grew dark. The air rumbled and turned cold. Bird dung fell like hail. Horses stopped and trembled in their tracks, and chickens went in to roost. "I was suddenly struck with astonishment at a loud rushing roar, succeeded by instant darkness," the ornithologist Alexander Wilson wrote after he encountered a pigeon flock along the Ohio River in the early 1800s: "I took [it] for a tornado, about to overwhelm the house and everything around in destruction." Wilson sat down to watch the flock pass over, and after five hours, he estimated that it had been 240 miles long and numbered over two billion birds. (Price 1999, p. 1; internally citing Wilson 1832, pp. 201–04)

Price continued:

> A typical wild-pigeon roost blanketed hundreds of square miles of forest. The underbrush died, the trees were entirely denuded of their leaves, dung piled up inches deep, and century-old trees keeled over under the cumulative weight of the nine-ounce birds. (Price 1999, p. 3)

This unfortunate creature was doubly cursed by both instinct and market forces. At the sound of gunshots, the frightened birds would flock together, making them an easy target for hunters. Worse yet for the bird's reproductive potential, each female produced only one egg per year.

Widespread commercial hunting did not begin until about 1840 although early New England settlers already hunted passenger pigeons. Within a decade the creature was in serious decline in New England:

> The last significant nesting in New England happened in 1851, near the town of Lunenburg, Massachusetts. The following year, Henry David Thoreau wrote: "Saw pigeons in the woods, with their inquisitive necks and long tails, but few representatives of the great flocks that once broke down our forests." (Steinberg 2002, p. 67; internally citing Foster 1999, p. 167)

By the 1860s, hunts of grand proportions became common in the Middle West (Tober 1981, p. 94). Consider just how grand these proportions were. James Tober, a student of Brown's, wrote:

> From Hartford, Michigan in 1869, 3 carloads per day were shipped to market for forty days, which yielded a total of 11,880,000 pigeons. Another Michigan town was reported to have shipped some 15,840,000 birds over a two-year period. From the Michigan nesting of 1874, a single railroad station is reported to have shipped 80 barrels per day, each containing from 30 to 50 dozen birds, for the length of the nesting season. Two reports from the Shelby, Michigan nesting of 1876 suggest that 350,000 and 398,000 birds were shipped per week. (p. 95)

> The last major nesting occurred near Petoskey, Michigan, in the spring and summer of 1878, with an estimated total shipment of 1,500,000 dead birds and 80,352 live from Petoskey station alone. (Tober 1981, p. 96; citing Roney 1907, p. 92)

This massive slaughter soon took its toll. According to Stephen Gould:

> By 1870, birds were reproducing only in the Great Lakes region. Hunters used the newly invented telegraph to inform others about the location of dwindling populations. Perhaps the last large wild flock, some 250,000 birds, was sighted in 1896. A gaggle of hunters, alerted by telegraph, converged upon them; fewer than 10,000 birds flew away. (Gould 1993, p. 54)

People comforted themselves by regarding the collapse of the population as a temporary phenomenon. In 1897, *Western Field and Stream* wrote that the birds were "as liable to return at any time as unexpectedly as they went." *Forest and Stream*, in 1899, supposed that the species would "live long in the land, but never again as a bird found in enormous numbers" (cited in Tober 1981, p. 94).

Soon thereafter the passenger pigeon disappeared from the planet. The last member of the species, named Martha, died in the Cincinnati Zoo on September 1, 1914, at the approximate age of 29 years. For the next couple of decades, purported sightings of passenger pigeons (like those of Elvis) trickled in, but none were verified (Price 1999, p. 48).

The tragic combination of market forces and instinct sealed this creature's fate. Recall that, following Hotelling, economic theory teaches that the price of the bird should have risen as its numbers dwindled, signaling to all concerned that they should respond to the looming scarcity by economizing on the resource. In fact, nothing of the sort happened with this unfortunate creature. According to Gardner Brown and Barry Field, "The passenger pigeon became extinct with hardly a ripple in its commercial price" (Brown and Field 1978, p. 241). Later, Brown added: "Since price did not rise to signal growing scarcity, there was no economic force inducing entrepreneurs to attempt to save the pigeon" (Brown 1990, p. 212).

According to economists who dismiss the threat of scarcity, a combination of new technology and substitution provides alternatives to scarce resources. In the case of the passenger pigeon, these forces actually contributed to the extinction of the bird.

In so far as substitution is concerned, people regarded the bird as a close substitute for chicken. According to Brown:

> The market price of passenger pigeons did not rise, because chicken was regarded as a close market substitute and the price of chicken remained stable during the passenger pigeon's demise. Since price did not rise to signal growing scarcity, there was no economic force inducing entrepreneurs to attempt to save the pigeon, because there was no evident economic scarcity rent to be earned. (Brown 1990, p. 212)

Even though the price did not increase, hunting the birds was so easy that the enterprise remained profitable, despite their dwindling numbers. Here technology contributed to the problem. The rapid spread of the railroad at the time meant that sellers could ship the birds on ice over a longer distance (Farrow 1995), thereby hastening the demise of the bird. In addition, the telegraph made the slaughter more "efficient."

Although Hotelling's elegant theory may give comfort to those who advocate market-based management of the environment, evidence that the price system will work in the way that he proposed is lacking— certainly in the case of the passenger pigeon.

Neither substitution nor technology helped prevent the extinction. The supply of chicken held prices down, preventing the market from signaling an impending shortage, while the railroad expanded the demand for the bird.

Looking at this case from a purely economic perspective, however, a cynic could assert that the scarcity problem was nonexistent. After all, because consumers could substitute chicken for passenger pigeons, the extinction caused them no hardship at all. Of course, resources have value over and above their capacity to serve an immediate economic need. They may have a potential that is presently unknown, as was the case with helium, which I will discuss in chapter 3.

In conclusion, the case of the passenger pigeon indicates that the warnings, which Hotelling theorized would signal a growing scarcity, do not always occur. Frequently, the price system fails to give even a hint of an impending disaster. The extinction of the passenger pigeon offers a particularly sad illustration of how markets fail to promote conservation.

The Tragedy of the Commons

The market figures prominently in two competing explanations for environmental disasters, including extinctions such as that of the passenger pigeon. According to the earlier sections of this chapter, markets pose an environmental danger. I described how market forces give people an incentive to use resources with abandon because they take little or no account of the future costs to society of wasteful practices.

A competing theory proposes that markets offer the best possible approach to providing environmental protection. Garrett Hardin, a conservative biologist, wrote the classic statement of this proposition during the salad days of the environmental movement in an article entitled, "The Tragedy of the Commons" (Hardin 1968). The "Commons" in the title referred to the land that traditional English villagers shared for grazing their animals.

With no evidence whatsoever, except for an obscure nineteenth-century pamphlet, Hardin insisted that the absence of property rights in the English common lands inevitably led to an environmental disaster. Based on his limited understanding of traditional English land-use patterns, Hardin declared that without private property, each individual would selfishly attempt to graze as many animals as possible on a finite area of land, putting excessive stress on the environment. Hardin's story has been so widely circulated that it has become commonly believed. Even serious environmental books frequently reprint the article.

Experts in British rural history dismiss Hardin's account. Specialists who have done extensive research about contemporary collective ownership also dispute Hardin's contention that such an arrangement will necessarily cause excessive use of the environment. They distinguish between open access systems where anybody is free to take all that they want and a commons, in which people work out rules for sharing a resource. These scholars have found that traditional societies frequently developed effective ethical codes to ensure both sustainable aggregate harvests and a relatively equitable distribution of access to resources. They report that traditional societies have created arrangements that are "far more binding on individual conscience than any government regulations could ever be" (Sethi and Somanathan 1996, p. 766). Rather than belabor the details of this subject, I would direct the reader to Elinor Ostrum's excellent introduction to the literature that she prepared for economists (see Ostrum 2000).

Of course, the power of Hardin's article had less to do with its historical veracity than its comforting message for those who wish to nurture faith in the market. The evidence that Hardin mustered was little stronger than an urban myth. No matter that he was wrong; no matter that these villages had institutions that actually prevented the overuse of the commons—Hardin's article continues to be read. The intended lesson is supposed to be that no reasonable alternatives to the market exist.

Grow or Die

Although Hardin contended that nonmarket societies are inevitably antithetical to sustainability, in fact, market societies present a far greater threat to sustainability. Just as riding a bicycle requires enough forward momentum to avoid a spill, a market economy must continue to grow or else it may risk crashing. Without the potential of growth, investment dries up. Without investment, the economy withers. Blair Sandler cleverly dubbed this characteristic of markets as GOD, "Grow or Die" (Sandler 1994).

Business is not alone in needing growth. Without growth, labor too will suffer within the framework of a market economy, unless output continues to grow. The incessant increase in productivity means that each year fewer and fewer workers are able to create the same quantity of goods and services. In addition, population tends to grow each year. The combination of the displacement of workers by technology and the increase in the population of workers means that output must grow enough to avoid growing unemployment. In the U.S. economy, this growth rate comes to about 2.5 percent each year.

Of course, this inherent necessity for growth eventually comes up against environmental limitations. For the most part, low prices for resources obscure the nature of these limits. Recall Thomas Nixon Carver's observation that farmers in the United States would not have ever made a profit if they would have had to reimburse the economy for the value of the soil fertility that they destroyed in the process of growing crops.

The destruction of soil fertility need not present an immediate barrier for a society. In the United States, for example, farmers would typically use up the soil fertility on their farms and then move further west. Where untapped land resources are unavailable, a nation can import food after its soil becomes too infertile. But for the world as a whole, such options are not available. Often an economy can transcend environmental limitations through technology, as in the case of the manufacture of artificial fertilizers to replenish the soil. However, these technologies cannot work indefinitely, because they also draw down resources.

The example of artificial fertilizers reminds us that the validity of Carver's remark is not restricted to agriculture; it holds for the economy as a whole. So, while the fortunate market participants pocket huge profits, the corresponding environmental damage represents a loss of even greater proportions reflecting the depletion, dispersion, and contamination of resources. At first glance, the inclusion of the dispersion of resources might not seem obvious. For example, per capita wealth of the third of the world's population living in the Indian subcontinent and in Africa below the Sahara has declined, even where conventionally measured growth occurred (Dasgupta 2001).

In chapter 3, I will discuss the importance of helium for high technology. When helium is used and released into the atmosphere, the atoms remain intact yet become less available for future use. Industry, of course, could recapture the helium from the atmosphere, but to do so is relatively expensive, both in terms of money and the resources required for the process.

The monetary cost of resources typically includes both the cost of extraction and a rent that goes to the supposed owner. The extraction cost is often typically relatively small, reflecting the cost of digging or pumping the resource from the ground. The rent may be much more than extraction costs but it would rarely, if ever, cover the full cost of restoring the resource.

Theoretically, the replacement of petroleum would involve growing crops and then heating them while they are held under great pressure. Of course, the energy required to grow the crops and cook them would be greater than the energy embodied in the artificial petroleum, not to mention the other resource costs of the manufacture of the artificial petroleum. As a result, efforts to replace the initial usage of petroleum would result in a net loss of energy. In short, full restoration is impossible.

On a more subtle level, economic activity also undermines what are sometimes called ecosystem services. Gretchen Daily defines these ecosystem services as "the conditions and processes through which natural ecosystems, and the species that make them up, sustain and fulfill human life. These services maintain biodiversity and the production of ecosystem goods" (Daily 1997a, p. 3).

In some cases, these environmental services parallel commercial economic activity. For example, farmers hire beekeepers to bring in hives to pollinate their trees. We could compare the harm done to bees, say by pesticides, with the amount that commercial operations would charge to do comparable work. In other cases, no comparable commercial activity substitutes for such natural services.

A number of researchers have attempted to calculate the value of ecosystem services. One widely circulated estimate put the value of natural services at about twice as much as the market value of the world's economic output (Costanza et al. 1997). Another recent study compared the value of five ecosystems before and after development. In every case, the loss of economic services, such as storm and flood protection, atmospheric carbon sinks, hunting, and tourism at least, outweighed the marketed benefits that came with conversion, often by a large amount (Balmford et al. 2002).

This study did not address the value of services that are not currently marketed as commodities. Without some of these nonmarketed services, such as the conversion of carbon dioxide to oxygen and plant mass, life itself would be impossible to sustain. In this spirit, Daily warned: "It is, of course, eminently clear that the total value of ecosystem services is infinite—we could not possibly live without them. But establishing sound ecosystem conservation policies requires determining the costs of destroying the next unit of relatively intact natural habitat" (Daily 1997b, p. 366).

Marsh's description of the complexity of the ecosystem stands as an eloquent reminder of the impossibility of accurate measurement. Daily, herself, went on to explain why any attempt to measure the value of habitats services faces insurmountable difficulties.

Resilience

The fate of the passenger pigeon illustrates a larger point about the depletion of environmental resources. Although the extinction of the passenger pigeon was not unavoidable, nobody seemed to have realized what was happening at the time. In the beginning, the population of these birds was so massive that the possibility of extinction probably would seem absolutely implausible.

Once widespread hunting became a matter of course, few people would have reason to believe that the effect of their individual behavior would have much of an impact on the overall population. The resilience of the population, which might have seemed almost limitless when the hunting first began, gradually eroded. This imperceptible deterioration continued until it was too late. All of a sudden, the pigeon disappeared.

Discontinuities of this sort are common in nature, but difficult to predict. We know, for example, that a healthy human body often can absorb shock after shock, seemingly impervious to the damage that chemicals or foreign organisms inflict upon it—at least for a while. At some point, however, as the intensity of these traumas increases the body loses its capacity to recover. Many ecosystems respond to shocks in a similar manner. At some point, cumulative damage will weaken the ecosystem so much that the slightest pressure can wreak havoc on it (Scheffer et al. 2001). Markets tend to value an ecosystem by the quantity of harvestable resources available. In the case of the population of a specific species, such as the passenger pigeon, an objective observer might be able to collect sufficient information to be able to evaluate the evidence of its future survivability. However, we must understand such numerical estimates in light of the fact that once a breeding population falls beneath a certain threshold, survivability of the species becomes questionable.

Today, probably not a day goes by without some species going extinct. The story of the passenger pigeon may seem more dramatic than contemporary extinctions because the demise of the species owed more to the direct hunting of the bird rather than a systemic undermining of its habitat. Ecosystems typically lack early warning signals of massive change that overhunting might possibly generate.

Gretchen Daily raised a question about the value of resilience in her book on the value of nature's services, observing: "A high-diversity system is assigned the same total value as a low-diversity system with the same number of functional groups because the probable added value of diversity remains poorly known and thus accounts for nothing at present" (Daily 1997b, p. 366). She went on to ask how much ecological stability and resilience might be worth. Unfortunately, no easy answers are forthcoming.

How can the market automatically generate price signals that prevent people from stressing the system to the tipping point at which it becomes vulnerable? I believe that markets are incapable of generating prices that take resilience into account for several reasons. To begin with, as I discussed earlier, markets tend to be focused on the near term, discounting future problems. In addition, markets focus on individual pieces of the puzzle of resilience. In other words, seen through the perspective of the market process, an ecosystem may impact with a number of markets—say a market for timber, a market for game, and a market for plants that could be harvested within it. Each of these individual markets generate prices, but no process exists to ensure that the sum total of these prices relates to the overall health of the ecosystem. Just as the individual hunter of the passenger pigeon had little reason to believe that his own activity was crucial for the fate of the bird, participants in these separate markets have no reason to consider the impact of their actions on the other markets, let alone on the non-priced elements of the ecosystem.

Rather than putting a value on resilience, the market system actually tends to create strong incentives to reduce the resilience of ecosystems, since simplified systems tend to reduce direct economic costs. For example, in the United States, seed companies bred virtually all the hybrid corn with a single gene, Texas Male Sterile, to save the trivial cost of hiring about 125,000 high school students to cut the tassels off the breeding stock. By removing some of the genetic variability of the corn plant, this technology reduced the resilience of corn, leaving it more susceptible to some system-wide pathogen. In this particular case, the corn crop lost its resistance to a strain of a fungus disease, *helminthosporium maydis*, commonly known as corn leaf blight (Perelman 1977, p. 47).

Although a few isolated scientific studies had warned that the sterility gene weakens plants, this problem escaped commercial agricultural interests until 1970, when an outbreak wiped out 43 percent of the crop in South Carolina. The agricultural sector feared that comparable losses were possible across the nation, but fortunately a favorable weather pattern held the losses to 15 percent for the nation (Perelman 1977, p. 47).

Interestingly enough, the seed industry, working together with the United States Department of Agriculture, is getting ready to commercialize a genetic modification to cause plants to become sterile to prevent farmers from replanting their seeds (see Perelman 2002, chapter 4). This ominous project goes well beyond the breeding of sterile hybrid corn. Whether the unintended consequences of this so-called terminator gene will also be correspondingly greater remains a matter of conjecture.

Concluding Remark

This chapter has tried to make the case that markets are ill equipped to manage natural resources. Next, I will turn to the nature of economic theory. That material will help to show why economists have been relatively insensitive to the problem of sustainability.

3

Value

Economic Logic

E conomics consists of two distinct layers of theory. The most superficial one comprises self-evident propositions that are virtually unquestionable. Within this context, economics teaches that an individual prefers more to less; that lower prices encourage consumption and discourage an individual firm from increasing production. All of these propositions would seem to represent common sense rather than some scientific insight.

Notice that each of these propositions refers to the behavior of an individual, acting in isolation. Economics based on such common sense sometimes works relatively well in simple situations. For example, you can feel fairly confident that if a large number of people move into town without a corresponding increase in the number of housing units, rents will increase.

Problems emerge when economists attempt to go beyond such commonsensical statements. The quest for a scientific foundation of economics revolves around the purported rationality of human beings. Rather than show how individuals actually behave, economists develop equations to describe a world in which every agent sets out to maximize utility or profit through ultrarational behavior. Economists find comfort in their assumption that human behavior is rational, even though that approach makes their work less applicable to the real world. At least, the mathematical formulation of this imaginary world has the look and feel of science.

Cognitive psychologists, who specialize in studying the way people actually behave, see the world quite differently. They are forever discovering the irrationality of human behavior. Of course, creating mathematical equations to predict irrational behavior is virtually impossible.

Even rational behavior can violate the tenets of economics. For instance, economists postulate that people will purchase goods at the lowest possible prices. In reality, high prices can actually encourage people to purchase a commodity because many people take low prices as a signal of an inferior quality. For example, a number of software developers found that they were only able to increase the market for their products after they raised their prices. In addition, consumers sometimes prefer to purchase goods with higher prices because of the snob effect—that other people would see their display of such goods as evidence of affluence.

Economists face more vexing problems when they try to move beyond postulating the actions of an isolated individual, yet a modern economy consists of a complex network of interactions among a large number of people. Economists have no way of capturing this complexity of human interactions. Instead, they are left to basing their reasoning upon highly simplified models that, more often than not, leave out essential elements of the subject matter.

Economists, however, rarely give any indication that their results are more tenuous when economists make the leap from common sense to a more abstract level of economics. Instead, they adopt an unmerited certitude supposedly befitting their scientific pretensions.

Part of the problem reflects the structure of graduate training in economics. Earning a Ph.D. in economics today is extraordinarily demanding. Students must master difficult mathematical and statistical techniques. Success in these endeavors is far more important than acquiring knowledge about the real world. What matters is an ability to propose an idea in a formal economic model, or better yet, to present some data that is consistent with the model, often only after finding clever ways to manipulate this data.

The model must be novel, but excessive novelty, especially on the part of a young economist, will bring a strong rebuke. So the road to success is to work within the mainstream, do something ever so slightly innovative, while displaying sophisticated mathematics or statistical techniques.

For a young economist to dare to venture too far afield would be foolhardy. Worse yet, the curriculum is so demanding that few graduate students could have the time to pursue broader intellectual interests. Once the student has sunk so much time and energy in an effort to master up-to-date technical skills, throwing them overboard would have to seem dauntingly risky. Instead, economists become protective of their academic investment.

Value Theory

When pressed to explain the basis of their theory, economists do not appeal to common sense, but rather to what they call value theory. At first glance, the economists' value theory seems reasonable enough. They conceptualize the economy as a network of relationships in which each supplier attempts to maximize its individual profits. Following Adam Smith, economists set out to show that the invisible hand of the market leads all concerned to the best of all possible worlds.

Robert Lucas, a Nobel Prize–winning economist, expressed this side of economics with a clarity that is unusual among economists:

> The central lesson of economic theory is the proposition that a competitive economy, left to its own devices, will do a good job of allocating resources. . . . This is the basic message of nineteenth century economics and has continued into the twentieth century. Recurrent depressions and occasional inflation were something of an embarrassment to this theory, but these tended to be brief and it was not unreasonable to hope that some reform of monetary institutions could be found that could eliminate or mitigate them. These beliefs were very widely shared in the pre-1929 capitalist economies, not just by a few economists but by the public at large. (Lucas 1979, p. 4)

Adam Smith offered a literary analogy to express his belief in market efficiency. The most influential economists of the nineteenth century were intent on making Smith's case in a more scientific manner. They set out to prove that in a competitive economy the combined efforts of the individual suppliers turn a given allotment of resources into a maximum output of value—ignoring for the moment that I am glossing over some of the finer points of value theory.

Value, at least in the economic sense of the word, is a strange concept. The term, value, originally seems to have begun as a simple expression for comparison of the relative worth of various commodities. In the hands of economists, value has become almost metaphysical. All the while, common usage of the word, value, easily slid from economic value to religious values, family values, and back to economic value again. Ironically, while the English language labels matters of real importance as invaluable, the market system tends to devastate any element that lacks a price, whether it be the air or the water upon which life itself depends.

Although the economists' version of value operates as metaphysically as Adam Smith's invisible hand, economists tend to treat value theory uncritically—with good reason. Whenever an occasional economist ventures into the methodological wilderness to give a deeper analysis, the result is a hopeless muddle.

For economists, value is supposed to convey something comparable to a scientific framework. Just as gravity allows physical bodies to exert force at a distance holding the planets in the solar system in balance, in the real economy, value relations between the multitude of firms and households supposedly hold the economy in balance.

Although the actions of firms and household will reciprocally affect each other just as gravitational forces of physical masses do, this process has none of the predictability of Newtonian physics. Instead, surges of wild and unpredictable speculative behavior buffet the economic system in a fashion that defies scientific explanation.

Ironically, Newton himself, despite his awesome scientific mind, as well as his position as the Warden of the Mint, invested £7,000 in the speculative mania of the South Sea Bubble. When asked about his foolish investment, he is reported to have said that he could calculate the motions of the heavenly bodies, but not the madness of the crowds (Carswell 1960, p. 131).

In a sense, value theory probably should have more in common with the weirdness of quantum theory than the elegant precision of Newtonian mechanics. As a result of ill-informed behavior, the economy experiences a seemingly random pattern of boom and bust. This outcome seems to refute the smooth functioning of the economy predicted by conventional economic theory.

Economists, however, casually explain away such unwelcome events by attributing them to noneconomic events, typically foolish government policies or irresponsible behavior by workers or their unions. If only markets had been freer to function, without some outside interference, nothing of the sort would have happened. Refuting this defense is impossible because no society has ever been foolish enough to give markets absolutely free rein.

Self-Expanding Value

Despite its questionable merits, this "scientific" value theory has far-ranging ramifications for economics. In fact, virtually all abstract economics rests upon an underlying theory of value. More than a century and a half ago, John Stuart Mill, probably the most influential British economist of the time, explained the vital importance of value theory for economics: "Almost every speculation respecting the economical interests of a society thus constituted, implies some theory of Value: the smallest error on that subject infects with corresponding error all our other conclusions; and anything vague or misty in our conception of it, creates confusion and uncertainty in everything else" (Mill 1848, p. 456).

So, despite the overwhelming importance of the concept of value for economic theory, economists typically eschew anything but the narrowest conception of value. When they do say anything at all about the basis of value theory, they typically satisfy themselves with some superficial remarks, then express their supreme confidence about the value of value theory.

Despite economists' reticence to delve deeper into the subject of value, Mill was absolutely correct about the importance of value theory for economic theory. Mill, however, also fell into the trap of overconfidence, continuing his evaluation of the role of value theory with an enormous blunder. Brimming with certainty, he boldly proclaimed:

> Happily, there is nothing in the laws of Value which remains for the present or any future writer to clear up; the theory of the subject is complete: the only difficulty to be overcome is that of so stating it as to solve by anticipation the chief perplexities which occur in applying it: and to do this, some minuteness of exposition, and considerable demands on the patience of the reader, are unavoidable. (Mill 1848, p. 456)

Mill's authority was insufficient to put questions about value theory to rest. However, rather than thinking more deeply about the subject, economists believed that they could make their theory more substantial by recasting it in a mathematical form, following the model of Newtonian physics.

By the 1870s, [mathematically-inclined] economists had succeeded in this task to the satisfaction of most of the profession, making the traditional term, political economy, seem antiquated. The profession embraced the more scientific sounding term, economics.

Given their heroic effort to model economics on physical laws, you might expect economics to resemble natural science. In fact, some of the economists who led the way in making economics more mathematical sought the approval of the most important nineteenth-century physicists regarding their application of the physicists' mathematical techniques. They proudly informed a few eminent physicists of what these economists believed to be their common interests.

Much to the economists' chagrin, the physicists did not reciprocate the respect that economists showered on them. They took umbrage with the economists, observing that their physical theories were built around conservation laws, such as the conservation of matter and the conservation of energy. They insisted that economics could not legitimately pretend to have much in common with natural science without some sort of conservation law (Mirowski 1989a, p. 271 ff.).

The physicist's conservation laws reflected a world strictly bound by the material limits of the environment. The economist's world knew no such bounds. Lacking a counterpart of the conservation laws, economists believed that the proper functioning of the market creates a surplus of value out of the blue.

Moreover, the economists' value was capable of infinite expansion over time. As long as society can put more labor and more capital to work and/or technology improved, the economists believed that output can continue to increase forever. The physicists balked at this aspect of economics. They insisted that the new economic theories had little in common with physics, despite some superficial similarity in some of the equations that their two disciplines used.

In looking at the world around us, the self-expanding nature of value might seem reasonable. Most people today have more stuff than their ancestors did. Think of the aggregate wealth of the community as its stock of houses, cars, clothing, and all the other commodities that contribute to its standard of living.

Over time, while the produced commodities continue to expand, the material base that makes these commodities possible continues to degrade. Gross National Product accounting makes an attempt to calculate the flow of the market values of the commodities that economy produces. The resulting statistics are very imprecise, but they do give a rough idea of the economic growth of markets. Unfortunately, nobody has ever made a comparable effort to estimate the other side of the balance sheet: the losses due to consumption or degradation of the natural resource base.

In fact, some of the losses of the resource base appear as an increase in wealth. For example, as land becomes scarce, its capitalized value increases, indicating an increase in wealth of those who own it. Similarly, the value of forests will increase as they get caught in the squeeze between a shrinking supply and increasing demand.

In addition, nonmarket aspects of life also go unmeasured. For example, the health impacts of polluted air or water or even the time lost in traffic congestion.

Sweeping Time Under the Rug

Despite Mill's confident optimism, as well as the ingenious efforts of later economists to give economic theory a scientific gloss, efforts to build a theory of economics around an abstract value theory floundered. The sort of mathematical economic theory that the economists developed might have made sense if the economy consisted of nothing more than a small, unchanging village in which people awoke each morning to take a fresh harvest of resources and convert them into a daily output.

Not only did this "scientific" theory banish money from the economy, in effect it eliminated time, making confidence in the economists' theoretical proof of efficacy of the economic process difficult to maintain. Let me explain.

In a modern economy, people invest in long-lived capital goods, such as railroads. Although capital goods can function for a long time, technology can destroy their economic values, often with maddening speeds. A realistic value theory would have to address the difficulty of comparing values of durable capital goods over time.

For example, substitute the example of bread for Adam Smith's woolen coat. Part of the process of making bread consists in conveying wheat in railroad cars. The reasoning behind an individual baker's decision whether or not to bake another loaf of bread to sell in the market is not very challenging. The conditions in the market today are probably going to be much like they were yesterday.

A comparable decision for investing in railroads involves enormous speculation. What grounds does anyone have for believing that the investment in railroads will be the ideal one? Perhaps a revolutionary new mode of transportation will become economical in a few years. Or the location of people or industry may move, eliminating much of the market for the railroad.

Expectations about such possibilities can have profound effects on current values. As John Maynard Keynes observed:

> It is by reason of the existence of durable equipment that the economic future is linked to the present. It is, therefore, consonant with, and agreeable to, our broad principles of thought, that the expectation of the future should affect the present through the demand price for durable equipment. (Keynes 1936b, p. 146)

Obviously in ordering a new loaf of bread to stock a grocery store, uncertainty about the future does not create nearly as much of a problem. The grocers need information about the public's eating habits over the next few days, while railroad executives have to concern themselves with the demand for transportation more than 30 years hence. Later, in this chapter, I will argue that economics discounts the future, making what happens 30 years from now largely irrelevant. The railroad example might seem to contradict that idea. The problem is that most heavy investments, such as railroads, cannot repay themselves in a short period of time. Typically they can only become economical if the company can spread the cost of the investment over a substantial period of time.

Those who are responsible for the decision to purchase plant and equipment have no way of ascertaining what the future demand for their product will be or if alternative technologies will make their investment obsolete before it can pay for itself.

The more permanent an investment is, the more that uncertainty pervades the decision-making process. But the efficiency of the overall process of making bread depends in part upon the efficiency of the transportation system that conveys wheat from the farmer to the miller to the baker and then to the final consumer.

The example of the railroad emphasizes the importance of understanding the complications of economic decision-making under uncertain conditions. This problem increases with the durability of the investment. It is insignificant for a loaf of bread that will be sold tomorrow; it will be a major factor in the price of a railroad.

For the most part, economists are understandably uneasy in having to confront the concept of time. Léon Walras, one of the great pioneers of modern economics, wrote: "Once the equilibrium has been established in principle, exchange can take place immediately. Production, however, requires a certain lapse of time. We shall resolve the second difficulty purely and simply by ignoring the time element at this point" (Walras 1874, p. 242).

Walras's solution to the problem of time might strike you as silly, but modern economists have not advanced much beyond his approach. They have applied sophisticated mathematical techniques, which give the impression of scientific analysis, but they do little to come to grips with the complexity that the concept of time requires. For example, in his introduction to a book of articles by John Nash, the mathematician who won the Nobel Prize in economics and made famous by the Academy Award winning film, A Beautiful Mind, Ken Binmore wrote: "Nash's 1951 paper [freed] economists . . . of the need they had previously perceived to spell out the dynamics of the relevant equilibrating process before being able to talk about the equilibrium to which it will converge in the long run" (Binmore 1996, p. xii). In other words, an abstract mathematical theorem shows how each of the decision makers in an unrealistic economy might instantaneously arrive at choices so that the outcomes for the economy as a whole will be consistent with one another.

Imagine that a team of anthropologists were to happen upon a tribe of primitive people who expressed such unquestioning confidence in such a nebulous concept. In addition, suppose this tribe would ostracize any members who would dare to question this concept. Modern observers would be likely to find such behavior irrational. However, since economists base their value theory upon the presumption of ultrarational behavior, they might seem to inoculate themselves against the charge of irrationality, except when you realize the limited scope of rationality that they accept. The absence of time in their theory is only one of many such defects.

Value Theory and Discounting

Orthodox economists would not accept my interpretation that they have banished time from their theory. Typically, economists appeal to a standard practice in speculative markets to find a way of getting around the difficulties presented by future uncertainties. Consider the formation of a price for a piece of real estate. Theoretically, the market valuation process has three dimensions. First, the participants in the real estate market have to estimate the range of possibilities for each potential payoff period in the future. For example, rents this year might be $50, $200, or $300, depending on circumstances. More generally, these numbers ultimately depend upon some combination of the expectations about both the future sales price and the rents that the property will earn prior to its sale to the next buyer.

Then, the prospective purchasers have to apply a probability to each of these possibilities to calculate an expected payoff for each future period. For example, in the three possible rental outcomes, there might be an 80 percent probability that the rents will be $200 and a 10 percent chance for both the higher and the lower possible rents. Given these probabilities, the buyer will calculate an expected return by multiplying the $200 outcome by 0.8 and the other two possible outcomes by 0.1, then adding these three numbers together to obtain the expected income, which will be $195.

Finally, the prospective buyer will have to discount each of these expected payoffs—meaning that she or he will take account of the fact that people prefer to have a dollar today relative to the opportunity to have that same dollar in five years. For example, if the enjoyment of the prospect of spending a dollar next year is worth only 90 percent as much as the opportunity to spend it today, then the discounted expected income from next year will be treated as being 90 percent as much as the $195. Similarly, a dollar two years from now will be considered to be worth only 81 percent—0.9 multiplied 0.9—as much as a dollar today. The rate at which the value of future enjoyment declines is known as the discount rate.

The basic idea of discounting—in the sense of preferring present to future enjoyment—is not just some fantasy of economists. Experimental psychologists have found that even animals exhibit behavior consistent with discounting (Ainslie 2001, p. 34). The widespread incidence of preference for present rather than future enjoyment does not prove the rationality of using a constant discount.

Discounting may be fairly useful as a crude rule of thumb for making decisions in the real estate market. In effect, then, the real estate market manages to collapse the entire future into a single number, known as a present value or a capitalization. On the basis of these calculations, speculators can come up with a figure that supposedly represents how much a property is worth. If the market price is below this present value, it represents a good investment. If not, a speculator will refuse to make a purchase.

Of course, the future revenues to be discounted are unknown. Instead, the speculator/investor must depend upon expectations, which are notoriously volatile. Wild swings in the stock market demonstrate how expectations about the future can move without reference to any real underlying information. Keynes claimed that the shares of ice producers in the U.S. were higher during the summer than in winter months (Keynes 1936b, p. 154) and that railway shares were highly sensitive to changes in weekly traffic returns (Keynes 1930b, vi, p. 360).

In such highly liquid markets, speculators can move huge sums of money with amazing rapidity. Sophisticated financial speculators attempt to make precise calculations of present values. By taking advantage of even slight differences between the market price and the estimated present value, speculators can hope to turn a profit. By leveraging their capital with borrowed money, a relatively small sum can finance a huge investment, this technique can be extraordinarily profitable when it works and disastrous when it does not.

In effect, sophisticated speculators try to find rational methods to profit from the irrationality of others. Economists assume that these rational investors can somehow rid the system of irrationality, bringing order to individual speculative markets.

Economists go one step further, fancifully assuming that for the economy as a whole, individual market participants making decisions based on discounted expected future revenues somehow or other magically result in an ideal outcome. Based on their abstract models, built on highly unrealistic assumptions, laissez-faire economists suggest that we should trust markets to arrive at a rational plan for using resources. The idea that discounting could allow a complex economy to coordinate its decisions in a way that the net effect will be to bring about an optimal management of resources over time strains the imagination. In fact, as I discussed in the context of Scoville's defense of land butchery, discounting turns out to be destructive when it becomes the basis for making complex, long-term choices with extensive impacts. Economists, however, rely on this theory because the simplification of reality allows them to construct mathematical models to describe markets, which are in reality anarchistic.

These models have two great attractions. For some, they allow their creators to demonstrate their mathematical virtuosity, which wins them considerable credit within the discipline. For others, these models provide ideological comfort because they are supposed to prove market efficiency. However, if the theory of discounting is defective, then these models of market efficiency become irrelevant except as a reminder of the way in which our theories become hostages of other motives.

Dynamic Market Efficiency

Such proofs of market efficiency are far from convincing. Present value calculations, whether justified or not, require an incredible simplification of the vision of the economic process. This technique skirts the question of time by reducing the complexity of the unknowable future to a simple number. In effect, the present values that lie at the heart of their models transform the dynamic economy into something that is mathematically equivalent to a static snapshot of the world. No matter how clever the models are, the real world that they are supposed to represent is dynamic to its core.

Notice the amount of information required in this admittedly simplistic example. Assuming a range of potential outcomes is not terribly difficult, but assigning realistic probabilities to each possibility staggers the imagination. Supposedly, rational investors investigate past history to determine the likelihood of each potential outcome. If you are concerned with finding the probability of drawing a particular card or throwing a particular combination with dice, running an experiment many times can provide relatively good information about the probabilities of any particular outcome.

In a real economy, past history can sometimes be informative about possibilities, especially in the short run, because certain aspects of the economy persist, sometimes even for decades. The problem is that nobody knows how long will pass before this past history will become irrelevant.

For example, today's weather might often be a fairly good predictor of tomorrow's, but eventually a rainstorm will interrupt a string of sunny days. If you dress for a sunny day based on yesterday's weather, your decision will not affect what happens to me or to anybody else. In contrast, in the economy, people are bound together by a herd instinct. If you speculate on the price of a stock going up, you will put some upward pressure on it. In doing so, you may make it seem more profitable for me to speculate on the same stock. As even more of us join in the speculation, investing in the stock may become still more attractive to others.

If enough of us get caught up in the speculation, the stock price takes on momentum of its own. People take the past history of increasing stock price as evidence of the rationality of further speculation, but eventually a rainy day interrupts the sunny weather.

The examples that I just gave are overly simplistic. The people who manage hundreds of millions or even billions of dollars do not merely predict that tomorrow will resemble today. They make sophisticated use of historical statistics. They obviously take into account the knowledge that the economy experiences booms and busts. They typically assume that the range of outcomes is distributed like a normal bell curve, with small changes more likely than major ruptures.

Unfortunately, the economy appears to be far more complex than the normal bell curve suggests. The economy seems to follow a somewhat distorted bell curve, which has fat tails relative to the normal bell curve. This particular shape indicates a much greater probability of dramatic changes than the normal curve predicts. Without getting too technical, I will merely say that conventional statistical techniques tend to underestimate the likelihood of dramatic ruptures.

The most important money managers also hire Ph.D. mathematicians, physicists, and economists to develop complex computer models to provide further information. But even this layer of sophistication is inadequate. The future always brings surprises that upset the plans of even the most brilliant speculators as well as the models of the greatest economists.

Long Term Credit Management

In 1997, Robert Merton and Myron Scholes won the Nobel Prize in economics for their sophisticated formula for valuing complicated financial assets. They extended their analysis to develop a technique for supposedly removing most of the risk from investment. By accurately valuing a variety of assets and carefully combining them, investors could supposedly insure themselves against risks. If the market moves one way, some of their investments will be so profitable that they will more than make up for the losses on the others that moved unfavorably. With such offsetting speculations, they could expect to profit no matter which way the market moved.

Every investment house worth its salt hired economists, mathematicians, and/or physicists to find opportunities for applying this technique. In 1994, these Nobel Prize–winning economists themselves joined a firm, Long Term Credit Management, inspired by their method (see Lowenstein 2000).

The company did magnificently. For four years, Long Term Credit Management earned an annual profit of more than 40 percent. Already, by 1995, Long Term had bets on $650 billion worth of securities: *Business Week* gushed that the fund's Ph.D.s would give rise to "a new computer age" on Wall Street. "Never has as much academic talent been given this much money to bet with," the magazine observed in a cover story published during the fund's first year (cited in Lowenstein 2000, p. 47). At its peak, the accumulated investments and profits of the owners totaled $7 billion and its investments in derivatives reached a staggering $1.3 trillion (Blustein 2001, pp. 307 and 315).

But then suddenly the firm stumbled. In 1998, Long Term Credit Management went bankrupt so spectacularly that many financial leaders were fearful that the implosion could completely undermine the world's financial system. Panic-stricken, many of the leading bankers and brokerage houses met at the New York branch of the Federal Reserve System to cobble together a $3.5 billion rescue plan.

Despite the fact that Alan Greenspan, chairman of the Federal Reserve Board, had already declared that the stock market was caught up in a fit of irrational exuberance, the Federal Reserve lowered interest rates in an effort to bolster confidence in the financial market. It succeeded, so much so, that the market, especially the NASDAQ stocks, skyrocketed to unprecedented heights.

Ironically, before the company disappeared, the professors believed that both their theoretical and financial success stood as proof of the absolute efficiency of markets. Admittedly, their models did work superbly so long as the financial world remained somewhat stable. Once the conditions represented by the fat tail of the bell curve began to appear, their models came unglued.

Long Term Credit Management went far beyond simply calculating present values, but its fate serves as a useful reminder that no matter how sophisticated calculations of future values may be, without exact knowledge of the future—which is of course impossible—these calculations remain nothing more than educated guesses.

If the Nobel Prize–winning economists can be so wrong on something as specific as the Russian bond market, how then can market processes as a whole be trusted to care for the natural resource base on which life itself depends?

Buridan's Ass

The fate of Long Term Credit Management illustrates a more general problem with present value calculations. Business commonly overestimates its likelihood of success. The end of each business cycle is littered with the remains of once high-flying businesses that had only recently represented a broadly admired model of success. Adam Smith attributed this tendency to human nature:

> The over-weening conceit which the greater part of men have of their own abilities, is an antient evil remarked by the philosophers and moralists of all ages. Their absurd presumption in their own good fortune, has been less taken notice of it. It is, however, if possible, still more universal . . . . The chance of gain is by every man more or less over-valued, and the chance of loss is by most men under-valued. (Smith 1776, I.x.b.26, pp. 124–25)

John Maynard Keynes suggested that although this excess of optimism might not be common to humanity as a whole, it might well be a necessary characteristic of people who engage in business. To succeed in business, one has to make decisions, even though the grounds for choosing one option over another may be lacking. In Keynes's words:

> Generally speaking, in making a decision we have before us a large number of alternatives, none of which is demonstrably more 'rational' than the others . . . . To avoid being put in the position of Buridan's ass [which died of starvation from being unable to choose between two equivalent

bales of hay] we fall back ... on habit, instinct, preference, desire, will, etc. (Keynes 1938b, p. 294)

For Keynes:

Most, probably, of our decisions to do something positive, the full consequences of which will be drawn out over many days to come, can only be taken as the result of animal spirits—of a spontaneous urge to action rather than inaction ..., so that the thought of ultimate loss which often overtakes pioneers, as experience undoubtedly tells us and them, is put aside as a healthy man puts aside the expectation of death. (Keynes 1936b, p. 162)

The behavior that Keynes described might make good business sense. A good number of those who follow their urge to action will succeed so long as the economy is vibrant, even though the inevitable recession will eventually winnow out a good number of them. However, the high mortality rate casts doubt on the purportedly efficient nature of markets. Within the natural world where evolution relies entirely on genetic mutations, a high mortality rate might seem inevitable. In industry, where people can consciously create new forms, the high mortality rate seems to be an extraordinarily wasteful method of managing the fragile endowment of natural resources upon which the economy, and even life itself, depends (see Perelman 1999b).

The financial system can bail out a Long Term Credit Management for a few billion dollars. Nobody knows how to recover depleted energy sources or to rescue devastated environments on a global scale.

Value Theory and the Future

Discount rates are unknown in the natural sciences. A molecule of oxygen tomorrow is identical to a molecule of oxygen today regardless of the preferences of individuals. This sort of reasoning may be foreign to science, but it is central to business calculations. In effect, business values natural resources as if they were no different than the paper that bond traders exchange (Brennan and Schwartz 1993).

Even if you grant that discounting is legitimate, the question remains: what then should the appropriate discount rate be? The theory of discounting presumes that people will make rational decisions regarding the future. The basis for this presumption is all but nonexistent.

First, most people, especially the young are notoriously oriented to the present rather than the future. For example, young people are less likely than a middle-aged person to ask a prospective employer about medical benefits or pensions. I recall how many years ago I would sometimes make my young daughter go to bed a few minutes early when she seemed particularly tired. Not infrequently, her response would be to tell me that I just ruined her life. In effect, losing a few minutes of playtime meant more to her at the time than the rest of her life. Of course, she was exaggerating, but not entirely so. The immediate future actually seemed far more important to her than what might occur a few months hence.

As I reflected on my daughter's response, I realized that I probably reacted in a similar fashion when I was her age. Supposedly, children place very little value on the future, because their brains are not completely formed until maturity. In effect then, children have a very high discount rate, even though they probably have no idea about what discounting means.

Like most people, as I aged, I became more future-oriented, but I recognize that I am still very impatient, even to the point of irrationality. Let me give a simple example to illustrate what I mean. Imagine a seemingly rational person hurrying to drive to his destination. He has a split second to decide whether to rush through an intersection where the yellow light is about to turn red. The opportunity to beat the light may save him a couple of minutes in transit time. It may also run the risk of a severe accident. Let's assume that the probability of an accident is 1/10 of 1 percent. Should such an accident occur, surely he would regret his decision and wish that he could turn back the clock to make the choice to wait for the red light to turn green. If other people would ask his advice, he would probably counsel them to be more patient. But now, pressed for time, rather than thinking through his decision in a broader perspective, he rushes to avoid stopping for the red light.

Like children, business also has a very high discount rate. Many corporations will abstain from any investment that does not promise an expected rate of return of 20 or 25 percent. With such a high discount rate, whatever happens 10, 15, or 20 years from now is inconsequential. Given that perspective, the long-term conservation of resources has virtually no importance whatsoever.

The Office of Management and Budget of the United States recommends a discount rate of 7 percent, much lower than business typically uses. Even at this lower rate, the value of the future quickly disappears.

Consider the following example: assume that the Gross Domestic Product of the world will be $8 quadrillion in the year 2200 in current dollars. Suppose next that we want to calculate that present value using the 7 percent discount rate. The answer is a mere $10 billion. In other words, it would not make sense for the world's present inhabitants to invest a mere $2 per person on a measure that would prevent the loss of the entire GDP of the world 200 years from now (Portney and Weyant 1999, p. 5).

I suspect that many people would believe that a $2 tax levy would seem to be a very small sum to prevent human extinction 200 years from now. Certainly, serious environmentalists would find this aspect of economic rationality shocking.

Discounting future values operates similar to interest rates, although they are not quite mathematically equivalent. A high discount rate, like a high interest rate, skews the price structure in favor of those whose income comes from ownership of capital relative to those who live from their wages.

For example, consider how high interest rates discourage people from acquiring housing. If you borrow $100,000 for a new house, with a 30-year mortgage you make 12 payments a year for 30 years. After 30 years, with an interest rate of 5 percent, you will have paid almost as much in interest as the value of the original loan. If the interest rate goes up to 10 percent, your total interest payments will amount to more than twice the value of the original loan. At 15 percent, the interest payments escalate to more than three and a half times as much as the original loan.

Of course, the relationship between the value of the original mortgage and the total repayment is far less extreme than a comparable calculation based on discounting. The reason for the difference is the dissimilar repayment schedules. Part of the typical house loan is paid off right away, beginning the very first month. If the house were purchased with a single lump sum payment 200 years from now, the total interest charge would tower above the initial loan with a magnitude just about as lopsided as the example of discounting the entire Gross Domestic Product of the world.

Hyperbolic Discounting

Let me mention another problem with the theory of calculating present values by discounting. Remember that the theory of discounting was supposed to reflect preferences inherent in people's psychological make-up. In so far as people prefer present enjoyment to future enjoyment, at first glance the theory appears to be on solid ground, but real human beings do not discount the future in the way that typical present value calculations presume.

In fact, the overwhelming evidence of both economists and experimental psychologists rejects standard present value calculations. For example, a recent survey of the subject concluded:

> The DU [Discounted Utility] model, which continues to be widely used by economists, has little empirical support. Even its developers—Samuelson, who originally proposed the model, and Koopmans [whom we will discuss later], who provided the first axiomatic derivation—had concerns about its descriptive realism, and it was never empirically validated as the appropriate model for intertemporal choice. Indeed, virtually every core and ancillary assumption of the DU model has been called into question by empirical evidence collected in the past two decades. (Frederick et al. 2002, p. 393)

In particular, although people apply high discount rates to events in the near future, they assign a much lower discount rate to the more distant future. For instance, even though the typical child might not give much thought to the future, most adults would cringe at the earlier example in which the world 200 years from now would have virtually no value whatsoever.

Economists refer to this tendency to use lower discount rates for the more distant future as hyperbolic discounting (Ainslie 1991; Angeletos et al. 2001). Even animals seem to exhibit hyperbolic discounting (Ainslie 2001, p. 34). You have probably seen hyperbolic discounting in action among your friends. People resolve to quit smoking or begin dieting in the future without making any immediate change in their behavior (see Akerlof 2002). In short, people may commonly place a high discount rate on the immediate future, adults do not apply the same discount rates to more distant events.

So while economic theory proposes that prices, including present values, reflect people's preferences, the standard calculation of discounted values would seem to conflict with people's actual preferences.

Economic theory teaches that the price system is necessarily efficient, in part, because prices are consistent with people's preferences. The hyperbolic discounting thesis seriously undermines the credibility of this thesis. First of all, hyperbolic discounting means that, starting today, people will behave as if tomorrow should be heavily discounted. By continuing to act in the same fashion over a long sequence of time, they will indeed be acting as if they have little regard for the future. Yet, if you were to ask people today if they think that the future should be so heavily discounted, they would reply negatively. This sort of behavior means that people will be unlikely to formulate a long-run course of behavior that would be consistent with their own preferences (see Strotz 1956). Economists used to attribute the excessive discounting of the future to pure irrationality. In one of the most famous statements about such irrationality, a noted British economist Arthur Cecil Pigou exclaimed:

> our telescopic faculty is defective.... [We] ... see future pleasures, as it were, on a diminished scale.... [P]eople distribute their resources between the present, the near future, and the remote future on the basis of a wholly irrational preference.... The inevitable result is that efforts directed towards the remote future are starved relatively to those directed to the near future, while those in turn are starved relatively to efforts directed towards the present. (Pigou 1920, p. 25)

Hyperbolic discounting suggests that the problem is not exactly irrationality, but a failure to connect short-term behavior with long-term consequences.

In contrast to people who do have a sincere, but possibly ineffectual concern about the future, recall that business operates under a crude discount vision that pays virtually no heed whatsoever to the long-term consequences of environmentally destructive behavior. In other words, under a system of profit maximization, business has no reason at all to consider a lower discount rate for the more distant future.

You might respond that business, by paying little regard to the future, is no different than the typical individual. Unlike most people, however, business, especially large business, explicitly plans for the future, often constructing projects that may take the better part of a decade to complete. The earlier example of forestry requires an even longer planning horizon. As a result, business typically has to consider explicitly some long-term consequences of its actions, but, for the most part, only insofar as its own narrow interests are involved.

George Ainslie, who may have put more thought into the concept of hyperbolic discounting than anyone else, has suggested that healthy individuals engage in a form of intertemporal bargaining, in which a variety of long-term interests and short-term interests compete with one another (Ainslie 2001). People who give little voice to their long-term interests are most liable to become prisoners of addictions. In a society where business is relatively free to treat natural resources wantonly in search of the highest possible profits, the bargaining power of those who identify with longer-term interests is very weak—comparable to people who are prisoners to their own addictions.

While business might rationally use present value calculations to maximize its private profits, the social rationality of assigning little value on the future is open to question. Although some people might act today without taking account of the longer-term future effects of their actions, they would balk at accepting the rationality of long-term business calculations that undermine the value of the future.

In conclusion, although the mathematical theory of discounting has an aura of scientificity, the notion of hyperbolic discounting suggests that the price system, rather than guiding society toward rational behavior, reinforces the tendency to undermine the future. The problem is not necessarily a defect in individual psychology, as Pigou suggested, but rather a flaw in relying on prices as the primary organizing principle for society.

Helium

No matter that present values are generally illusory. Present value calculations serve a vital purpose for economic theory. Once the world is reduced to present values, economists can treat the world as if the future does not exist: each decision becomes a once-and-for-all choice without any regard for the future other than what the price system was already signaling.

Concerns about resources have no place within this framework. If a real danger of resource scarcity were looming on the horizon, markets would recognize that fact. The price structure would induce firms to take action by economizing on the resource and by developing alternatives.

The treatment of the national helium reserves illustrates this troubling relationship between discounting and scarcity. Helium is a remarkable substance. Because it is inert, it does not combine with other substances. Because of its perceived military importance in dirigibles, during the 1920s the United States began to collect helium under a federal monopoly.

Helium has properties other than being lighter than air. No other element can reach the low temperature of liquid helium. This property makes it useful in a broad array of high-tech industrial, research, and medical technologies, such as fiber-optic cables and magnetic-resonance imaging systems (National Research Council 2000).

The government later established a facility in Texas to store crude helium (National Research Council 2000). The Texas location is not accidental. Although atmospheric helium is plentiful, it is dispersed. Extracting this helium from the air is a very expensive proposition since only minute quantities of helium exist within a fairly large volume of air. The sedimentary rocks that form the gas carry about one part per million of uranium. According to Kenneth Deffeyes, "During the slow decay to lead, each uranium atom spits out six to eight alpha particles. An alpha particle in physics is identical to the nucleus of a helium atom in chemistry. The helium gas that we put in party balloons is simply used alpha particles" (Deffeyes 2001, p. 66).

In contrast to its dispersion in the atmosphere, helium in natural gas deposits is relatively concentrated. Some natural gas deposits have helium concentrations as high as 8 percent, making them the most economical source of this element (National Research Council 2000, p. 40). Separating helium from natural gas costs only about 1/1000 as much as obtaining it from the atmosphere (Koopmans 1979).

In 1960, Congress amended the Helium Act, which had originally authorized the helium depository. This new legislation eliminated the federal monopoly of helium, although the Bureau of Mines continued to collect helium. Several companies in the United States entered the market to collect and sell the gas. These companies sold their excess helium to the federal government, which stored it in the National Helium Reserve in Texas.

Private consumption of helium reached a low point in the 1970s, even though private production was still vigorous. As a result, the government continued to accumulate more helium in the reserves until around 1980. With the build-up of federal stockpiles, conservatives singled out the helium reserves as a particularly egregious example of government waste (see Stroup and Shaw 1985). Christopher Cox, the California Congressman who led the fight to privatize helium labeled the reserve: "The poster child of Government waste" (Verhovek 1997).

In 1996, Congress eliminated the National Helium Reserve, leaving the management of helium to the free market and the likes of Enron, Exxon, and Panhandle Eastern Corporation. Well, not exactly, the free market. The law required that the government gradually dispose of its helium over a couple of decades to prevent privatization from decreasing the price that the private producers charge. The promised cost savings have yet to appear.

The American Physical Society, a prominent group of physicists, has warned that the privatization plan is dangerous, because it has no requirement that a large stockpile will be maintained (Verhovek 1997; Powell 1996). Helium demand is now increasing at about 10 percent per year. The supply may be largely depleted by 2015, the date by which Congress proposes to phase out the reserve.

Indeed, a federal report says that the current trends indicate that shortages will appear within less than 20 years, unless private business develops new technologies. However, these experts are confident that business will somehow meet the challenge, although they give no indication of what this new technology might be (National Research Council 2000).

Discounting Helium

The helium story is interesting in several respects, especially, taken in conjunction with the role of natural gas. As is well known, natural gas is probably the least environmentally destructive fossil fuel. Of course, the consumption of natural gas is not without problems, over and above the damage involved in moving it from its natural state to the place where it is ultimately burnt. In addition to obvious costs of the depletion of the gas itself and the contribution to global warming, the careless consumption of natural gas causes the dissipation of helium.

In this sense, the helium story brings us back to the theme of extraction versus production, but with a twist. Ironically, this same helium, which is being squandered because of the inattention to storing it for the future may well prove to be a vital part of high technology that could possibly lead to significant savings in energy, including natural gas.

In addition, the helium story serves as a useful reminder of the complex pathways of cause and effect typical of most environmental systems. Push in any direction and unexpected consequences crop up. In contrast, the contemporary profit system works with an appallingly simple mindset. Here is a resource that can benefit some corporations. Just give it to them to exploit without much thought about the ultimate consequences and all will be well.

The economist who may have given the most attention to the question of helium is the late Tjalling Koopmans, whom I noted in the discussion of hyperbolic discounting. Koopmans was a distinguished theoretical economist and winner of the 1975 Nobel Prize in economics. He proudly associated himself with the study of pure economics. He violently denounced those economists who relied on empirical data, without first carefully situating it in abstract theory (Mirowski 1989b). He was so fanatically committed to abstract economic theory that he even "seriously opposed ... fine writing in economics, not a common crime in our field. According to his code of scientific honor, mere elegance must not give ideas an unfair boost" (Samuelson 1989).

In 1978, Koopmans delivered the presidential address to the American Economic Association (Koopmans 1979). His lecture concerned the difficulties that economists had in communicating with natural scientists. Koopmans was not speaking out of ignorance of the ways of natural science. In fact, he had earned a degree in quantum physics. Koopmans explained to a meeting of the American Physical Association in 1979 that he initially decided to switch from physics to economics because he "felt the physical sciences were far ahead of the social and economic sciences" (cited in Mirowski 2002, p. 251).

By the time that he gave his lecture, Koopmans seemed to think that economics had advanced to the point where he could confidently recommend that scientists learn to accept the economists' approach.

In effect, harkening back to Adam Smith's account of the complex production process behind the appearance of a single coat, Koopmans attributed a superiority to economics over natural science. Whereas a scientist might be inclined to think of a helium policy in terms of the use or the production of helium, the economist uses monetary values to capture the systemic ramifications of a helium policy. In Koopmans's words:

> In the present context, an important trait of the neoclassical (economic) model is that it does not postulate one sole primary resource, be it labor, energy or any other, whose scarcity controls that of all other goods, and which thereby becomes a natural unit of value for all other goods. (Koopmans 1979, p. 7)

Instead, as Lionel Robbins observed in his influential study of economic methodology, the economy is a "complex of 'scarcity relationships'" (Robbins 1969, p. 19). Within this context, prices take into account a wide array of factors, rather than a single objective, such as the conservation of helium.

In his address, Koopmans related his experience working on the report to the Helium Study Committee of the National Research Council. Most of Koopmans's discussion of helium merely dealt with technical questions regarding the supply and the extraction of helium. The one point that Koopmans kept returning to was the scientist's insistence that "Btu's are the same everywhere and at all times" (Koopmans 1979, p. 8). Koopmans wanted to teach the scientists that discounting future benefits, which lay behind the calculations justifying privatization, was rational.

Even if you grant the importance of discount rates, nobody knows how to select the appropriate discount rate for determining whether or not responsibility for collecting and storing helium should be privatized. Some discount rates would have been consistent with privatization. Other lower rates would not. Koopmans never mentioned how to decide on the correct discount rate. Nor did Koopmans indicate that he had any inkling of the possibility of hyperbolic discounting. In fact, the absence of an adequate theory of discounting represents a major challenge that stands in the way of the scientific aspirations of economists.

Tjalling Koopmans, the National Research Council, and most economic and political forces aligned themselves against those who express any concerns about sustainability. Presumably, if a problem occurs, they proposed that the resulting profit opportunities will create sufficient incentives to generate a solution. Their proposed solution is not sustainable, but instead an outcome in which the system efficiently maximizes discounted present values. Unfortunately, they did not have a clue as to what that discount rate should be.

No Easy Answers

I do not want to give the impression that the solution to environmental problems lies in merely discarding economic analysis. Economists have raised legitimate concerns about a wholly environmental approach to organizing human activity. I would say that the example of helium illustrates just how difficult protecting the environment is, whether it be by using the price system to ration resources or by using some sort of regulatory mechanism to accomplish the same goal. Before the age of dirigibles, probably neither environmentalists nor economists thought of helium as an important resource. Helium was just there. It had no economic purpose and no price. It did not seem to support any sensitive habitat or endangered species.

The early ignorance of the importance of helium suggests a more general phenomenon. The fact that we have learned so much about the environment recently suggests that we have only scratched the surface in our understanding of the complex web of life.

The appropriate reaction to ignorance should be an effort to take care to do no harm. This approach, however, has a different meaning in the context of economics than it does with respect to ecological considerations. Ecologists would have us be careful to protect the environment, even if such an approach might hamper economic activity. Economists would advise us to avoid interfering with the economic process without strong evidence that some serious ecological harm could occur.

Many economists have emphasized the inability of a single planner to comprehend the complexity of an economic system. For example, Friedrich von Hayek won a Nobel Prize in economics largely for proposing that the sum total of business people, each operating in his or her narrow area of specialization, could create a system of information superior to what any individual planner could accomplish. In effect, the price system supposedly assembles this information and then, like a giant computer, develops an outcome superior to what any planning organization could devise.

Supposedly, letting market rules dictate all decisions is rational within the context of this theory. Following this logic, Koopmans was correct in asserting that the price system probably reflects a wider range of influences than a typical environmental planner could take into account. Unfortunately, the price system excludes a wide range of information. It primarily reflects discounted commercial values. Environmental considerations generally fall from the picture, even though many environmental resources may eventually have substantial economic value. As a result, the price system provides a very distorted picture of reality.

A fatal defect in the price system makes this distortion even more serious. Almost a half century ago, economists discovered that the efficiency of the price system is very fragile, in the sense that it can give appropriate signals only under very restrictive conditions. First, mainstream economic theory depends upon highly unrealistic assumptions that have no counterparts in the physical world. The conditions required for perfect conditions are impossible to meet.

In addition, this theory is extraordinarily fragile. If a single element of the system does not conform to these unrealistic assumptions, the whole system can loose its coherence. For example, in a world close to perfect competition, if only two prices deviate from their optimal equilibrium values, whether because of government regulation or inadequate information, correcting both of these prices will make the economy perform better. However, adjusting only one of these prices to its equilibrium level can actually harm economic performance (see Lancaster and Lipsey 1956).

While the economists have a point when they maintain that the price system reflects a wide range of influences, they typically neglect to mention that it also ignores a wide range. In conclusion, while the price system may claim a certain degree of inclusiveness, prices are unlikely to guide the economy into an environmentally rational direction, especially since the price system is prone to exclude crucial environmental considerations.

So, while mainstream economic theories might make sense in an abstract fantasy world in which even the future can be known with certainty and no single producer is big enough to have any influence on price and environmental effects are unimportant, in the real world these theories lack any justification.

The Absence of Realism

Even with a host of unrealistic assumptions, economists failed to prove that markets necessarily lead to the best of all possible outcomes, even within the abstract world that they hypothesized. Consequently, they lowered their sights, attempting to show that the resulting output would be such that no possible reorganization of the economy could make any individual better off without harming another—a far more modest objective.

Despite the absence of realism in their abstract mathematical theories, these economists, led in the English-speaking world by William Stanley Jevons won over the majority of their own profession. A host of factors contributed to their victory. First, framing their work in mathematical terms made it appear more scientific—lending an aura of prestige to their work comparable to the natural sciences. Moreover, the seemingly scientific formulation of these theories made them unassailable, except by those who had the mathematical expertise to understand the underlying assumptions.

Second, these economic theories, cast in mathematical form, concluded that markets were the only way of organizing economic activity efficiently, or as D. McCloskey once wrote, "The Market, God Bless It, Works" (McCloskey 1978, p. 21). In this spirit, Gerard Debreu, wrote in his book, *Theory of Value*, which won him a Nobel Prize in economics: "The two central problems of the theory [of value] are (1) the explanation of the prices of commodities . . . and (2) the explanation of the role of prices in an optimal state of an economy" (Debreu 1959, p. vii). This conclusion made followers of conventional economics welcome in a world in which business interests played the dominant role.

Finally, the increasingly technical sophistication that economists used to present their theories created an illusion of progress, even though they made virtually no scientific headway in furthering their understanding of the economy.

What is Capital?

Whenever economists begin to feel confident that they finally have a good enough command of their material to embark on a deeper examination of their work, disturbing questions present themselves, causing obvious discomfort. The theory of capital is no exception. For example, value theorists see capital as a lumping together of all sorts of capital goods. Theoretically they would measure each of these individual capital goods with precise present value calculations. Even though such calculations are impossible in reality, economists get around such complications by making unrealistic assumptions about the capital stock. In this way, economists can treat long-lived capital goods as if they were no different from a loaf of bread that would be both baked and consumed within a few days—in effect banishing the complexities of time and uncertainty from their theory.

When economists attempt to go beyond naïve present value calculations, they run into difficulty. For example, Knut Wicksell, one of the two most influential economists of the early twentieth century, wrote to Alfred Marshall, who was even more influential:

> the theory of capital and interest cannot be regarded as complete yet. As I have tried to show several times ... so long as capital is defined as a sum of commodities (or of value) the doctrine of the marginal productivity of capital as determining the rate of interest is never quite true and often not true at all. (Wicksell 1905, p. 102)

Alfred Marshall himself recognized a further dimension of the challenge of measuring capital, suggesting: "Capital consists in great part of knowledge and organisation" (Marshall 1890, pp. 138–39). Of course, such magnitudes defy measurement.

Almost a century after Wicksell wrote, Barkley Rosser, an economist from James Madison University, remarked that economists cannot even agree on what capital is, let alone its value:

> What really is capital and what does it mean for value, growth, and distribution? Is it a pile of produced means of production? Is it dated labor? Is it waiting? Is it roundaboutness? Is it an accumulated pile of finance? Is it a social relation? Is it an independent source of value? The answers to these questions are probably matters of belief. (Rosser 1991, p. 125)

The reader who is unfamiliar with some of the terms that Rosser used need not worry too much. Let me assure you that each of the characterizations of capital that he mentioned represents a quite different perspective. A decade and a half before Rosser wrote, a British economist, Christopher Bliss, predicted that the answers to Rosser's questions were not likely to be forthcoming:

> When economists reach agreement on the theory of capital they will
> shortly reach agreement on everything. Happily for those who enjoy a
> diversity of views and beliefs, there is little danger of this outcome.
> Indeed, there is at present not even an agreement as to what the subject
> is about. (Bliss 1975, p. vii)

He went on to explain:

> capital is many things to different men. To the rentier it is a claim on
> income now and in the future. To the entrepreneur it is some necessary
> inputs. To the accountant it is entries in a valuation account. To the
> theorist it is a source of production and a component of the explanation
> of the division of that production. (Bliss 1975, p. 7; see also Hicks 1973,
> p. 83 for a similar assessment)

Few economists took note of Bliss's pessimistic realism. Instead, each
school of economics continued to deploy its own idiosyncratic theory of
value without much concern for realism. Yet almost all economists agree
that the key to a healthy economy is the accumulation of capital—
whatever that elusive stuff may be.

Value Theory and Economic Efficiency

People who study such markets realize that present value calculations do
not offer anything like objective indicators of value. Instead, market
prices are susceptible to irrational forces. This irrationality should not be
surprising. After all, the future remains unknown.

Lacking an objective measure of the future, psychological factors exert
a powerful effect on the values of stocks or real estate. Waves of optimism
or pessimism frequently sweep across these markets driving the prices up
or down, creating boom and bust cycles.

Although intuition and emotion typically exercise more influence in
most deals than outright knowledge, abstract economic theory unrealistically assumes that everybody behaves in a supremely rational manner.
However, even if the speculators had perfect information about the future
performance of this property, the subjective influence of the discount rate
would still intrude.

Economists do not make the assumption of rationality based on evidence about the real world. Instead, this assumption is necessary for the
economists to make the theory work the way that they want it to. So they
make the assumption of rationality, even though it makes their analysis

unrealistic and even irrelevant to the real world. Without rationality, they would be unable to "prove" that the economy works efficiently.

Besides outright irrationality, rapid change in technology or market conditions can and often does pull the rug out from earlier calculations, even if investors had applied cold rationality to their calculations. In the wake of such changes, assets may no longer be suitable for their original use. The value of such assets need not necessarily disappear entirely. Creative investors can sometimes find ways to redeploy them. For example, when the military cut back on its aerospace expenditures in the 1980s, General Dynamics sold a wind tunnel to Micro Craft, which now rents the facility for $900 an hour to businesses, such as bicycle helmet designers and architects who wish to gauge air flows between buildings (Douglass 1994).

In a more recent example, Iridium invested $5 billion in an elaborate satellite phone system. After only six months of operation, the company folded in what was one of the largest bankruptcies in history. The company then proposed to crash its 70 satellites into the oceans, until the military breathed life into the system by offering a two-year $72 million contract (Chang 2000; Nelson 1998).

While this system has proved to be of limited use as a commercial, civilian communication network, it seems to be ideal for measuring the electrical currents in the upper atmosphere. This information might seem to be esoteric, but the flow of charged particles from the sun fluctuates a great deal. When these auroral currents become unstable, they can disrupt radio signals, damage power grids, and drag down satellites (Chang 2000). In the end, the Iridium investment might well have turned out to be a good use of resources, even if the original investors may not have benefited. Later, during the invasion of Iraq in 2003, this same phone system became a mainstay of the reporters following the military.

Had the expectations of the investors in Iridium been met, the world might have hailed them as visionary. Instead, they were left with egg on their face. Notice, that the redeployment is often just as unexpected as the conditions that had earlier undermined the value of the investment.

Of course, one cannot dismiss the economists' work out of hand, regardless of its lack of realism. After all, their word remains highly influential.

The Wreck of Value Theory

Another unrealistic assumption of value theory is called "decreasing returns," meaning that each unit produced will cost more than the previous unit. Of course, anyone familiar with modern manufacturing knows that costs tend to decrease with the scale of production. John R. Hicks, who later won the Nobel Prize for economics, observed that the assumption of the decreasing returns alone would be virtually fatal if economic theory were to be held to an objective standard. For Hicks, "It is, I believe, only possible to save anything from this wreck . . . if we assume that the markets confronting most of the firms with which we shall be dealing do not differ very greatly from perfectly competitive markets." He asks "But why should anyone care about the wreckage?" (Hicks 1946, p. 84).

Hicks's evaluation of economic theory appeared in a book that had been read by virtually every graduate student in economics for a number of decades. Students devoted many hours to learning the mathematical intricacies of economic theory found in this book, but few ever paused to note the author's stark dismissal of the realism of this theory.

Instead, having devoted so much time and energy to mastering this mathematical theory of value, economists tend to be protective of their investment in acquiring this knowledge, regardless of the questionable realism of value theory. So, economists still put great stock in value theory even though they are usually discreet enough to stow it away from public view.

The recent run-up in the NASDAQ dot.com stocks illustrates just how tenuous the capitalization process is. Investors, believing that Internet stocks had an almost unlimited profit potential, bid up the prices of these stocks to what in retrospect were ridiculous heights.

Given the high discount rate typical of financial markets, these stock prices seemed to make no sense whatsoever unless profits would become quite large. However, few of these companies made any profit whatsoever. Investors seemed to be unmoved by the absence of profits. Investors even seem to have taken the rate at which these companies lost money as a signal of future prosperity.

Value as a Mental Construct

Some economists attempt to simplify value theory by reducing the value of any good to a merely subjective value—what a good is worth to an individual, or in the jargon of economics, utility. At first, subjective value seems to be in line with common sense. This interpretation of value implies that, in effect, each individual person has her or his own set of values.

These utilities remain unobservable. Value ultimately resides within the individual and is subject to potentially unstable, individual whims. Nobody can measure how much I like ice cream or classical music.

Purchases are the only evidence of preferences. All the economist can do is to follow these purchases and to take the price at which a good changes hands as evidence of value.

This theory provides a useful, but abstract description of how a large number of individual agents affect each other through market relations, but does little to help anyone understand the workings of an actual economy. It only suggests that if each person is free to buy or sell what she or he considers to be most advantageous for herself or himself, then the outcome for society as a whole will be optimal. Economists typically wield this theory to warn that because the system is so complex any tampering with the market will cause irreparable harm. So the best the economist can do is to insist that society do nothing to interfere with the market.

This conclusion requires several extraordinarily strong and unrealistic assumptions. For example, people cannot affect each other, except through market exchanges. In effect, then, the consequences of pollution or depletion are assumed away. Besides, within this framework, goods that are not bought and sold do not register as values. Here again, matters such as pollution and depletion, need be of no concern.

Perhaps the most important result of adopting subjective value theory was the mindset that it created. Since value was subjective, it seemed to exist disconnected from the material world. This perspective fed into the hype regarding the so-called new economy in which value supposedly reflected the pure creativity that went into the product. Only a couple of years before deceptive financial maneuvers brought down Enron and a slew of other major companies, Greenspan proclaimed:

> All the new financial products that have been created in recent years, financial derivatives being in the forefront, contribute economic value by unbundling risks and reallocating them in a highly calibrated manner. The rising share of finance in the business output of the United States and other countries is a measure of the economic value added from its ability to enhance the process of wealth creation. (Greenspan 1999)

With hindsight we can see that much of this value existed only in the minds of participants in the financial markets, unrelated to any counterpart in the real world.

Tulipomania

In my earlier discussion, I related the idea of self-expanding value to the upsurge in the production of material goods. From that perspective, at least the increase in value corresponds to something in the real world.

The break in the linkage between value and the material world allows the self-expansion of value to go well beyond anything that could be explained by apparent increases in productivity. This phenomenon is most apparent during speculative bubbles.

Here again, the experience of the Dutch is instructive. In 1634, the Dutch became infatuated with the Tulip, a plant native to Turkey. Because the tulip multiplies asexually, growers could not increase the supply nearly as fast as the demand grew. Consequently, the value of tulips, measured by their market price, skyrocketed:

> In 1634, the rage among the Dutch to posses them (tulips) was so great that the ordinary industry of the country was neglected, and the population, even to its lowest dregs, embarked in the tulip trade. As the mania increased, prices augmented, until, in the year 1635, many persons were known to invest a fortune of 100,000 florins in the purchase of forty roots. It became necessary to sell them by their weight in perits, a small weight less than a grain. (Mackay 1841, p. 90)

A single Semper Augustus fetched a price of 5,500 guilders, equivalent to more than 100 ounces of gold (Garber 1989a, p. 53). The market, of course, eventually crashed.

Later commentators referred to this speculative frenzy as tulipomania. Peter Garber began studying this phenomenon shortly after the October 1987 stock market crash. According to Edward Chancellor, another student of speculation, Garber's work "was written with the intention of heading off proposed government regulation of stock futures markets" (Chancellor 1999, p. 24). Garber attempted to explain that the speculation had a rational basis. However, even he had to admit that the one-month 20-fold price surge for common bulbs in January 1637 does defy explanation (Garber 1989b, p. 556).

Fictitious Value

The lessons of tulipomania were lost on later generations. Periodic euphoria seems to be endemic to market economies. This failure is especially dangerous because the difficulty of getting a handle on underlying values increases in the course of economic development.

Over time, the connection between ownership of resources and economic well-being became increasingly less direct. To begin with, as economies advanced, the share of wealth represented by land began to recede. A few capitalists amassed immense fortunes that towered over what workers could earn in wages. Later, stock exchanges allowed ownership to become even more indirect. Eventually, the control of paper assets alone was sufficient to convey great wealth. At first, these paper assets bore some relationship to material goods. A person who owned a stock issued by a railroad had nominal ownership of a share of the railroad. Even a railroad bond represented a claim on the physical wealth of the railroad—in the sense that if the railroad did not honor the bond, the bondholder would have the right to a claim on the railroad's physical assets.

At year-end 1995, book value of the S&P 500 stocks accounted for only 26 percent of market value of the underlying companies. In other words, intangible assets were worth three times the value of tangible assets, such as buildings and equipment (Kelley 2001, p. 46).

Some of this intangible property later turned out to be fictitious, disappearing with the end of the great NASDAQ bubble, which burst as spectacularly as the Dutch tulip market. Much intangible wealth, however, represents intellectual property rights that exercise a powerful hold over society.

For example, the material goods that Microsoft controls are trivial compared to the market value of its intellectual property. As a result, the company earns a profit margin of 85 percent on its Windows products (Abrahams 2002). Only a small part of the 15 percent of the price that covers the costs of the product goes to actual manufacturing expenses. Other costs, such as marketing, are far greater.

Microsoft is not alone in this respect. However, much of the presumed value of the intellectual property of the dot.coms was imaginary. Nonetheless, the great dot.com bubble pushed the NASDAQ index to 4,800 in March 2000. Giddy with the success of the stock market, pundits began predicting that the stock market would soon reach even more fanciful levels. Publishers marketed books with titles, such as *Dow 36,000* (Glassman and Hassett 1999), *Dow 40,000* (Elias 1999), and *Dow 100,000* (Kadlec and Acampora 1999).

The speculative run on the NASDAQ market did not last indefinitely. By April 2001, the meltdown had sunk the index to below 1,640. By late March 2001, an estimated $4.6 trillion worth of value that the NASDAQ had enjoyed in March 2000 had evaporated (Vickers 2001).

Retrospectively, the eventual collapse of a speculative bubble might seem to offer evidence that in the long run value returns to a level that is consistent with the underlying material basis. Of course, nobody can precisely identify the underlying material basis of value, even in retrospect.

The enthusiasts of the dot.com bubble believed that the soaring stocks were justified in terms of material fundamentals. They argued that the computer, the Internet, and modern communications technologies had so revolutionized the productive system that future earnings would more than justify what the skeptics believed to be excessive stock prices.

The idea that speculative bubbles occur from time to time and then disappear suggests that rationality is the norm, except for the periodic lapses that cause the bubbles. I do not know of any grounds for believing that rationality is the norm in speculative markets.

Nobody has a firm basis for identifying what the appropriate value of a speculation should be. Even after the NASDAQ market crashed, observers continued to debate whether the market was still overvalued or whether investors had overreacted and driven stock prices below what market analysts considered to be their fundamental values.

Economists typically write about bubbles as if they were anomalies. I would argue, instead, that bubbles are extreme cases of a common phenomenon. A thick fog of ignorance and uncertainty engulfs the future. Lacking adequate knowledge, people can only rely on educated guesses or follow others who might seem to have better information. This situation leads to a kind of herd behavior, which is conducive to bubbles.

Some bubbles grow to grotesque sizes. Others are more modest and pass unnoticed. But these bubbles are everywhere, not just among stock or bond traders or option dealers. In a market economy, virtually every investment is a speculation, whether opening a restaurant or investing in some complicated financial instrument.

The Illusion of Weightlessness

Many seemingly informed people, including Alan Greenspan, the chairman of the Federal Reserve System, fed the stock market bubble of the late 1990s. He proposed that the economy was entering a new phase in which it could transcend traditional material limitations. Greenspan himself effused about the potential of the supposed new economy in which information would be the driving force.

The popular promoters of the idea of new economy breathlessly referred to a weightless economy (see Coyle 1998). Tom Peters, the management guru, derided old-line businesses as "Lumpy-object purveyors" (Peters 1997, p. 16). Even Alan Greenspan is fond of rhapsodizing about how modern production techniques are making the economy lighter and lighter:

> The world of 1948 was vastly different from the world of 1996. The American economy, more then than now, was viewed as the ultimate in technology and productivity in virtually all fields of economic endeavor. The quintessential model of industrial might in those days was the array of vast, smoke-encased integrated steel mills in the Pittsburgh district and on the shores of Lake Michigan. Output was things, big physical things. Virtually unimaginable a half century ago was the extent to which concepts and ideas would substitute for physical resources and human brawn in the production of goods and services. In 1948 radios were still being powered by vacuum tubes. Today, transistors deliver far higher quality with a mere fraction of the bulk. Fiber-optics has [*sic*] replaced huge tonnages of copper wire, and advances in architectural and engineering design have made possible the construction of buildings with much greater floor space but significantly less physical material than the buildings erected just after World War II. Accordingly, while the weight of current economic output is probably only modestly higher than it was a half century ago, value added, adjusted for price change, has risen well over threefold. (Greenspan 1996)

The initial prophet of weightlessness was George Gilder. More than a decade earlier than Greenspan's pronouncement, flush with the victories of the Reagan revolution, Gilder extravagantly proposed: "The central event of the twentieth century is the overthrow of matter. In technology, economics, and the politics of nations, wealth in the form of physical resources is steadily declining in value and significance. The powers of mind are everywhere ascendant over the brute force of things" (Gilder 1989, p. 18).

For Gilder, weightlessness served as a decisive refutation of Karl Marx's emphasis on labor. In Gilder's view, ideas—what now more commonly would fall within the purview of intellectual property—rather than the physical effort of workers creates wealth and value. This devaluation of blue-collar labor resonated in the fulsome praise heaped upon the rise of the new economy, supposedly driven by ideas and information. Greenspan's description of weightlessness, was more measured and less blatant, but not qualitatively different from Gilder's.

The downplaying of the material world—including both nature and labor—reinforced the feeling that value could expand without limits, creating an enormous gulf between the respective perspectives of economics and natural science.

Shortly after the NASDAQ bubble burst, California began to experience severe shortages in electricity. One popular culprit was supposed to be the

Internet—the central figure in the fantasy of a weightless economy—which was accused of gulping as much as 8 percent of the national electricity load (McKay 2000). While the media repeated this estimate as a fact it was highly inflated—so much so that even the *Wall Street Journal* referred to it as "All Wet" (Wessel 2002)—it still stood as a reminder that even the weightless economy depended upon substantial material inputs.

The California energy system, which supplies much of the so-called weightless economy, depends to large extent upon natural gas and hydro-electric power, which, in turn, depends upon rainfall. A lack of rainfall, along with cynical corporate manipulation, was a major factor in the California electricity crisis of 2000.

The production of the materials that make up the weightless economy consume huge complexes of material resources. Consider the omnipresent computer chip. A typical 2-gram silicon chip requires 1.6 kilograms of fossil fuel, 72 grams of chemicals and 32 kilograms of water. Some of the chemicals, such as solvents called polychlorinated biphenyls (PCBs), are toxic (Williams et al. 2002).

The direct use of water represents only a tiny fraction of the water costs of producing microchips. Many of the chemicals involved in the manufacturing process for these marvelous devices are serious toxins that can render large bodies of water unsafe. Those who enthuse about the weightless economy never mention the material basis of the technological wonders that represent the foundation of the weightless economy.

Because of the close nexus with water, the electricity system interacts closely with both agriculture and aquatic ecologies. This complex network of energy, agriculture, fisheries, and the rest of the environment stand in sharp contrast to economic analysis, where the impact of an entire industry collapses into a single price. In fact, virtually all economic models rule out such interactions, except for price effects, in order to make the mathematics tractable.

But Then, What is Productivity?

Although fraud and swindle were relatively familiar to those who had a passing acquaintance with the history of business, the dot.com bust and the larger corporate unravelings that followed occurred in a relatively unique environment for several reasons. First, the linking of executive pay to stock prices created a stronger incentive for the manipulation of earnings. Second, although corporate boosterism is far from new, the unprecedented consolidation of the media meant that critical perspectives were marginalized to an extent previously unknown. Additionally, techniques of corporate public relations had become exceedingly sophisticated. These two factors led to a political environment in which the corporations' prerogatives went unchallenged.

In an earlier age, while business-oriented political figures may have been dominant, some more critical people, although not occupying central stage, still had a political voice. During this great boom at the end of the twentieth century, the political environment had marginalized criticism to the point of effectively silencing it. News broadcasts would cheer the stock market as it reached new heights. Nobody dared to question the underlying substance.

The dean of the Yale School of Management, Jeffrey Garten, later admitted: "Even those of us at business schools are implicated. It's not like the educational establishment sounded any warning. We were cheerleaders, too" (cited in Pearlstein 2002). According to Garten:

> I think it is fair to say that there was nobody in the business community who is not implicated in this in some way. . . . Not the executives who were under the excruciating pressure of having to meet quarterly earnings targets, no matter what. Not the lawyers and the accountants and bankers who were forced to compete furiously to get and keep clients. Not the regulators who became so intimidated by all the exuberance in the air. Certainly not the underwriters or the analysts or the credit-rating agencies or you in the press. (Cited in Pearlstein 2002)

Lacking any significant challenge, business managed to have Congress eliminate a slew of regulations, including those designed to protect investors. Business accompanied every request for change with a promise to enhance productivity as well as its own profits. In this way, society as a whole was supposed to share in the benefits.

A final factor was crucial. Never before had financialization gone so far. By financialization, I mean a delinking of the financial from the material basis of the economy. Financialization is not new. In the nineteenth century, the Chicago Board of Trade exercised great influence in agriculture by allowing people to buy and sell the rights to buy or sell agricultural products at a future date for a specified price. Enron, for example, grew to spectacular heights by devoting itself to buying and selling rights to buy and sell everything from energy to optical fiber bandwidth. Their trades were so complex that virtually no one could understand them. As a result, investors were left to accept the company's word that the enterprise was performing magnificently.

In an earlier age, investors could gauge the health of the economy by looking at material measures, such as railroad shipments. In an age of financialization, investors were mostly left to look at the abstract financial indicators to get a handle on economic conditions. This situation put investors at the mercy of unscrupulous manipulators.

Manipulation, of course, is hardly new, but the context had changed. At the turn of the nineteenth century, manipulators were out in force, but a large number of small but influential muckraking publications were exposing some of the abuses. Fraud still existed, but access to critical information had the potential to hold it in check. Today, nothing comparable exists.

In hindsight, a good deal of the profits turned out to be imaginary, as was the productivity that supposedly generated the profits. I do not mention this imaginary productivity merely to flog corporate malfeasance. The gross manipulations in the course of this stock bubble provide a dramatic demonstration of the arbitrary nature of many economic measurements.

Intellectual Property and Productivity

The companies that earn the most profit—the core of the so-called new economy—tend to rely on intellectual property. The world of intellectual property is absolutely inconsistent with the traditional vision of economics (see Perelman 2002). People cannot use up intellectual property in the same way that people destroy fossil fuel when they burn it. In fact, the more people use intellectual property, the more useful it becomes.

In addition, intellectual property is not scarce in the same sense that natural resources are. The law, however, creates an artificial scarcity of intellectual property, supposedly to encourage the creation of still more intellectual property. In fact, the efforts to protect this artificial scarcity of intellectual property will stifle the further development of intellectual property—not necessarily tomorrow or the next day, but the deleterious effects are inevitable (see Perelman 2002).

The world of intellectual property is not weightless by any means. The protection of the monopolistic profits of purveyors of intellectual property depends heavily on the full weight of the law. Because of these inflated profits, the marketers of intellectual property appear to be highly productive.

More often than not, the corporate owners of these intellectual property rights have played little, if any, role in its actual creation.

Frequently, the real creators work for public agencies, such as the government or universities. Although public institutions may have funded the creative work, the law permits private corporations to claim ownership for themselves (see Perelman 2002). Even where the paid staff of the corporate owner creates intellectual property, typically the major contribution of corporate management is to lobby government to find ways to strengthen its intellectual property rights. This process has a great deal to do with the worsening distribution of income in United States today (see Perelman 2001).

4

Patience

Discount Rates and Morality

The study of economics runs in two opposing directions. On one hand, it is an attempt to understand how the economy works. On the other hand, it is a justification of the market society.

These conflicting objectives of economics make the subject of discounting more confusing. On the ideological side, economists present wealth as a reward for those who save and invest. The comfortable situation of the affluent is supposedly a reasonable compensation for those with the good sense to maintain a low enough discount rate to provide for the future.

In contrast, poor people supposedly undermine their own interests with excessively high discount rates. Economists have long derided the poor on this account. For example, John Rae, a brilliant Scottish political economist, who migrated from Scotland to Canada, was convinced that the failure of the poor to provide for the future condemned the poor to a state of perpetual poverty (Rae 1834, p. 200). He regarded the small quantity of household utensils in the working-class homes as proof that such people had an excessive discount rate—although he used another term (Rae 1834, p. 202). He complained that the poor squandered their funds on alcohol and tea instead of better pots and pans, which could have allowed them to reduce the amount of food that they waste (Rae 1834, pp. 202–04).

Rae was convinced that the nature of North American society was not conducive to a low discount rate. He lamented that Scottish farmers no longer built stone fences like they once did in their homeland after they came to North America. Instead, they satisfied themselves with wooden fences or living hedges (Rae 1834, p. 206).

Although a stone fence requires considerably more time and effort to build compared with other forms of fencing, once completed it needs almost no maintenance. The wooden fences or living hedges, in contrast, demand additional periodic repairs or replacement. Over a long enough period of time, the upkeep of these less permanent technologies will certainly exceed the extra cost of building a more permanent stone structure.

Rae attributed the willingness to invest in something as durable as stone fences to a strong sense of morality. Not surprisingly, he attributed the highest degree of morality to his Scottish ancestors, while Chinese and Indian people, along with the lower classes, suffered from varying degrees of moral deficiency (Perelman 2000a). More recently, Eric Posner has proposed that negative behaviors that lead to promiscuity, smoking, drinking, less education, crime, and addiction all reflect a high discount rate (Posner 2000, pp. 36–37).

Of course, providing for the future is much easier when you are already blessed with great wealth. In the present-day United States, poor people typically pay more for equivalent goods and services than the rich (Ehrenreich 2001). Even worse, the poor person, living near the edge of survival, rarely enjoys the luxury of being able to plan for the distant future. Instead, the future may appear as an abyss of utter desperation. Lacking hope, forgetting the future might seem preferable to preparing for it.

John Rae might conclude that giving in to despair might be self-defeating. Had the expenditure on drink been saved and then spent wisely, the poor person might have been able to make some progress. In his eyes, the poor person might seem to be the victim of his own irrationality. Indeed, Rae's own fondness for the bottle seems to have played a part in his dismissal as a teacher (James 1965, p. 95).

From the perspective of the poor person, Rae's approach might not have made as much sense. Efforts to provide for the future may have only raised false hopes that were sure to be shattered, given the frequency with which wage disaster seems to strike. The cost of the seemingly inevitable disappointment greatly outweighs the slim possibility of making some headway. Within that perspective, the choice squandering of scarce resources on drink may be more understandable.

Although wealthy people may be more likely to save for the future than those who are less well off, the extent to which people from any social strata are inclined to save may change over time. For instance within the culture of the United States, excessive frugality is the subject of ridicule.

In contrast, despite Rae's condemnation of traditional societies for their neglect of long-term investments, they are notoriously frugal. For example, the mother of the founder of the enormous Mistui organization was reputed to have collected discarded sandals and horseshoes, which woven from straw, could be used as building material for plaster. She had paper strings, with which men and women tied their hair, picked up, spliced, and wound into big balls for use in the store. A leaky wooden dipper became a teapot pad (Horide 2000). Even if the family had fabricated the story to create a mystique about its values, the very idea that such behavior would win favor among the Japanese suggests how high the esteem for frugality might have been.

Even in the United States, prior to the 1920s, society regarded consumer credit unfavorably (Olney 1991, pp. 120–21; Manning 2000, pp. 108–14). Massive advertising campaigns broke down the resistance to borrowing. With the expansion of credit, consumer spending boomed in ways that would have been otherwise unthinkable. With the outbreak of World War II, saving accumulated, in part, because it was supposed to be patriotic and in part, because the trauma of the Depression put a premium on precautionary savings. Perhaps more important, many factories converted to the production of military equipment causing most large ticket items, such as automobiles, to become unavailable.

Saving as a percent of disposable personal income, which stood at 10.9 in 1982, fell rather steadily until it became negative in the second quarter of 2000 (President of the United States 2001, table B-32, p. 313).

Profit Rates and Discount Rates

Although the conventional rhetoric celebrates the morality associated with a low discount rate, it also holds other forces in high esteem that increase the effective discount rate for society as a whole. Specifically, market society regards a high profit rate as an important indicator of economic health.

Although the prevailing rhetoric associates low discount rates with virtue, the same culture that praises that aspect of patience also celebrates high rates of profit as evidence of economic health. Market society even reveres those individuals who succeed in earning high profits. Yet in a market society, profit rates are necessarily connected to the operative discount rate for society as a whole—so much so, that, in effect, a high rate of profit is tantamount to a high discount rate.

In theory, competitive forces should cause the profit rate to fall toward the discount rate. Instead, the prevailing discount rate seems to rise upward toward the profit rate.

To explore how high profit rates trump low discount rates, consider the economic forces that require the depletion of forests. In a market society rational investors seek the highest possible profit. Because the production of mature forests takes many decades, investing in the regeneration of forests is uneconomic.

The earlier discussion about the future having very little value unless the discount rate is very low is relevant here. The immediate cost of replanting a forest comes in undiscounted dollars. The future cost of caring for the forest as it matures does not appear quite as burdensome because those costs will be discounted.

Finally, after say 30 years, the mature forest is ready to harvest. By that time, the discounted value of the wood is so low that the project looks unprofitable unless the value of the trees would be fantastically high.

Strange as this reasoning might seem when applied to a forest, in fact, foresters seem to have been the originators of this logic. Let me put the foresters' role in context. While the modern environmental movement has made some headway in raising the awareness of the ecological importance of forests, for centuries governments had been viewing forests mainly as a revenue source, aside from their importance as a supplier of timber for ship-building, state construction, and fuel.

Given the importance of the forests, the idea began to take hold that "proper" management could improve on the bounty that nature offered.

By the middle of the nineteenth century, the German foresters had become leaders in the "scientific" management of forests (Scott 1998, pp. 11–12). Martin Faustmann, a German forester who was searching for ways to increase the efficiency of forest production, seems to have been the first person to develop the mathematical analysis of profit maximizing over time (Faustmann 1849; Lo"fgren 1983; and Mitra and Wan 1985).

The theoretical elegance of his mathematical procedure represented a breakthrough in economic thinking. Unfortunately, Faustmann achieved his analytical result by treating the complex forest ecosystem as if it were merely a simplified factory for producing a homogeneous output of wood:

> In [this] state "fiscal forestry," ... the actual tree with its vast number of possible uses was replaced by an abstract tree representing a volume of lumber or firewood .... Gone was the vast majority of flora: grasses, flowers, lichens, ferns, mosses, shrubs, and vines. Gone, too, were reptiles, birds, amphibians, and innumerable species of insects. Gone were most species of fauna, except those that interested gamekeepers. (Scott 1998, pp. 12–13)

In effect, the forests would grow with the mathematical precision of a financier's maturing bond. In all fairness, Faustmann was not alone in this respect. He was only formalizing the sort of logic that John Richards applied to the economic infeasibility of maintaining older oak trees because of their slow rate of growth. Regardless of its origin, foresters around the world followed Faustmann's logic by planting a monoculture of the fastest-growing wood they could find. Gifford Pinchot, the second chief forester of the United States and often admired as an early icon of U.S. environmentalism, was trained in German forestry. The British hired a German forester, Dietrich Brandes, to assess and manage the great forest resources of India and Burma. "By the end of the nineteenth century, German forestry science was hegemonic" (Scott 1998, p. 19).

The results were less than positive. In their natural state, the health of the trees depended upon a complex symbiotic network of living organisms, including fungi, insects, mammals, and flora. One student of the German experiment noted:

> It took about one century for them [the negative consequences] to show up clearly. Many of the pure stands grew excellently in the first generation but already showed an amazing retrogression in the second generation. The reason for this is a very complex one and only a simplified explanation can be given.... Then the whole nutrient cycle got out of order and eventually was nearly stopped. (Plochmann 1968, pp. 24–25; cited in Scott 1998, p. 20)

The foresters attempted to rectify the situation by artificially creating habitat for a few selected species that they thought could restore the health of the forest, but they still attempted to maximize yields by growing a single species of trees rather than allowing the natural diversity to return. As might be expected, they were not successful (Scott 1998, p. 21).

More modern foresters began to concern themselves with questions of sustainability. Some even went so far as to suggest that discount rates should be irrelevant in determining forestry practices. Paul Samuelson, a Nobel Prize–winning economist, rebuked them for their naïveté (Samuelson 1976, p. 473). For Samuelson, economic logic must prevail over biological concerns. Only with a zero discount rate will biology and profit-maximizing behavior coincide:

> The higher the effective rate of interest, the greater will be the shortfall of the optimal rotation compared to the age that maximizes steady-state yield. As the interest rate goes to zero, the economists' correct optimum will reach the limit of the foresters' target of maximum sustained yield. (Samuelson 1976, p. 472)

Notice the distinction between "the economists' correct optimum" and the "foresters' [presumably naïve] target." Nowhere does he even consider the possibility that economic behavior might do well to adapt itself to the underlying biological system.

The Discount Rate as an Arbiter of Investments

Discount rates do not just overrule biology; they also discriminate between types of economic schemes. Our earlier example about house mortgages may help to clarify how discount rates weed out certain kinds of projects while favoring others. Recall how interest payments on the mortgage increase substantially with the rate of interest. For example, at 5 percent, a 30-year mortgage for $100,000 will require a monthly payment of $537. At 15 percent, the monthly payment soars to $1264. Just as a higher interest payment can make the mortgage unaffordable, a high enough discount rate can make any undertaking uneconomic.

Now, remember that the earlier mortgage payment example seemed far less extreme than the example of discounting the entire product of humanity because regular mortgage payments commence after one month. Unlike the mortgage example, the forest will earn nothing until the trees reach maturity, even though the forest business may have to cover costs every month until the trees are ready to harvest.

At a lower discount rate, the future benefits will appear more valuable relative to the present and less distant benefits. For example, at a zero discount rate, you would simply add up all the costs of regrowing the trees and compare those costs with the market value of a mature forest.

The forest example illustrates how a high discount rate can weed out those investments that are most forward-looking and selects those with the more immediate payoffs. Unless the discount rate or the costs of regenerating the forest are extremely low or the future value of the timber is extraordinarily high, such an investment may prove to be unattractive in purely monetary terms.

Even worse, as early as the first decade of the twentieth century, some economists had realized that small changes in the discount rate can cause perverse switches in what the most economical technology would be (see Velupillai 1975; and Fisher 1907, pp. 352–53). For example, suppose that two alternative technologies exist. At one interest rate, the first is most economical. At a slightly higher interest rate, the second can become more economical. At a still higher rate, the first technique becomes more advantageous once again. As a result, any link between the discount rate and economic rationality becomes questionable at best.

Even if the manager of a company responsible for the care of the forest realizes the ecological importance of maintaining a sustainable harvest, outside investors will demand that he pursue policies aimed at the highest possible profit. In such an environment, business deems efforts to provide for the future uneconomical.

So we are left with a paradoxical situation. Behavior consistent with a low discount rate, indicating a high value placed upon efforts to provide for the future in the form of saving, supposedly is a credit to both individuals and societies. Yet this same society also seeks out the highest rate of profit, a behavior that punishes business practices that might best provide for the future.

This paradox does not present a problem at all within the context of economics. In fact, economists see the picture of consistency because they measure their world in monetary terms. Through their lens, the future only exists in accountants' books. John Maynard Keynes put his finger on this perspective, writing:

> The "purposive" man is always trying to secure a spurious and delusive immortality for his acts by pushing his interest in them forward into time. He does not love his cat, but his cat's kittens; nor, in truth, the kittens, but only the kittens' kittens, and so on forward forever to the end of catdom. For him jam is not jam unless it is a case of jam tomorrow and never jam today. Thus by pushing his jam always forward into the future, he strives to secure for his act of boiling it an immortality. (Keynes 1930a, p. 330)

Shredding the forest for a quick profit means that investors will have more money to put into another project, whether it be drilling for oil or mining precious metals.

From the perspective of economics, depletion is irrelevant, because everything can substitute for everything else. If wood is scarce, you can use plastic or steel. If those commodities become difficult to obtain, we can invent something else to use in their place. Only money is unique because it offers a permanent store of value that allows you to move your wealth from one sector to another.

Rather than concerning themselves with the consequences of depletion, economists bask in a vision of continual accumulation. The increasing number of things that consumers enjoy, the escalating book value of corporations, and, most of all, an accumulation of monetary wealth, all serve as irrefutable evidence that the economy is providing for the future in the best possible way, even while the future may be irrevocably slipping away piece by piece.

The Social Context of Discount Rates

A high discount rate is embedded within the society as a whole. It is neither entirely good nor bad in itself. Let me use a personal example: the land surrounding the town where I live contains a number of stone fences, built much like those that John Rae described. Workers painstakingly gathered rocks and then piled them on top of one another to construct these fences without any mortar to hold them together. Except where vandals have destroyed these fences, they have survived intact for more than a century.

Much as I admire these fences, when I pass them I do not associate their construction with a particularly low discount rate. Instead, I think about the poor workers whose efforts were valued so cheaply that the landowners could afford to have them do such backbreaking work for a pittance. Had their labor been more expensive, the landowners certainly would have devised a more makeshift form of fencing.

In addition, while the permanence of these structures may appear as a virtue, it also represents a form of inertia. The placement of the fence may have been appropriate for one kind of land use, but an obstacle to another. Even if the fence still has utility, its presence may well inhibit the construction of a more appropriate technology.

Turning to another example, the existence of a variety of railroad gauges in the nineteenth century delayed the creation of a national railroad network. The legacy of obsolete capital supposedly created an even heavier anchor for the British economy. For example, in 1915 Thorstein Veblen proposed that the German economy was able to surpass the English economy because the British built their economy around early technologies. He charged that the British rail gauges were too narrow and that the layouts of the old English towns were ill suited to the transportation needs of a modern industrial system (Veblen 1915, pp. 130–31). In addition, later economists would note that high investment in steam and gas inhibited British use of electrification (Levine 1967, pp. 123–34). As a result, the British were "paying the penalty for having been thrown into the lead and so having shown the way" (Veblen 1915, p. 132).

A decade and a half later, Leon Trotsky returned to the subject of the German economic achievements. For Trotsky, the very backwardness of the economies of Germany and the United States was an advantage, which allowed those countries to leapfrog Britain (Trotsky 1932, p. 3). Again, in the 1960s, in an age when modernization seemed to be within the reach of the colonial regions of Asia, Latin America, and Africa,

Alexander Gerschenkron revived Veblen's theory, suggesting that with the proper institutional framework, backward economies could enjoy a rapid economic development (Gerschenkron 1962). More recently, Alice Amsden suggested that the success of the countries of East Asia during the 1970s and 1980s was due, in part, to the advantages of late development (Amsden 1989).

Following the logic of Veblen and the others who attributed the British decline to a prior commitment to long-lived capital goods, a low discount rate may presage relatively stagnant economic conditions in the future. Of course, nothing prevents the individual owner of a railroad from replacing it, but to do so will not necessarily be profitable when the railroad is part of a larger network. In that case, modernization might require the coordinated efforts of a large number of different business interests.

High Wages and High Discount Rates

While many observers associate the inertia from long-lived capital goods with Britain's fall from world economic leadership, conditions in the United States were different. Old stone fences and even the obsolete railroads were not typical of the U.S. economy. From the very beginning of the U.S. economy, the rapid replacement of capital goods struck visitors as exceptional. The continual pressure of high wages made relatively new plant and equipment quickly become obsolete.

Economists use the expression, induced innovation, to describe this rapid adoption of new techniques to counteract rising wages. The extent of induced innovation struck many visitors to the United States. For example, Alexis de Tocqueville, the famous French aristocrat, who toured the country in the early nineteenth century, reported:

> I once met an American sailor and asked him why his country's ships are made so that they will not last long. He answered offhand that the art of navigation was making such quick progress that even the best of boats would be almost useless if it lasted more than a few years. (de Tocqueville 1835, p. 453)

About the same time, the Secretary of the Treasury "reported in 1832, that the garrets and outhouses of most textile mills were crowded with discarded machinery. One Rhode Island mill built in 1813 had by 1827 scrapped and replaced every original machine" (Habakkuk 1962, p. 57; and the numerous references he cites).

The anticipation of early retirement in the United States was so pervasive that manufacturers in the United States built their machinery from wood rather than more durable materials, such as iron (Strassman 1959a, p. 88). Later in the nineteenth century commentators echoed de Tocqueville's observation that technology in the United States was designed to be short-lived (Schoenhof 1893); for example, the Cornell economist, Jeremiah Jenks asserted:

> No sooner has the capitalist fairly adopted one improved machine, than it must be thrown away for a still later and better invention, which must be purchased at a dear cost, if the manufacturer would not see himself eclipsed by his rival. (Jenks 1890, p. 254, cited in Livingston 1986, p. 39)

In 1889, Andrew Carnegie acknowledged: "Manufacturers have balanced their books year after year only to find their capital reduced at each successive balance.... Combinations, syndicates, trusts—they are willing to try anything" (Carnegie 1889, p. 142).

Eventually, business became more able to protect its investments as the increasing capital requirements diminished competitive forces and massive immigration reduced the cost of labour relative to capital. More important, business learned to combine into trusts, cartels, and monopolies, which curtailed competition.

Carnegie was uniquely contemptuous of the trusts, because he was able to outcompete his rivals by ruthlessly pursuing new technology to a degree unknown at the time. When his assistant, Charles Schwab, reported a superior design for a rolling mill, Carnegie ordered him to raze and reconstruct an existing mill, even though it was only three months old (Livesay 1975, p. 117).

Commentators typically attributed the rapid technical change that they witnessed in the United States to a shortage of labor, which kept wage rates high relative to other countries. They were not exactly correct. High wages, along with the prospect of continual increases in the wage rate, drove business to invest in short-lived technologies, with the expectation that newer technologies would displace them in the near future. The resulting rapid technical change, in turn, created conditions that allowed workers to win even higher wages, reinforcing the demand for still more investment in technical change.

Business also followed a second strategy to cope with its perceived labor shortages by bringing massive waves of immigrants to alleviate the perceived labor shortage. The more that immigration relieved the pressure on wages the less incentive business had to strive for improved efficiency.

The massive influx of immigration was insufficient to snuff out technical change in the industrial states of the northern United States. For example, although Carnegie skillfully used immigration to create ethnic differences to divide his workers, he still profited handsomely from investing in technical change.

In 1875, Captain William Richard Jones, manager of Carnegie's massive Edgar Thomson works in Pittsburgh, explained, "We must steer clear of the West where men are accustomed to infernal high wages. We must steer clear as far as we can of Englishmen who are great sticklers for high wages, small production, and strikes. My experience has shown that Germans and Irish, Swedes and what I denominate Buckwheats (young American country boys), judiciously mixed, make the most effective and tractable force you can find" (Bridge 1903, p. 81).

The South developed a more brutal method of using immigrants to hold down wages. There, an abundant supply of slaves kept labor artificially cheap, eliminating the urgency to improve technology. Even after the slaves achieved formal freedom, the brutal application of Jim Crow laws kept black wages artificially low. Low black wages, in turn, dragged down the wages of white workers. Lacking the pressure of high wages, the South remained technologically backward well into the twentieth century.

I do not mean to suggest here that restrictions on immigration are necessarily unhealthy for an economy. In fact, you can easily make a case that the immigrants promoted technical change by creating a rapidly expanding market that allowed manufacturers to take advantage of economies of scale. However, when business uses immigration as a weapon to keep labor in check, the direct results will be detrimental.

Wages, Discount Rates, and Growth

The effects of high wages and an elevated discount rate that struck de Tocqueville, along with many other visitors to the United States, were closely related to a third phenomenon: an abundance of inexpensive resources. For example, English business leaders reportedly prided themselves on the durability of their capital goods. This attitude may have been related to the scarcity of timber in their country, which made the choice of manufacturing long-lived metal equipment more attractive.

In contrast, business in the United States tended to favor wooden construction, which was more conducive to rapid scrapping. Recall the nineteenth-century report from the Secretary of the Treasury about the widespread scrapping of relatively new machinery.

The relationship between wages and the abundance of resources also astonished European visitors, as well as observant inhabitants of North America. Because land was so cheap, workers supposedly could earn enough to purchase their own farms. As a result, employers had to pay a high wage in order to attract employees. Consequently, a successful manufacturing industry in the United States was supposed all but impossible. For example, Benjamin Franklin observed:

> Land being cheap in that Country, ... hearty young Labouring men, who understand the Husbandry of Corn and Cattle, ... may easily establish themselves there. A little Money sav'd of the good Wages they receive there while they work for others, enables them to buy the Land and begin their Plantation. (Franklin 1782, pp. 607–80)

Quite likely, Franklin did not really believe that high wages would create an insurmountable impediment to the development of manufacturing in United States. He may have only been angling for protective tariffs and subsidies that would have given manufacturing some extra advantage (see Perelman 2000a, pp. 264–65). In any case, his prognosis for manufacturing in the United States was well off the mark. As de Tocqueville vaguely understood, high wages promoted the efficiency that became the hallmark of manufacturing in North America.

In fact, high wages, in combination with an elevated discount rate and an abundance of inexpensive resources, created a fourth characteristic of a successful economy—rapid technological change. This configuration seemed to represent the best of all possible worlds, except for one consideration that, until recently, typically passed unnoticed—the reliance on the continual depletion of a limited system of natural resources.

The origin of inexpensive resources need not be domestic. The example of Holland in the seventeenth century reminds us that countries can draw upon resources from other parts of the world. I suspect that an economy will be more sensitive to depletion the more it relies on local resources.

In a sense, then, the social conditions that give rise to the farm worker paradox are self-defeating since high wages can promote growth. However, the benefit of keeping the poor in poverty is only partly economic. The people who sit on the top of the economic pyramid enjoy both the social distance between themselves and ordinary people as well as the economic luxuries that they have at their disposal.

Earlier, I had made the case that an elevated discount rate, especially to the extent that it is associated with a high interest rate, tilts the distribution of wealth and income in favor of those who control the most capital. High wages can, at least partially, offset the discount rate, putting the pressure for growth on the resource base.

Growth, even slow growth, is predicated on an abundant resource base. Once scarcities kick in, further growth and even the possibility of a constant GDP may be unattainable, depending on how severe the scarcities are.

In chapter 5, I turn to the possibility of using resources more efficiently.

5

Environmental Efficiency

Markets and Environmental Efficiency

According to the iron logic of economics, markets supposedly avoid the Tragedy of the Commons by assigning higher prices to relatively scarce commodities. This form of rationing encourages people to find ways of economizing on scarce resources.

Some economists have even claimed that privatizing public resources is the most effective means of ensuring conservation. In some cases, a number of environmentalists have partially agreed. For example, in mostly arid California, both the state and federal governments supply farmers with subsidized water that is so cheap they can irrigate their fields with abandon. At the same time, the cost of bottled water is more expansive than a comparable measure of gasoline. If the price of agricultural water were raised, farmers would certainly use it more sparingly.

By appealing to this same logic, corporations are winning control of the water supplies throughout much of the world. In the process, they often make water unaffordable for the poor, as we saw in discussing the tragedies of privatization in Bolivia and South Africa.

The anomaly between the subsidized water for California farmers and the unaffordable water for the poor of Cochabamba or South Africa reflects a relatively steady hypocrisy regarding the market. The rich and powerful advocate that the rest of the world submit to the discipline of the market, but they expect absolutely no interference with the subsidies that they enjoy. So while in most contexts, economists, along with powerful business interests, insist that consumers pay market prices for resources, corporate interests tend to resist the application of market discipline to their own behavior.

In the United States, the government not only offers cheap water to powerful agribusiness interests, delivered through an expensive, publicly built system, but it subsidizes virtually every influential corporate interest. For example, while the government charges some money to timber companies for access to the public lands, these payments cannot come close to covering the cost of building roads into the forests to facilitate hauling the lumber to market. Ranchers and mining corporations get land for almost nothing. Yet, we hear little or nothing about the Tragedy of the Commons in the official discussions of these corporate giveaways. This tragedy inflicts harm on the common people as well as the common land.

From some quarters, we hear that the answer to the hypocrisy regarding the market should be to impose market discipline on corporations, as well as the rest of society. In this book, I have tried to show why markets tend to be neither efficient nor equitable.

The example of water takes the argument considerably farther. While some people undoubtedly waste enormous quantities of water, whether in ostentatious displays or careless production techniques, many of the poorest people in the world lack access to the minimum water required to sustain a healthy life. The high price of some "designer water" will not create undue hardships for people with access to healthy tap water, but when the price system excludes people from a necessity of life itself, it has lethal consequences.

Every society imposes limits on what people should legitimately treat as a commodity. In the United States, people are not free to buy and sell sex, drugs, or human organs (see Radin 1996). Why then should the poorest of the poor be forced to pay for water?

Overcoming Waste

Despite the hypocrisy regarding the market, rising prices can encourage conservation. In general, in thinly populated societies with abundant natural resources, people casually discard goods that would elsewhere have considerable value. For example, Adam Smith reported:

> At Buenos Ayres, we are told by Ulloa, . . . [a]n ox . . . cost little more than the labour of catching him.
> Mr. Hume observes, that in the Saxon times, the fleece was estimated at two-fifths of the value of the whole sheep, and that this was much above the proportion of its present estimate. In some provinces of Spain, I have been assured, the sheep is frequently killed merely for the sake of

the fleece and the tallow. The carcass is often left to rot upon the ground . . . . If this sometimes happens even in Spain, it happens almost constantly in Chili, at Buenos Ayres, and in many other parts of Spanish America, where the horned cattle are almost constantly killed merely for the sake of the hide and tallow. (Smith 1776, I.xi.b.7, p. 164; and I.xi.m.6, pp. 246–47; see also Juan and Ulloa 1748; and Hume 1778, i, p. 226)

As societies put more pressure on the environment, either through the expansion of population or the increasing demands of industrial production, they must learn to use resources more intensively. Recall how Josiah Tucker had proposed that a more populated society would take care to recycle urban wastes back to the countryside to restore the fertility of the soil.

Charles Babbage, a remarkable thinker who prematurely tried to construct the first computer in the early nineteenth century, described the incredible diligence with which people would gather up the waste products from a horse slaughtering plant at Montfaucon, near Paris:

1. The hair is first cut off from the mane and tail. It amounts usually to about a quarter of a pound, which, at 5d/lb, is worth 1.25d.
2. The skin is then taken off, and sold fresh to the tanners. It usually weighs about 60 lb., and produces 9s to 12s.
3. The blood may be used as manure, or by sugar refiners or as food for animals . . . . A horse produces about 20 lb. of dried blood, worth about 1s.9d.
4. The shoes are removed from the dead horses . . . The average produce of the shoes and shoe-nails of a horse is about 2 1/2d.
5. The hoofs are sold partly to turners and combmakers, partly to manufacturers of sal ammonia and Prussian blue, who pay for them about 1s 5d.
6. The fat is very carefully collected and melted down. In lamps it gives more heat than oil, and is therefore demanded for enamelers and glass toy makers. It is also used for greasing harness, shoe leather, &c; for soap and for making gas; it is worth about 6d per lb. A horse on an average yields 8 lb. of fat, worth about 4s, but well fed horses sometimes produce nearly 60 lb.
7. The best pieces of the flesh are eaten by the workmen; the rest is employed as food for cats, dogs, pigs, and poultry. It is likewise used as manure, and in the manufacture of Prussian blue. A horse has from 300 to 400 lb. of flesh, which sells for from 1l. 8s. to 1l. 17s.
8. The tendons are separated from the muscles: the smaller are sold fresh, to the glue makers in the neighbourhood; the larger are dried, and sent off in greater quantities for the same purpose. A horse yields about 1 lb. of dried tendons, worth about 3d.
9. The bones are sold to cutlers, fan makers, and manufacturers of sal ammoniac and ivory black. A horse yields about 90 lbs., which sell for 2s.

10. The smaller intestines are wrought into coarse strings for lathes; the larger are sold as manure.
11. Even the maggots, which are produced in great numbers in the refuse, are not lost. Small pieces of the horse flesh are piled up, about half a foot high; and being covered slightly with straw to protect them from the sun, soon allure the flies, which deposit their eggs in them. In a few days the putrid flesh is converted into a living mass of maggots. These are sold by measure; some are used for bait in fishing, but the greater part as food for fowls, and especially for pheasants. One horse yields maggots which sell for about 1s. 5d.
12. The rats which frequent these establishments are innumerable, and they have been turned to profit by the proprietors. The fresh carcass of a horse is placed at night in a room, which has a number of openings near the floor. The rats are attracted into it, and the openings near the floor are closed. 16,000 rats were killed in one room in four weeks, without any perceptible diminution of their number. The furriers purchase the rat skins at about 3s. the hundred. (Babbage 1835, pp. 393–94)

The simple, labor-intensive methods that Babbage described are incompatible with a modern, high-wage economy. Nonetheless, business could create industrial equivalents of the activities that Babbage described by using modern technology to recapture and reuse what would otherwise be waste. Indeed, in Upton Sinclair's novel, *The Jungle*, based on meticulous journalistic research, he described the process in a fictional plant:

No tiniest particle of organic matter was wasted in Durham's. Out of the horns of the cattle they made combs, buttons, hair-pins, and imitation ivory; out of the shin bones and other big bones they cut knife and toothbrush handles, and mouthpieces for pipes; out of the hoofs they cut hairpins and buttons, before they made the rest into glue. From such things as feet, knuckles, hide clippings, and sinews came such strange and unlikely products as gelatin, isinglass, and phosphorus, bone-black, shoe-blacking, and bone oil. They had curled-hair works for the cattle-tails, and a "woolpullery" for the sheep-skins; they made pepsin from the stomachs of the pigs, and albumen from the blood, and violin strings from the ill-smelling entrails. When there was nothing else to be done with a thing, they first put it into a tank and got out of it all the tallow and grease, and then they made it into fertilizer. (Sinclair 1906, pp. 44–45)

Lip Dwellers and Cockroaches

While successful efforts to reuse and recycle are, in principle, admirable, such efforts also pose risks—especially in so far as biological materials are concerned. The redistributing of the organic matter provides openings for pathogenic organisms to gain a new toehold. The spread of the mad cow disease perhaps offers the most dramatic illustration of the sort of dangers that I have in mind.

Modern industrialized slaughterhouses produce far more potential waste than Babbage or even Sinclair could have ever imagined. Left untreated, these animal remains can create a health hazard by nurturing vermin or by harboring dangerous bacteria. The utilization of these waste products could potentially create a sizeable benefit for society.

Instead of enticing rats to enter for the benefit of poor scavengers as in Babbage's account, specialized rendering companies collected waste products from the cattle slaughterhouses and converted much of them into animal feed. This strategy made excellent sense, except for one problem: a primitive biological structure, known as a prion, which causes brain impairment and eventually death. Turning the remains of the slaughtered animals containing these prions into feed passes on the prions to other animals. Worse still, from the standpoint of human beings, people who eat animal products made from these infected animals also pick up the prions, leaving them vulnerable to mad cow disease.

The problem of mad cow disease would not have been nearly as severe in a simpler, relatively localized agricultural system. True, the remains of a slaughtered carcass, with prions having already begun to destroy its brain, might infect people in a localized agricultural system just as surely as in a modern, globalized system. However, the problem would be more likely to remain localized in the simpler system. Once the outbreak became recognized and people were able to identify the source of the problem, the slaughter of a relatively small number of animals could suffice to stop the spread of the disease.

In contrast, in a modern agricultural system, both live animals and their processed flesh move over long distances. Packers then mix together the flesh of innumerable animals. A single 4-ounce ground beef patty may contain pieces of animals from more than a thousand different carcasses based on analyses performed in four U.S. beef packing plants and six beef-grinding plants (Smith et al. 2000). These animals might originate in a number of different states or even different countries.

To make matters more complex, the prions require a considerable time to destroy a brain. Decades may pass before the symptoms become apparent. All these factors make identification of the exact cause of the outbreak virtually impossible. Despite the difficulty of identifying the cause of an outbreak, it still would remain localized.

In the case of mad cow disease, a tight environmental system transports harmful organisms into cycles where they would not otherwise be.

The waste created by the failure to take advantage of apparent efficiencies may be slight compared with the risks.

The tragedy of mad cow disease represents a more general problem than the contamination of meat. As modern, industrial societies put more demands on the environment, the technologies that are supposed to increase the efficiency of resource utilization also create risks.

Similarly, the origin of new strains of influenza seems to arise out of one of the tightest systems of environmental efficiency ever devised: Asian farming systems that bring ducks, pigs, and people into close contact. The viruses multiply in the birds, then jump to the pigs, where they rapidly mutate. Every decade or two a mutation capable of creating a pandemic develops—the most lethal of which was the 1918–1919 influenza epidemic that killed at least 40 million people (see Scholtissek and Naylor 1988).

Mad cow disease offers another dramatic illustration of the risks associated with tight environmental systems. Until recently, nobody had any idea that prions even existed. Such discoveries are not unique. For example, scientists recently found a new creature, wholly unrelated to any previously known species. This creature lives only on the lips of one particular type of lobster (Morris 1995). Although this form of specialization is remarkable, it could also leave the lip dwellers vulnerable to even a slight change in their environment. For example, some external environmental change may cause the lobsters to migrate. While this new location might be more favorable for the lobsters, it may not support the continued existence of their tiny lip dwellers.

Of course, not all flora and fauna are as specialized as the lip dwellers. For example, in stark contrast, the cockroach is a model of adaptability. It appears to have no specialization whatsoever. Instead, the cockroach seems capable of adapting itself to virtually any conditions.

The more society has to adapt to extreme resource scarcity, the more it comes to resemble the lip dwellers rather than the cockroach. For example, the Inuit people, living in harsh conditions with limited resource availability, have marvelously adapted themselves to their environment. Their specific adaptive strategies would be of little use in more temperate environments. Relying as they do on relatively few essential resources, a substantial decline in any one of them could threaten the Inuit's survivability.

But What is Waste?

The U.S. economy spewed out 209 million tons of garbage in 1995, or a bit less than 1 ton per person according to data from the United States

Environmental Protection Agency (1999). Doug Henwood, editor of the invaluable *Left Business Observer*, informed me that New York City alone produces 26,000 tons of garbage every day (New York City Department of Sanitation). Both of these estimates exclude the innumerable tons of garbage strewn about as litter, which may never arrive at an official garbage dump. Even more ominously, the economy bombards the environment with enormous quantities of toxic waste products.

Eliminating waste is, no doubt, a noble goal. Waste products not only create harmful effects, but they may also represent lost opportunities to utilize potentially productive resources. Few modern corporations gave much thought to their waste stream—at least until they came under regulatory pressure. Left to themselves they take the attitude that once the waste leaves their pipes and smokestacks, effluent need not be of any concern, except in the relatively unlikely case that a court finds the company liable for damage.

Henry Ford was an exception. He devoted an entire chapter of his book, *Today and Tomorrow*, to describing the lengths to which his company went to either reduce waste or to put it to good use. The company transformed scrap wood into containers and backing for upholstery; slag from blast furnaces was used in making cement; broken shovel handles became handles for screwdrivers. Two men devoted most of their time just to repairing mop buckets (Ford 1926, pp. 91–97).

Ford even attempted to use soybeans as an input in as many automobile parts as possible. By the mid-1930s, a bushel of soybeans went into the paint, horn button, gearshift knob, door handles, window trim, accelerator pedal, and timing gears of every Ford car (Lewis 1995; also see Institute of Technology 1935).

My college roommate's father recounted what became my favorite example of a Ford economy. During the 1920s, he worked for Timken, a company that supplied ball bearings for Ford. The orders from Ford required that Timken ship their product in wooden crates that were made according to strict specifications. Then Ford had his workers carefully disassemble these crates, drill a few holes in them and then install them as the floorboards in his cars.

The Division of Labor and System Vulnerability

The case of the Sumitomo glue factory, a highly integrated system, suggests a related vulnerability from what we might call "network risks." In this case, the system lacks any redundancy. When one element fails, the system can no longer function. Part of what would be lost in efficiency with a smaller-scale, more distributed strategy of glue production would be gained in resilience.

Michael Kremer referred to this phenomenon as the "O-ring production Function," alluding to the Challenger space shuttle disaster, where the failure of the O-ring caused the entire crew to perish (Kremer 1993). Recall our earlier example of spare tires. Under normal conditions, a car would be more "efficient" without any provision for a spare tire. The extra space and energy used to carry a spare tire is wasted—except, of course, for those unexpected occasions when one of the tires fails and the spare becomes a necessity.

Ignoring for the moment the real possibility that a tire failure can prove fatal, most people carry a spare tire in their cars because they prefer to reduce the risk of being stranded without a spare. In effect, a flat tire represents a type of O-ring failure in the sense that the typical car is not a particularly effective form of transportation without four functioning tires. Generalizing from the tire example, in many situations in which uncertain conditions preclude knowledge of future demands, efficiency over the long run requires a certain degree of redundancy.

One strategy for preventing an O-ring-like failure is to ensure that absolutely nothing goes wrong. Within an engineering system, attention to every detail might prevent most failures, but even the best engineers and production systems cannot entirely eliminate the risk of problems. Of course, devoting excessive attention to every detail, especially when failures do not create horrible results, represents a form of waste. The expression, checking and double-checking, suggests that care represents a form of redundancy.

Redundancy becomes increasingly important because modern society depends ever more on complex systems that are, by their very nature, brittle. Small mistakes can lead to big problems (Perrow 1984). No matter how careful responsible people might be, especially when systems must function within a natural environment instead of controlled laboratory conditions, unanticipated events can cause breakdowns.

All too often, corporations are willing to forgo the laborious tasks of double-checking. Instead, they find it profitable to outsource work, often to the lowest bidder. In this arrangement, the subcontractor has the responsibility for the errors, but in order to win the bid, it also has a financial incentive to keep its labor costs to a minimum.

In a famous case that sadly illustrates the risks involved in this arrangement, an airline, Valuejet, outsourced its maintenance rather than having its own employees perform the work. The contractor employed low-paid, low-skilled, Spanish-speaking workers and then supplied them with unintelligible, contradictory safety manuals, and unavailable safety equipment. Horrendous breakdowns in communications only made matters worse. While this strategy might seem to be cost effective in the short run, the company's luck could not hold out forever. Regulators never paid much attention to the potential risks until one of the planes tragically crashed killing all the passengers and the crew (Langewiesche 1998).

Rather than having their own unionized workers perform tasks, companies often contract out to independent companies with lower labor costs. Normally, the strategy will be cost effective, but occasionally serious accidents will occur snuffing out the lives of hundreds of people at a time. While people might rationally choose to accept a certain degree of redundancy, such as a spare tire, a business seeking to maximize immediate profits sees less reason to provide for redundancy.

The deregulation of energy in California illustrates this indeterminacy of efficiency. Energy demands fluctuate. Demand surges during what are known as peak energy periods. In California, energy demands increase during the summer when air conditioners run full blast. During these peak energy periods, shortages of energy sometimes occur. Some entities signed contracts that gave them lower rates for their electricity in return for temporarily reducing their demand when shortages occur.

Under deregulation without any provision for reserve capacity, the state had to pay enormous prices to meet the needs of the state. This arrangement allowed the handful of energy suppliers to withhold power to drive rates up. For example, in California in April 2000, the wholesale power at peak times when electricity is most expensive was about $36 a megawatt-hour. By April of 2001, well before peak summer demands, the price reached $300 per megawatt-hour. By May 20 and May 21 of that year, peak power for delivery at the California–Oregon border rose even further to $345 per megawatt-hour. At one point, the State of California paid one power purchaser $1,900 per megawatt-hour.

In recent years, many business pundits have made a virtue of system vulnerability. This fad began in the 1970s, when the Japanese economy was setting the pace for the rest of the world. At the time, Japanese business popularized the just-in-time production technique. The idea was to run a production system as tightly as possible. The constant stress of being near an O-ring type break down required that all workers remain at a heightened state of alertness. This practice would expose weaknesses in the system, allowing the company to become more and more efficient. The fashionable just-in-time production soon spread across the U.S. business world.

This quest for efficiency might seem commendable, except that the just-in-time strategy makes the most sense on an assembly line where conditions are relatively stable. Small events can provide challenges that can reveal potential improvements in productivity. In the case of a more extreme upheaval, the slackness of a more traditional production system will probably prove advantageous.

Financial stringency has imposed the just-in-time system where it is least appropriate. For example, hospitals in the United States are currently under severe cost pressures. One technique, for cutting costs is to run emergency rooms on a just-in-time inventory basis. In this way, hospitals do not have to pay for more supplies than they typically need. Because hospitals can predict fairly well how many people normally come in for treatment during a typical week, this strategy may usually prove to be efficient.

In addition, as many hospitals eliminate emergency rooms, the system as a whole is beginning to run on a just-in-time basis. The remaining operations will be running more near capacity on a typical day. The problem is that not all days are typical. At infrequent and unpredictable intervals, catastrophes will occur for which the hospital will have an inadequate capacity to meet urgent needs. So, by running emergency rooms nearer full capacity and with a tight inventory of supplies, they are left unprepared for the times when they are most needed.

The hospital will not bear the ultimate cost of the lack of preparedness. Instead, the people who cannot find proper treatment will be the ones to suffer. In hindsight, the hospital may recognize that the relatively minor cost savings from inventory reduction may not come close to justifying the personal losses resulting from the shortsighted cost savings.

In chapter 7, I emphasize how military casts aside the sort of thinking that guides markets when facing life and death situations. The case of redundancy is no exception to this rule. Seymour Hersh cited a high-ranking officer who reflected on the military's attitude toward redundancy: "The military is not like a corporation that can be streamlined. It is the most inefficient machine known to man. It's the redundancy that saves lives" (Hersh 2003).

Corn Leaf Blight

Supposedly, one of the greatest triumphs of agricultural research was the development of hybrid corn. A closer look at the history of hybrid corn suggests a note of caution as well.

The technique of hybridization requires the production of two separate pure strains of corn, which are then crossed to produce the hybrid seed. To effect the crossbreeding, workers had to remove the tassels from one strain to make sure that it would pollinate with the other breed. Manually cutting the tassels of corn used to cost seed growers between $100 and $200 per acre. To avoid this cost, seed growers turned to plant breeders. In 1925 scientists observed an onion plant in Davis, California, with no male organs (Saini and Davis 1969). By 1931, corn breeders discovered the same trait in a corn plant (Horsfall 1975). In 1945, another line of male sterile corn was discovered in Texas. This gene, dubbed Texas Male Sterile or Tms, was incorporated in all hybrid corn. Breeders added another gene discovered by D. F. Jones, which restored the tassels in subsequent generations. This development in plant breeding eliminated the need for the 125,000 high school students who earned some extra money cutting tassels from the corn.

In 1958, one of the giants in corn breeding, Donald F. Jones, discoverer of the restorer gene, warned his fellow workers that they were courting disaster in their reliance on genetic engineering: "Genetically uniform pure line varieties are very productive and highly desirable when experimental conditions are favorable and the varieties are well protected from pests of all kinds. When these external factors are not favorable, the results can be disastrous due to some new virulent parasite" (cited in Horsfall 1975, p. 110).

Three years later two researchers in the Philippines confirmed Jones's warning (Mercado and Lantican 1961). They found that a fungus, *helminthosporium maydis*, virulently attacked corn containing the Tms gene. Other corn was relatively immune. American breeders ignored this omen.

By 1970, no more warnings were needed. *Helminthosporium maydis* violently struck the U.S. corn crop. The resulting corn leaf blight destroyed about 15 percent of the national corn crop. South Carolina lost about 43 percent of its crop, and Illinois, where about one-quarter of the nation's corn crop is grown, lost about 24 percent.

Large as these losses were, they were far less than what might have occurred had the weather not suddenly taken a favorable turn during the growing season. Even so, the 1970 losses from this fungus cost the nation about $1 billion.

Seed growers should have worried that male sterility was already known to alter the transport and synthesis of DNA and RNA in the male organs of plants (Saini and Davis 1969). When *helminthosporium maydis* struck, it upset the workings of the mitochondria, small oddly shaped bodies whose action allows chemical reactions to take place inside the cells that house them (Miller and Koeppe 1971). Somehow, the incorporation of the male sterile gene weakened the resistance of the mitochondria to the fungus. Other corn plants were relatively immune.

The hybridization of corn also seems to have lowered its nutritional qualities. According to William Albert Albrecht, once the head of the Department of Soil Science at the University of Missouri:

> in 1911, before the hybridization practice was common, the mean concentration in this feed grain was reported at 10.30% for a single grain. By 1950, the top grade among five then listed contained 8.8%, while the lowest had 7.9%. By 1956: among 50 tested corn grains from the outlying experiment fields of the Missouri Experiment Station, one sample of these hybrids reached a low of 5.15% of "crude" protein, or a value of just half what it had been 45 years ago. (Albrecht 1959)

When hybrid corn was first introduced, the livestock industry complained about the poor performance of hybrid corn as a feed. Since then the industry had to supplement the corn with soybeans and fish meal (Perelman 1977, p. 47).

Later, the protein content of corn began to increase somewhat as a result of more intensive fertilizer use, but not back to its earlier level. The effects of fertilizer, however, also seem to have altered the mix of protein, decreasing the levels of lysine and tryptophan (Anon. 1977).

I do not mean to condemn plant breeding as such. Many of our most desirable harvests differ greatly from the indigenous plants from which they have descended. Over the centuries, farmers have bred many wonderful properties into their crops. They did so through a slow process of trial and error. Because different farmers followed a different breeding strategy, for any given region the harvest had a considerable degree of genetic diversity. As a result, a disease or a predator that might destroy some susceptible plants might come up against resistance in others. However, when breeders become too ambitious and try to produce a uniform crop with an excessive degree of genetic uniformity, they risk disasters, such as the corn leaf blight.

6

Back to the Farm Worker Paradox

The Context of the Farm Worker Paradox

In the early days of economics, or political economy as it was then called, the farm worker paradox hardly appeared paradoxical. The vast majority of economists, prior to and in the early days of the Industrial Revolution, advocated a world in which all but a select few people would work as many hours as possible for a subsistence wage. Women, children as young as three, religious orders, and convicts all appeared as cheap sources of labor power (Perelman 2000a).

Consider the words of Bernard Mandeville: "in a free Nation where Slaves are not allow'd of, the surest Wealth consists in a Multitude of laborious Poor" (Mandeville 1723, p. 287). In a similar vein, Smith's contemporary, the Reverend Townsend, writing as "A Well-Wisher to Mankind," wrote:

> [Direct] legal constraint [to labor] . . . is attended with too much trouble, violence, and noise, . . . whereas hunger is not only a peaceable, silent, unremitted pressure, but as the most natural motive to industry, it calls forth the most powerful exertions . . . . Hunger will tame the fiercest animals, it will teach decency and civility, obedience and subjugation to the most brutish, the most obstinate, and the most perverse. (Townsend 1786, pp. 404 and 407)

Some of Smith's contemporaries also insisted that a small group of affluent people must have the means to purchase the goods that the majority produced. The aristocrats seemed to be more than willing to take on that role. Egalitarian thoughts never crossed the minds of the privileged classes whose ideas constituted the intellectual heritage of the age. How else could the wealthy enjoy their prosperity except through the poverty of the masses?

So, while the farm workers whom Adam Smith observed wracked their bodies in obscure poverty, the aristocratic landlords ostentatiously displayed their lavish wealth. This situation seemed to be the natural order of things.

True, a handful of economists, such as Adam Smith, did occasionally seem to express what might seem to be some mild egalitarian sentiments, but, in the case of Smith, his real purpose was not really egalitarian at all. Instead, he was intent on preaching quiescence. Like modern economists, he attributed rural poverty to the absence of market norms. He wanted the poor to believe that acceptance of market norms would lead to a modest prosperity for the working class (see Perelman 2000b, chapter 9).

The fairness of the system that Adam Smith advanced rested on a questionable foundation—that the existing distribution has some basis in justice. Landownership, however, rarely has honorable origins. The great French novelist, Honoré de Balzac, once perceptively observed: "The secret of great wealth with no obvious source is some forgotten crime, forgotten because it was done neatly" (Balzac 1991, p. 103).

Adam Smith displayed clear insight into the calculations that go into the perpetrations of such a crime:

> But the ambitious man flatters himself that, in the splendid situation to which he advances, he will have so many means of commanding the respect and admiration of mankind, and will be enabled to act with such superior propriety and grace, that the lustre of his future conduct will entirely cover, or efface, the foulness of the steps by which he arrived at that elevation. (Smith 1759, I.iii.3.8, p. 64)

Indeed, some crimes are only vaguely remembered and largely forgiven—at least in the eyes of the law. Typically, those who were the most powerful, whether they were members of the existing society or invaders, were able to lay claim to land by virtue of superior force. If nobody could wrest the land away from them, they could pass their land on to their heirs. After a few generations, the bloody origins of ownership began to become clouded and maintenance of existing property relations became the fundamental principle of justice.

In countries where modern imperialist powers have only relatively recently confiscated the indigenous people's land, say in the last 150 years, the role of force in determining the pattern of land ownership is fairly obvious to anyone who cares to study such matters. For example, I live on property that the Spaniards once stole from the Native Americans. The Spaniards, in turn, lost the land in the Mexican revolution, only to have the United States capture it later. Because my part of the state was too dry to attract many Europeans, the Mechoopda continued to occupy it until improvements in transportation finally made the land profitable to farm commercially. Then the Mechoopda had to give way to more powerful interests. Certainly, I am overlooking some other less far-reaching thefts of this land, but the fact remains that virtually no land ownership in the world has either honest or honorable origins. Regardless of the violent origin of ownership, the law sanctifies any current property rights and threatens to punish anybody who would think of dispossessing the "rightful" owner of the day.

Winning possession from a previous occupier is sufficient justification for property rights. For example, John Marshall, writing for an unanimous U.S. Supreme Court in 1823, noted, "The potentates of the old world found no difficulty in convincing themselves that they made ample compensation to the inhabitants of the new, by bestowing on them civilization and Christianity." Marshall seemed to be content to accept that exchange. He gave further justification, observing that England had authorized Cabot and others to take possession of lands, "notwithstanding the occupancy of the natives, who were heathens, and, at the same time, admitting the prior title of any Christian people who may have made a previous discovery." Since the United States was the successor to England, the same sovereign rights passed to the new nation (Johnson V. Mcintosh 8 Wheat. 543). This ruling still stands as the law of the land.

In other countries, where successful invaders have not been able to hold on to confiscated land for many centuries, untangling the pattern of ownership is more complicated. In either case, neither justice nor economic efficiency seems to have any relationship to the distribution of land.

Resolving the Farm Worker Paradox: First Attempt

Control over resources, beginning with land, was the primary source of individual wealth, even in the early capitalist world. Mere ownership of the land, regardless of its origins, distinguished Adam Smith's farm workers from their superiors. In that world, each class earned a reward supposedly commensurate with its productive contributions: the landlords for their land and the workers for their labor. Or, a third party with the wherewithal to employ the workers could pay rent to the landlord with the expectation that his workers could produce enough of a surplus to provide him with a profit after covering the expense of both wages and rents.

Undaunted by such considerations, early economists attempted to explain away inequality by devising clever rationales for the unequal distribution of the ownership of land (e.g., see Turgot 1766). They began by assuming that private property in land was a natural phenomenon. This assumption is questionable. Territoriality, unlike property rights, may be almost universal. Animals frequently claim territory for their own, either as individuals or as part of a group, but the modern concept of private property is entirely different; it allows the owner to sell the land voluntarily to another—something unknown in the animal world.

After all, many cultures never acknowledged private property in land. For example, when Peter Minuet famously "purchased" Manhattan Island from the Lenapes for $24 worth of trinkets, the sellers probably had no understanding that they were engaging in a commercial transaction. They may have been willing to allow the settlers to use the land and they may have accepted a gift, but the rights to usage were a matter of hospitality. I suspect that they saw the situation as somewhat like the exchange that occurs when a guest brings a bottle of wine for the hosts before settling down for dinner, without any intention of claiming property rights to the chair.

Next, to buttress their suggestion that the basis of landholdings may have some grounds in justice, these economists fancifully assumed that the land was once distributed equally. Then, they proposed that as population gradually increased, ownership became increasingly subdivided among the descendants of the original owners. Over time, the sizes of these subdivided holdings would become unequal, with children from smaller families having more land. Some of the inheritors of very small parcels would be unable to sustain themselves from the land. They would have to resort to working for those few, who by dint of talent and diligence, managed to accumulate more property.

So, according to this fabulous tale, everybody eventually got what they deserved and resources fell into the hands of those most capable of making productive use of them. This attempt at a resolution of the farm worker paradox flies in the face of the popular characterization of the great landlords as lazy and dissolute. Recall how many landlords were so out of touch with their land that to induce them to visit their properties the British Parliament felt compelled to give them special hunting privileges. This negative interpretation of the contributions of those landlords had greater claim to veracity than the comforting economic rationalization.

All the while, the rich did everything in their power to rig the system so that the poor remained in poverty.

Fossil Fuels and the Farm Worker Paradox

The belief that the masses should necessarily remain in poverty continued through the early decades of the nineteenth century. Later, in the final decades of the nineteenth century, as factories began to harness the power of fossil fuel more effectively, an entirely new set of problems emerged. Until the Industrial Revolution, the key to increased productivity was to find methods of making workers labor longer and harder. Technological changes occurred but the pace was painfully slow by modern standards. The Industrial Revolution created entirely new possibilities. The last part of the nineteenth century saw the realization of these possibilities.

Fossil fuel was the key to the Industrial Revolution. True, some industries had already harnessed inanimate power in the form of wind and water. Indeed, some of the early textile mills relied on waterpower, but the number of available sites with suitable water was both very limited and seasonal.

The opportunity to turn fossil fuel into a power source seemed to offer an unlimited source of energy. The widespread availability of fossil fuels meant that, to a large extent, workers no longer drove the machines; instead the machines drove the workers. Employers still had to tap into streams of workers, but not nearly as much as traditional methods of production would have required.

Once England began to shift to fossil fuels, the economy could transcend the limits normally imposed by a system of production dependent on traditional organic sources. For example, population in England grew by approximately 280 percent between 1550 and 1820. In contrast, all the major countries of Continental Europe grew by roughly 80 percent (Wrigley 2000, p. 118).

By the mid-nineteenth century, these fossil fuel–based technologies created an unprecedented rate of technical change. John Lukacs provided some perspective on this assertion, writing:

> Napoleon could progress from the Seine to the Tiber no faster, and no differently, than could Julius Caesar two thousand years before: yet a century later one could travel from Paris to Rome in less than twenty-four hours in a comfortable sleeping-car. The locomotive, the steamship, the motorcar, the submarine, the airplane; the radio, the telegraph, the telephone—they were all invented and put into practice before 1914, the only post-1914 invention of this kind having been television. Of course, there is a difference between the supersonic jet plane and the Wright Brothers' contraption, but it is a difference in degree not in kind. (Lukacs 1968, pp. 306–07)

The telegraph represents another interesting example. Although recent writers enthuse about the Internet, the transition from the pony express to the telegraph was a far more dramatic innovation than the creation of the Internet. One popular writer even referred to the telegraph as the Victorian Internet (Standage 1998).

These revolutionary technological improvements brought a whole new set of problems in their wake. To begin with, although the harnessing of fossil fuels put to rest most concerns about scarcity by the late nineteenth century, the new technologies also created anxiety about the disruption resulting from excess production.

A rapid succession of technological changes made possible dramatic reductions in costs. For example, the Bessemer process reduced the price of steel rails by 88 percent from the early 1870s to the late 1880s; electrolytic refining reduced aluminum production costs by 96 percent; synthetic blue dye costs fell by 95 percent from the 1870s to 1886 (Jensen 1993, p. 835). Most of these technological improvements had a fatal drawback for the corporations: they required a much bigger scale of operation than earlier methods of production. To gain a competitive edge with these technologies, businesses were erecting colossal economic enterprises that collectively had the capacity to produce far more than the public could afford to buy (see Perelman 1996). As businesses flooded the market with an excess supply of goods, they drove prices down toward the cost of production. These production costs, however, did not include the cost of the plant and equipment.

To make matters worse, as I have already noted the rapid succession of technological improvements forced many companies to scrap capital goods long before they could pay for themselves, even with much higher prices. The most famous example may have been Andrew Carnegie's decision to raze and reconstruct a three-month-old steel mill once he learned of a superior technology (Livesay 1975, p. 117).

Within the competitive environment of the time, corporations tripped over one another to lower costs in order to capture a greater market share, or even just to maintain their previous position. The major alternative to the wholesale scrapping of capital goods was to keep wages down. Waves of new immigrants together with repressive government actions held wages in check for the mass of workers. Recall how Captain Jones developed his "recipe" for "judiciously" mixing different national and ethnic groups for Carnegie.

Here again, the apparent solution created a new problem. While low wages are a benefit for an individual employer, a pervasive policy of lowering wages restricts the size of the market creating further difficulties for business. As a result, instead of bringing prosperity to modern industry, as mentioned earlier the new fossil fuel–driven technologies created conditions of excess production and deficient demand, leaving a trail of widespread bankruptcies. Plummeting farm prices made economic conditions even worse, since about half the population was still rooted in the agrarian economy.

Despite the economic problems of industry, the gap between rich and poor widened. The stark contrast between the productive capacity of the economy and the miserable conditions of the working people who produced the goods was painfully obvious to anybody who cared to look.

Business tried to overcome the barrier of limited markets by prodding governments to use their influence to expand markets overseas. Business also successfully encouraged the government to build up the military, especially the Navy, which was seen as crucial in opening up new markets and preventing industrialists from other economies from making incursions into lucrative markets.

This strategy created still another contradiction. Because all the governments of advanced capitalist nations attempted to expand their foreign markets in the same way, they continually jostled against each other. By the early twentieth century, this competitive scramble to find and protect new markets intensified. Soon, the inevitable clashes got out of hand, leading, to a great extent, to World War I.

Capitalist Apologetics

The immense productive capacity of the economy cast a dark shadow over the embarrassing gap between the poverty of the masses and the conspicuous consumption of the elite. Unions were gathering strength despite a hostile legal structure. In addition, business repeatedly launched violent attacks on union members. States frequently also felt compelled to call upon the National Guard to quell protests. At other times, employers hired private armies, such as those that the Pinkerton Detective Agency supplied.

Warning signs about rising discontent were everywhere for the affluent classes. Making matters even more precarious, the giant factories required large numbers of workers to live and work in nearby neighborhoods. This massing of dissatisfied workers presented a far greater threat to employers than the more dispersed arrangement typical of traditional technologies. In addition, international events did not provide much comfort for the wealthy. For example, right after 1871, workers in Paris took over the municipal government, supposedly inspired by Karl Marx's recently published *Capital*.

In this highly charged atmosphere, the leading economists were intent on calming the passions of those who were enraged by the inequities around them. Economists around the world attempted to reformulate economic theory in an effort to refute Marx and prove that the economic system was just.

For example, fear of the "working classes, with their growing numbers and powers of combination" seems to have motivated the theories of William Stanley Jevons, whom we have encountered before (Jevons 1866, p. 43; see also Dobb 1973; Meek 1967 and 1973; and Henderson 1955). At the same time that Jevons was developing his theory of value in England, Léon Walras was moving in a similar direction in Switzerland (Wicksell 1934, pp. 73–74). So was Carl Menger in Austria. Their attempted refutation of socialist tendencies consisted in refining the theory of value to show that the Invisible Hand of laissez-faire leads to the best of all possible worlds.

John Bates Clark, the most important economist in the United States at the time, also stepped into the breach by attempting to explain away the farm worker paradox. We have the testimony of Clark's son and sometimes coauthor, John Maurice Clark, himself an economist of note, that the "key fact" in his father's work is that "his statements are oriented at Marx, and are best construed as an earnest, and not meticulously qualified, rebuttal of the Marxian exploitation theory" (Clark 1952, p. 610).

In the introduction to his most famous book, *The Distribution of Wealth* (1899), Clark explicitly stated his objective. He was disturbed by the popular sentiment that labor was exploited. In his words: "The indictment that hangs over society is 'exploited labor'" (Clark 1899, p. 4). He set out to disprove that perspective by demonstrating "that the distribution of income was controlled by a natural law, and that this law, if it worked without friction, would give to every agent of production the amount of wealth which that agent creates" (Clark 1899, p. v). In this way, "free competition tends to give labor what labor creates, to capitalist what capital creates, and to entrepreneurs what the coordinating function creates" (Clark 1899, p. 3). And, of course, those who own resources, such as land, earn what they "contribute."

In fact, Clark's "proof" consisted of nothing more than an abstract theory that depended upon absurdly unrealistic assumptions. Despite its theoretical shortcomings, Clark's conclusion was so comforting that his theory became a central part of modern economic dogma. In celebration of his contributions to conventional economic theory, the American Economic Association awards the John Bates Clark Medal once every two years to "that American Economist under forty who is adjudged to have made a significant contribution to economic thought and knowledge."

One logical consequence of Clark's approach was that the structure of ownership was a matter of indifference—meaning that power relationships were irrelevant. This idea also took hold among economists. In the first years of the twentieth century, Knut Wicksell, the highly influential Swedish economist mentioned earlier, took up this theme: "We may, therefore, assume that the landowner will hire labourers for a wage . . . or that the laborers will hire the land for rent" (Wicksell 1934, p. 109). In either case, the outcome for the workers and landowners would be the same. Almost a half century later, Paul Samuelson, the Nobel Prize–winning economist whom we have encountered several times already, writing in an article devoted to an attempted refutation of Marx, restated the idea about the indifference of institutional arrangements: "Remember that in a perfectly competitive market it really doesn't matter who hires whom" (Samuelson 1957, p. 894).

Those who do the hiring obviously have power over the employee. No matter. Rather than an exercise of power, economists only see voluntary arrangements. Two highly respected economists compared the relation between employer and employee to that between shopper and grocer. They maintained that just as shoppers can fire their grocers by patronizing a different store, employers can chose to do business with different employees. "Telling an employee to type this letter rather than to file that document is like telling my grocer to sell me this brand of tuna rather than that brand of bread" (Alchian and Demsetz 1972, p. 778).

Other economists take this sort of fanciful thinking to an even more absurd level by describing obviously coercive measures as voluntary. For example, Greg Clark—no relation to John Bates Clark as far as I know—proposed that "factory discipline [was] successful because it coerced more effort from workers than they would freely give . . . . The empirical evidence shows that discipline succeeded mainly by increasing work effort. Workers effectively hired capitalists to make them work harder" (Clark 1994, p. 128).

Clark was referring to the sort of theory proposed by Clark Nardinelli, who, presumably in all seriousness, declared that children in the factories would voluntarily choose to have their employers beat them: "Now if a firm in a competitive industry employed corporal punishment the supply price of child labor to that firm would increase. The child would receive compensations for the disamenity of being beaten" (Nardinelli 1982, p. 289). Similarly, Steven Cheung maintains that riverboat pullers who towed wooden boats along the shoreline in pre-Communist China agreed to hire monitors to whip them to restrict shirking (Cheung 1983, p. 5).

To be fair, the economists, even Greg Clark, Cheung, and Nardinelli, never went so far as to suggest that ownership had no effect whatsoever. If the workers owned the land instead of having to rent it or work on the land as hired laborers, certainly their incomes would be higher. Samuelson and Wicksell only asserted that given any existing structure of ownership, it made no difference who hired whom. Nonetheless, the implication was that neither the structure of ownership nor power relationships was a matter of central importance. In this manner, they reinforced the notion that market forces were fair.

Fighting for Justice—For the Railroads

John Bates Clark could not have really believed that his theory of economic justice represented a serious scientific effort. In fact, Clark had the chameleon-like ability to change his views according to circumstances. After a brief period of youthful Christian socialism, Clark reinvented himself as a vigorous defender of the status quo—at least for labor.

Despite his call for workers to reconcile themselves to the justice of the market, Clark continued to see the market imposing undue hardships on those who deserved better, however, at this stage in his career, the supposed victims were not workers, but the largest U.S. corporations, especially the railroads. All around him, he saw markets self-destructing in a frenzy of cutthroat price wars.

Railroads were the dominant nonagricultural industry in the late nineteenth century. They represented 60 percent of all the listed stocks on the New York exchange (Chernow 1990, p. 67). In the 1880s, railroads built almost 74,000 miles of lines. In the process, they "hastily threw up lines that were not needed, through miles and miles of wilderness, merely to insure that another railroad would not claim the territory first" (Faulkner 1959, p. 145).

In the face of this wild overinvestment, competitive forces rapidly eroded prices. The railroads reported revenue per ton-mile falling from 1.88 cents in 1870 to 1.22 cents in 1880. In 1890, it had reached 0.94 cents. By 1900 it had fallen to 0.73 cents (Kolko 1965, p. 7).

Arthur T. Hadley, who served both as president of Yale University and the American Economics Association, and who was perhaps the foremost specialist in railroad economics, observed:

> Railroad competition may exist everywhere, somewhere or nowhere. If it exists everywhere, rates are reduced to the level of movement charges, and there is nothing to pay fixed charges . . . . If there is competition somewhere, the competitive point will have rates based on movement expenses, and the others will have to pay fixed charges. This constitutes discrimination. If we have competition nowhere, this either involves a pool, or amounts to the same thing. (Hadley 1903, pp. 142–43)

When Hadley wrote, "there is nothing to pay fixed charges," he was really saying that although prices might cover the direct cost of carrying the freight, they were far short of what would allow the railroads to pay off their bond holders or to reinvest in new capital goods when their old equipment required replacement. Railroads that could not afford to repay their debts were headed for bankruptcy. Indeed, railroad bankruptcies spread throughout the economy. Over 30 percent of domestic railroad mileage fell into receivership in the 1870s; 15 percent in the 1880s; and 25 percent in the 1890s.

When railroads began to fail again in 1893, major suppliers, such as the steel companies, followed. In just the first six months of the year, 32 failed. Stock market and bank crashes were not far behind (Faulkner 1959, p. 145).

As competition left widespread bankruptcy in its wake, business took measures to reduce competition by forming trusts, cartels, and monopolies. The leader in this movement was J. P. Morgan—so much so that people began to use the word, "Morganize," to describe the massive industrial reorganizations intended to minimize competition in industry after industry.

Despite his theoretical advocacy of competition, Clark approved of the anticompetitive restructuring of big business so that trusts, cartels, and monopolies would be allowed to dominate the economy. In discussing the instability competition was creating for modern industry, Clark reverted back to the rhetoric of his earlier Christian socialist days when he opined: "Individual competition, the great regulator of the former era, has, in important fields, practically disappeared. It ought to disappear; it was, in its later days incapable of working justice" (Clark 1887, p. 147). By justice, Clark presumably meant justice for the railroads and the other large corporations.

The Economic Attack on Competition

So, Clark's work moved in two opposite directions. When advocating the economic justice of markets, he contended that competitive forces offered everybody exactly what they deserved. When making specific policy recommendations to business and government, he warned that competition would destroy the economy and lead to bankruptcy for modern industries with high fixed costs, such as the railroads.

Apparently, Clark did not see any contradiction between arguing that individualist competition was moral and that stifling individualistic competition through trusts, cartels, and monopolies was also moral. Gabriel Hauge, a noted economist, once asked Clark's son about this apparent inconsistency in his father's writings. John Maurice Clark replied in a letter on December 16, 1937, "Your inquiry raises the question of a change in my father's attitude.... I do not think my father was conscious of any change in his basic attitude" (cited in Dorfman 1971, p. 13).

In effect, both types of morality that Clark strenuously advocated—on the one hand, satisfaction with the status quo for the workers who may have felt exploited in their situation and, on the other hand, an even more powerful system of exploitation in the form of trusts, cartels, and monopolies—were consistent with a desire to make the world more comfortable both for the great enterprises of the day and the elite who owned them.

Clark was consistent in another respect in calling for both competition and its elimination. He justified both policies by appealing to common sense, as well as justice. For example, in advocating the organization of business through trusts, cartels, and monopolies, Clark proclaimed:

> Combinations have their roots in the nature of social industry and are normal in their origin, their development and their practical working. They are neither to be depreciated by scientists nor suppressed by legislation. (Clark 1888, p. 11)

Notice that Clark described a "social industry." In this regard, he also sharply differed from the standard atomistic vision of neoclassical economics in which individual choices represent the foundation of the economy.

Within this monopolistic environment, competition may no longer be effective in regulating the powerful, but it still could exert considerable force on the weak. As Clark observed earlier in his career:

> Sometimes, as in railroad operations, competition works sluggishly, interruptedly, or not at all; sometimes, as in the transactions of labor and

capital, it works for a time, one-sidedly and cruelly, and then almost ceases to do its work. (Clark 1887, p. 207)

If railroad competition was not strong, the reason, of course, had nothing whatsoever to do with inherent market forces; instead, weak competition meant that the railroads had been successful in organizing to suppress competition among themselves. Weakened competition meant that more wealth flowed to the corporations and less to the people who actually produced the wealth, thereby intensifying the farm worker paradox.

Human Capital

Presumably, the aforementioned capitalist apologetics were intended to lead people to accept the proposition that since the system supposedly performs so equitably, only the wildest radical would ever dare to question the existing structure of ownership, property rights, and income. Given this perspective, farm workers, like everybody else, justifiably earn exactly what they deserve. A more realistic perspective might accept that the farm workers' personal circumstances might have played a significant role in this outcome. From that vantage point, an objective observer would have to take into account those factors that may have prevented the farm workers from enjoying the sort of privileged linguistic, educational, and social experiences that could have allowed them to transcend their situation.

In the real world, such opportunities allow more fortunate individuals to present themselves as belonging in the middle and upper classes—meaning that they appear to deserve easy access to better employment opportunities. The details of such matters are not of much concern to most economists; they are mostly left to the sociologists or to those few economists who work in what is now a mostly neglected corner of the field of labor economics.

Are we to believe that the only reason that women or different racial and ethnic groups earn less is supposedly because they are less productive? Professional sports offer a wonderful laboratory to see how discrimination works. Unlike most businesses, both salaries and performance records are public. Premier players command premier salaries in the National Basketball Association regardless of race. Superstars, such as Michael Jordan, transcend race becoming basketball players rather than black basketball players. Lesser athletes, however, especially those who are not on the starting team, earn a premium for being white. This factor is stronger for teams located in predominantly white locations, such as Salt Lake City, than for teams in places like Detroit, with a larger black population (see Brown et al. 1991; Kahn and Sherer 1988; and Kahn 2000).

I do not intend to attempt to give a complete or even a detailed explanation of exactly how the market determines wages, but merely to point to some of the nonmarket factors that affect labor markets. Prior to World War II, labor economists devoted considerable attention to this subject, but the profession soon marginalized that sort of work, emphasizing sophisticated tools that supposedly prove how efficiently labor markets work (Teixeira 2002). The causes that keep the children of the poor mired in poverty soon fell from view.

Let me begin by critiquing what is probably the economists' favorite explanation for the unequal distribution of income. While economic theory acknowledges that hard work finds a reward in the marketplace, educated work is generally far more lucrative. Just as a capitalist earns profits from investment in plant and equipment, so too workers supposedly earn compensation for something that the economists call human capital. This income from human capital represents a premium in excess of what workers would earn from brute labor alone. Workers supposedly accumulate this human capital through a combination of education and workplace experience, over and above their innate talents.

Of course, economists could never measure this human capital nor can they explain the precise process by which the act of sitting in a classroom transforms itself into productive capacity. Could the credentials that students earn just be providing a convenient signal for prospective employers?

For example, young people with a high school diploma on average earn the same wage regardless of their academic achievement (Bishop 1991b, p. 115). As a result, students who do not expect to advance beyond high school have no incentive to work hard in school (Bishop 1991a, p. 237). This outcome suggests that employers just take the diploma as a signal rather than bothering to evaluate what students got from their education.

Could education merely make students feel more empowered and thus entitled to demand more compensation? Admittedly, on a national level, greater education is associated with higher levels of productivity, but that elevated productivity may be the cause of the increase in education. Highly productive societies may choose to devote larger amounts of resources to education.

Despite these questions, economists seem to assume that employers somehow can find ways to evaluate workers' human capital accurately, and that they then pay, just as John Bates Clark assumed, the appropriate compensation for the human capital that workers bring to the workplace. So, while the farm workers might be putting in commendable efforts on the job, lacking human capital, economists teach that they cannot expect much more than a subsistence wage.

When economists have trouble statistically testing their models of human capital theory, they typically tweak their models by invoking some "unobserved variable." One of the most fashionable unobserved variables is tacit knowledge—knowledge that workers somehow pick up from experience rather than formal training. Tacit knowledge is tacit because it cannot be accurately described.

Farm work—indeed much traditional work—employs a good deal of tacit knowledge. For example, Ernesto Galarza, a remarkable pioneer in helping farm workers to organize unions, described the tacit knowledge of those farm workers who, to the untrained eye, might seem to be among the least skilled in the economy—those who pick the fruits and vegetables. In Galarza's words:

> [T]hose who persisted in stereotyping all harvest hands as "unskilled" failed to acknowledge many skills that proper handling of tomatoes or cantaloupes or peaches required. These skills, practiced with the economy of motion and effort that only experience can bring and refined into a kind of wisdom of work, the domestics possessed . . . .
> Field labor was a blur in which the details of field harvesting and the skills it required went unrecognized. To pick a ripe honeydew requires a trained eye for the bloom of tinted cream, a sensitive touch for the waxy feeling of the rind, and a discriminating nose for the faint aroma of ripeness. In the asparagus fields, the expertness of the Filipino cutters was obvious to all but those who hired them. (Galarza 1977, pp. 29 and 366)

Unfortunately, the tacit knowledge of farm workers counts for little, because the economic value of tacit knowledge, like virtually everything else in the labor market, has a class content. As Steven Shapin has written, "skill is knowledge without a voice" (Shapin 1990).

Factors that Affect Earnings

At first glance, the human capital explanation makes some sense. We have all heard stories about people who managed to beat the odds, catapulting themselves by means of education, experience, and hard work from humble beginnings into the ranks of the rich and powerful. We remember such stories, of course, just because they are so rare. For the most part, such successes would have been impossible without some unlikely event that gave the achiever in question the opportunity to prove his or her worth. Others, coming from relatively privileged conditions, sometimes somehow even manage to sink down to the lower ranks.

These extraordinary stories of economic mobility tend to confuse the basic process that determines how most people fare in society. In general, however, despite such exceptional cases, class origins still serve as a relatively good predictor of individual economic outcomes.

From their Olympian heights, those who comfortably bask in wealth casually proclaim that hard work alone will suffice to move up the economic ladder. For example, George Gilder, who spent many of his early summers with David Rockefeller and his family, wrote as if he knew something about the personal efforts required for success. Not one to mince words, he acknowledged, "The first principle is that in order to move up, the poor must not only work, they must work harder than the classes above them" (Gilder 1981, p. 84). But, of course, typically, even brutally hard work is insufficient to lift the poor out of poverty. Had Mr. Gilder stopped to inquire, I suspect that most farm workers could have enlightened him about the prospects for success for those at the bottom of the socioeconomic ladder.

The fact is that for the most part, the personal qualities of rich and poor alike will have an only modest impact on the outcomes of their encounters in the labor market. Perhaps most important, the children of the poor will not usually have entrée into prestigious educational establishments, even at the primary level. For example, children whose adopted parents are better off have much better educational prospects than other children whose adopted parents are less affluent (see Sacerdote 2002).

Jonathan Kozol's heartbreaking account of the gross inequities between the education of the poor and the rest of society provides convincing evidence of the handicaps borne by the less privileged (Kozol 1991). For example, in New York, low-poverty school districts receive an average of $2,152 more per student in state and local revenues than high-poverty districts do, despite the fact that teaching poor children is more challenging than teaching affluent children (The Education Trust 2002).

Besides being denied the education commonly enjoyed by the children of the rich, the children of the poor will never have access to the contacts that allow the more affluent to successfully navigate the labor market with a minimum of effort. The role models whom they encounter will be less likely to inspire economic success. The children of the poor will have more difficulty in acquiring the confident self-image that allows more affluent youth to believe that good positions are a virtual birthright (see Darity et al. 1997).

Tragically, the children of the poor will face even more terrible barriers, over and above the social and cultural factors that limit their social and economic mobility. For example, they are more likely to come in contact with toxins that will produce deleterious effects on their mental and physical development. In short, most of the poor, and even most of the children of the poor, will remain poor, while most of the rich along with their children will continue to enjoy affluence.

Led by the Nobel Prize–winning economist, Gary Becker, economists believed that economic mobility in United States was relatively high (Becker 1988). More recently, economists have come to realize that Becker's results were mistaken because the short time horizon he used created a distorted measure. Unfortunately, they have not made much headway in unraveling the reasons why the children of the poor remain poor (Bowles and Gintis 2002; Mazumder 2002).

Economists do know that economic mobility in the United States is relatively limited. Dividing the population by family income, the movement from the lowest to the highest 20 percent is fairly modest at best (Gottschalk and Danziger 1998). Moreover, the extent of economic mobility declined substantially during the 1990s from where it had been during most of the second half of the twentieth century (Wysong et al. 2002).

The Obstinacy of Economics

The complexity of the process of wage determination defies any simple explanation. Although we can point to some statistical regularities, such as the greater probability that most of the poor will remain poor, no simple explanation could ever unravel the complex process that determines wages. Many factors enter into wage determination that ostensibly have nothing whatsoever to do with productivity; for example, race or gender. Many of these factors intertwine in one way or another with class and social status.

Economists also find that characteristics such as obesity affect wages, even where it should have nothing to do with productivity. With no knowledge of workers' qualifications, outsiders can do a fair job of ranking their wages by just looking at their photographs (Hamermesh and Biddle 1994; Biddle and Hamermesh 1998).

Economic theory, however, tends to accept simple, but abstract, models that prove that labor markets work more or less the way John Bates Clark theorized. To make matters worse, economists have gone out of their way to undermine the prospects of any progress in coming to grips with the role of class, or even patterns of ownership, in economic outcomes. I don't mean that economists actually conspire to suppress such studies. The problem is not the intent of economists, but the mindset required to be considered a legitimate economist. In all sincerity, economists define "good economics" as the creation of abstract models, which for all practical purposes rule out all effects of class.

To elaborate on this problem, let me turn to the insight of George Stigler, a winner of the Nobel Prize in economics. Stigler was a very conservative economist. He was also extremely combative. For example, in a celebratory article about his teacher, Thomas Sowell described Stigler's style of intellectual debate as a "Demolition Derby" (Sowell 1993, p. 787). Yet Stigler, an implacable enemy of any doctrine that strayed from the conservative faith, acknowledged:

> It could be argued that there is one powerful factor making for conservatism: the inability of a very radical young economist to get a desirable university post. It is indeed true that a believer in the labor theory of value could not get a professorship at a major American university [because] professors could not bring themselves to believe that he was both honest and intelligent . . . The main reason for the conservatism [of economists] surely lies in the effect of the scientific training the economist receives. He is drilled in the problems of *all* economic systems and in the methods by which the price system solves these problems. (Stigler 1959, pp. 527 and 528)

Within this intellectual environment, a statistical model that "explains" why the current pattern of wages is beneficial is considered good economics; a study that looks at the actual experiences of people at the bottom end of the income pyramid will never be published in a "major" economics journal.

Even proving that social factors, such as class, are worthy of economists' consideration is all but impossible. At this very moment, I was just reviewing a series of E-mail exchanges on a list for economic historians, one of the least doctrinaire fields within economics. A number of prominent researchers in the discussion are contending that several hundred years ago women must have been half as productive as men because they were paid half as much. They were energetically dismissing all suggestions that factors such as discrimination could have played a role.

Of course, nobody engaged in that debate had information about how people actually made decisions centuries ago; instead these economists simply relied on the way that their abstract reasoning led them.

Norms of Compensation

According to the theory of John Bates Clark, each group should earn exactly what they deserve. Standing in opposition to Clark's theory is a long-standing belief that relative pay reflects shifting cultural norms rather than some objective standards of productivity. For example, Plato told Aristotle that no one should make more than five times the pay of the lowest member of society. J. P. Morgan said 20 times (Crystal 1991, pp. 23–24).

Jean Fourastie looked at the trends in earnings in France between 1800 and 1948. He reported:

> The salary of a councilor of state increased by a factor of at least 40 from 1800 to 1948; the salary of a professor at the College de France by 100; the average salary of an office boy in a government agency by 220; the hourly wages of laborers in provincial cities by more than 400. (Fourastie 1960, p. 30)

Someone might be capable of providing a scientific account of the changes in productivity growth that caused these trends in pay, but such an explanation escapes me. Instead, I suspect that the same sort of forces that created the French Revolution led to a more egalitarian—or, perhaps more correctly, a less grotesque—distribution of income.

From colonial times to World War I, the United States experienced a long-term trend toward increasing inequality. From the Great Depression through the 1960s, the trend rapidly shifted, leading to greater equality—not just in the United States, but also in most industrialized economies. This tendency toward egalitarianism went into a sudden reversal somewhere around 1970. Some countries, such as the United States, moved quicker than others, but the trend seemed to be relatively widespread. Within the United States, the increase in the wealth of the Forbes 400 richest people soared by an average $1.44 billion each year from 1997 to 2000.

The disintegration of the Soviet Union undoubtedly contributed to this tendency of increasing inequality, even though the trend had begun before the breakup. The United States no longer seems to have a need for projecting a minimal facade of egalitarianism, since countries that might have otherwise been attracted to the Soviet model, no longer have that choice.

Something else was afoot. It may have begun as rationalization, but it soon evolved into a strongly held belief: talented executive superstars were the key to corporate success. The flip side of this perspective was that the people further down the corporate ladder—especially those near the bottom—were merely interchangeable parts. Since executive leadership rather than employees' efforts was supposedly responsible for the bulk of their productive contributions, these lesser beings had little grounds to claim much compensation for the productivity of the corporation. Even though the economy seemed to be booming in the late 1990s, real hourly wages for nonagricultural workers in 2002 still lagged behind the levels that they had reached in 1974 (President of the United States 2002, table B-47).

The Other Side of the Farm Worker Paradox

On one side of the disparity represented by the farm worker paradox, we observe the abysmal standard of living of the people who do the basic work that makes life possible; on the other, is the obscene income and wealth that those who control the giant corporations enjoy.

The extent of this disparity is not a matter of inevitability. In the 1960s and early 1970s, the economic distance between managers and workers, while not insignificant, was far less extreme than today.

In 1968, the chairman of General Motors, James M. Roche, was the highest paid executive in the country, earning $795,000. At the time, the average worker earned $5,602 (Anon. 1999). In 1974, one of the most respected students of executive compensation estimated that the typical chief executive officer (CEO) of a large U.S. corporation was earning total compensation (excluding perquisites and fringe benefits) that was around 35 times the pay of an average manufacturing worker (Crystal 1991, p. 27).

Around that time, mainstream economists began to question whether high-level corporate managers really earned their keep. Some denounced the managers of large corporations for acting as self-interested individuals who manipulated corporate resources in order to earn the highest possible incomes for themselves at the expense of shareholders (Jensen and Meckling 1976).

The economists' main complaint did not specifically condemn the managers as individuals. In effect, the managers were acting in line with what economists would expect. The problem, according to the economists, was that the managers' incentives did not coincide with the interests of the shareholders who were the nominal owners of the corporations. For example, managers wanted to make the corporations grow to justify higher salaries, but growth for growth sake does not always make economic sense. Sometimes, the managers could serve the shareholders better by selling off assets and distributing the proceeds to them. The economists called for changing the managerial incentives so that their rewards would reflect how much value—not just growth—that the executives added to the shareholders' wealth.

The concern with divergent interests of management and the owners of corporations was hardly new. Over two centuries ago, Adam Smith raised the same questions about the corporate structure. He singled out the East India Company, showing how its structure permitted "the negligence, profusion, and malversation of their own servants" (Smith 1776, V.I.e, p. 755). In 1932, in the midst of the Great Depression in the United States, two members of President Roosevelt's brain trust, Adolf Berle and Gardiner Means, published *The Modern Corporation and Private Property*. The central thesis of this highly influential book was that managers were running the giant corporations in their own interest.

Despite the lack of originality, the more recent article about corporate compensation resonated. The business press and Wall Street enthusiastically concurred with the economists' complaints about managerial compensation. They all agreed that corporations should restructure managers' pay so that earnings reflected stock prices rather than the size of the firm.

Strangely enough, none of the participants in this discussion about managerial compensation connected the disconnect between managerial salaries and productivity to the farm worker paradox. Although the prevalent opinion was that the top salaries did not reflect managerial productivity, nobody questioned whether the lower paid workers earned salaries commensurate with their productivity, except when complaining that unions allowed unproductive workers to gouge excessive pay from their helpless corporate employers.

Under this new regime, executives took pains to make sure that their stock prices grew. As a result, corporate managers' earnings swelled to unimagined heights over the next decade. By 2001, *Business Week* published an article appropriately titled, "We're Back to Serfs and Royalty," suggesting a contemporary version of Adam Smith's farm worker paradox. The article reported that since 1980, the average pay of regular working people increased just 66 percent, while CEO pay grew a whopping 1,996 percent. The earnings of CEOs at 365 of the largest public companies averaged $13.1 million in 2000, roughly 531 times more than their average employees (Gill 2001). A study by *Fortune*, estimated that the top 100 CEOs earned 1,000 times the pay of an ordinary worker (Krugman 2002). In other words, in a couple of hours these CEOs earn as much as a regular working person earns in a year.

The ratio between after tax CEO earnings and those of the average worker rose even faster. For example, during the second half of the twentieth century, the wealthiest people in the country have seen their taxes fall rapidly. For example, Charles E. Wilson of General Motors was the best-paid CEO of 1950, earning $626,300. Without any exceptional deductions, his federal tax would have been $462,000, leaving him only $164,300 (Phillips 2002, p. 76.)

Many of these corporate executives brazenly abused their office, using the corporate treasury rather than their own lavish salaries to enhance their lifestyle. For example, the bankrupt Tyco Corporation bought lavish perqs for CEO, Dennis Kozlowski, including a $6,000 umbrella stand and a $15,500 sewing basket (Anon. 2002).

Even in retirement, corporate executives can continue to enjoy lavish benefits. For example, former General Electric CEO, Jack Welch, is a case in point. His divorce proceedings offered the public a glimpse into his retirement perks, including his use of a Manhattan apartment owned by GE, floor-level seats to the New York Knicks, courtside seats at the U.S. Open and Wimbledon, a box at the Metropolitan Opera, a box at Red Sox games, a box at Yankee games, four country club fees, security services in all four homes and limousine services while traveling, as well as discounts on diamonds and jewelry settings (see Fabrikant 2002). All this was over and above a $9 million a year pension plan. According to legal documents, Welch spends an average of $8,982 per month for food and beverages, $1,903 for clothes, $5,480 for country club memberships, and $52,486 for gifts. His personal assets of $456.2 million are about half the gross domestic product of Monaco (Silverman 2002).

Welch's predicament is ironic. Business reporters used to refer to Welch as Neutron Jack in recognition of his management style, which resembled a neutron bomb that destroys living beings but leaves material assets undamaged. In particular, he won this moniker for his ruthless attack on labor costs.

Some people justified the extent of the obscene inequality symbolized by bloated executive compensation. For example, the *Economic Report of the President* for 2002 praised these new arrangements, claiming that they are efficient because they ensured that the interests of managers and the corporation for which they worked were properly aligned (President of the United States 2002, p. 102). Yet the objective link between executive productivity and pay remained unproven—especially because soon afterward the earnings of some of the supposedly best corporations in the United States proved to be fraudulent.

Managerial Productivity

Putting aside the question of fraud for the moment, let us look more closely at some of the problems associated with the thesis that managerial pay reflects productivity. First, corporations frequently heap lavish rewards on managers even while their business is faltering or even failing (Lublin 2002; Luttwak 1999, pp. 1–2).

Even where corporations are prospering, we can still ask if the increase in pay is actually in line with managerial productivity. For example, total compensation of CEOs of U.S. companies with $200 to $500 million in annual sales in 1990 dollars more than doubled between 1984 and 1996, even after taking inflation into account (Abowd and Kaplan 1999, p. 146). Are we to believe that executives in the United States suddenly became more than twice as productive within little more than a decade? Why do the CEOs in the United States earn more than two and a half times as much as their German counterparts and five times as much as those in Sweden (see Abowd and Kaplan 1999, p. 146)?

In addition, we can ask ourselves what managerial productivity really means. A major component of the supposed productivity achievements of management in recent decades seems to be the ability to defeat labor rather than developing techniques for more efficient methods of production. In the last years of the twentieth century, stocks repeatedly soared immediately after managers announced job cuts (see Phillips 2002, pp. 150–51). Perhaps the most respected corporate leader at the time, Jack Welch of General Electric, earned the affection of the business community largely for his zeal in eliminating jobs.

How productive is the strategy of attacking labor? Andrei Shleifer and Lawrence Summers, who later became Secretary of the Treasury during the Clinton administration, wrote an aptly titled article, "Breach of Trust" (1988), analyzing the wealth supposedly created in the takeover of Trans World Airlines. Judging by the increase in the company's stock price at the time, the takeover added enormous value to the firm.

Even so, Shleifer and Summers observed that this value did not seem to reflect any creativity on the part of management. Instead, the firm merely imposed wage cuts on its employees. Admittedly, the way the market evaluates economic outcomes, imposing wage cuts without undermining performance actually counts as an increase in productivity. But even if we accept that merely curtailing wages and benefits represents an improvement in productivity, the market may have been a bit hasty in its evaluation of the productivity of management's move. In 1991, only a couple of years after the publication of "Breach of Trust," and again in 1995, the airline went into bankruptcy, suggesting that the productivity of the executives was short-lived, or more likely imaginary.

In light of the TWA example, we might say that real productivity advances did not cause the intensification of inequality associated with the farm workers paradox. Instead, we could even think of the intensification of the farm worker paradox as causing the supposed improvements in productivity. In other words, the direct assault on wages and benefits was a primary factor in creating the impression that productivity was advancing.

I suspect that rising inequality in the distribution of income will ultimately have a substantial negative effect on productivity. Proof of this hypothesis may be difficult to come by—at least for a while. Let me turn to an example from the labor market for professional athletes to suggest the nature of the perverse effect of inequality on performance.

Professional sports teams can concentrate their payroll on a few superstars, supported by a cast of athletes who earn comparatively little. Alternatively, they can have a less hierarchical system in which salaries do not differ nearly as greatly. A study, published in *The Academy of Management Journal*, found that professional baseball teams that adopted a more egalitarian arrangement performed better during the period 1985–1993 (Bloom 1999).

In a sense, this result may seem counterintuitive. Why should paying more to substitute players who appear in relatively few games and less to the superstars have a significant positive effect on the performance of a baseball team? I believe that the answer has to do with the chemistry of the team. A highly hierarchical wage structure tends to create jealousies among the players. In addition, to the extent that athletes will earn much more for their individual performance rather than their contribution to the team, they may be inclined to perform in ways that will improve their own statistics rather than contributing to winning games. In effect, players may tend to compete with each other for salary increases rather than competing against opposing teams. In such an environment, players may even find themselves tempted to undermine the performance of teammates.

In baseball, the extent to which players have to coordinate their performance with those of their teammates is far less than in other sports, such as basketball or football. For example, baseball players typically have the individual responsibility of catching a ball hit in their direction. In basketball, players have frequent choices about whether to pass the ball to a teammate or to shoot the ball themselves, adding to their individual statistics. Each player must be able to anticipate the other's moves.

The Futile Quest for Managerial Productivity

This study of the productiveness of more egalitarian salary structures in baseball covers a period that coincides with the beginning of the explosion in the executive compensation. Unlike the scholars of baseball performance, management experts emphasized the importance of superstars:

> Five years ago, several executives at McKinsey & Company, America's largest and most prestigious management-consulting firm, launched what they called the War for Talent. Thousands of questionnaires were sent to managers across the country. Eighteen companies were singled out for special attention, and the consultants spent up to three days at each firm, interviewing everyone from the C.E.O. down to the human-resources staff. McKinsey wanted to document how the top-performing companies in America differed from other firms in the way they handle matters like hiring and promotion. But, as the consultants sifted through the piles of reports and questionnaires and interview transcripts, they grew convinced that the difference between winners and losers was more profound than they had realized. "We looked at one another and suddenly the light bulb blinked on," the three consultants who headed the project—Ed Michaels, Helen Handfield-Jones, and Beth Axelrod—write in their new book, also called *The War for Talent*. The very best companies, they concluded, had leaders who were obsessed with the talent issue. (Gladwell 2002)

Enron was the most enthusiastic proponent of the McKinsey message. The CEO himself was a former McKinsey partner. The business press wrote breathless profiles of the company. It seemed to be doing everything right. Then Enron ended in a colossal failure.

The problem goes further than the obsessive emphasis on rewarding those who inhabit the upper reaches of the corporate pyramid. Within that pyramid, corporations identify the success of the organization with the CEO. Rakesh Khurana published a detailed study of this phenomenon entitled, *Searching for a Corporate Savior* (Khurana 2002).

CEOs, such as Ken Lay of Enron or Jack Welch of General Electric, became superstar celebrities. Corporate boards looked for talented individuals to lead their organizations into the promised land of perpetual prosperity.

This quest was fraught with problems. Nobody knew exactly what qualities such a corporate leader was supposed to have. Consequently, they narrowed down their search to a small population of executives already associated with successful ventures. With a powerful demand bidding for the services of a small number of people, executive salaries soared.

The likelihood of anointing an outsider to be the successor of a departing CEO weakened loyalties of the senior executives—a process similar to what may have happened to the baseball teams that emphasized superstars. In Khurana's words:

> One of the most serious casualties of the apotheosis of the charismatic CEO is often the dedication and loyalty of top managers. To presume, as the charismatic succession process implicitly does, that a single individual deserves more attention and rewards than are bestowed on anyone else in the organization ignores the reality that organizational performance is driven by more than one person. (Khurana 2002, p. 196)

Of course, I cannot prove conclusively that increased inequality in pay contributed to airline bankruptcies, such as that of TWA, or to the spate of corporate accounting frauds, such as Enron. After all, unlike sporting events, where judging winners and losers is relatively straightforward, business results are muddier. For example, business can cook the books to hide deep problems from the general public—at least for periods of time.

The murkiness of financial and economic measurements brings us full circle back to the farm worker paradox. When the economy is performing well, pundits are quick to credit the superior productivity of the people running the major institutions, thereby justifying the gross inequalities of society. They are less prone to apply the same reasoning when the economy flounders. Upon such occasions, they are more likely to appeal to the collected duty of everybody—including the poorest of the poor—to share in the unpleasant burdens of the moment.

Passive Ownership and the Farm Worker Paradox

For the most part, workers' "human capital" usually counts for little in the modern, financialized world. Much of their ownership of human capital merely reflects a capacity to make a physical contribution to the social production process. The modern fashion is to denigrate the production of material goods relative to those who invent financial innovations or create information. Recall our earlier discussion of the rhetoric of the weightless economy and the lumpy-object purveyors.

Of course, some of the people engaged in nonmaterial production efforts do make significant contributions to society. But what about the class of people who exist as rentiers, people whose livelihood depends on the collection of interest, rents, or dividends? How can their rewards square with the theory of John Bates Clark? These people have no real connection with the production process? Richard Tawney forcefully made this same point in his *The Acquisitive Society*:

> The characteristic fact, which differentiates most modern property from that of the pre-industrial age . . . is that in modern economic conditions ownership is not active, but passive, that [for] most of those who own property to-day . . . it is not a means of work but an instrument for the acquisition of gain or the exercise of power, and that there is no guarantee that gain bears any relation to service, or power to responsibility . . . . Ownership and use are normally divorced . . . . The greater part of modern property has been attenuated to a pecuniary lien or bond on the product of industry, which carries with it a right to payment, but which is normally valued precisely because it relieves the owner from any obligation to perform a positive or constructive function. (Tawney 1926, pp. 61–62)

The passivity of ownership was already clear in Adam Smith's days. Let me return to the subject of the exclusive hunting privileges of the aristocracy. At the time, so many of the great landlords lived in the city that Parliament did not dare to revoke the aristocracy's virtually exclusive right to hunt in Britain. The members of Parliament supposedly feared that their hunting privileges were necessary to encourage those absentee landlords to visit their lands from time to time.

Maybe the Game Laws, which prevented the vast majority of people in England from hunting, remained in force because so many of the parliamentarians were themselves aristocratic absentee landlords. Let us take them at their word and accept that they decided as they did to improve the quality of passive ownership.

Aristocratic hunting created havoc in the countryside, over and above the lives lost when innocent children got caught in the traps intended to prevent poaching or the thousands of people jailed or transported for infractions of the Game Laws. From the standpoint of production, hunting was very destructive. The Game Laws prohibited farmers from eradicating animals that ate their crops, while they enabled the gentry to hunt the foxes that helped to keep such creatures in check. To make matters worse, the hunters would wantonly trample crops in pursuit of their quarry. This legislation was responsible for the loss of as much as one-quarter of the crops in some counties (see Perelman 2000a, chapter 3).

No doubt, those on the bottom found themselves most disadvantaged by this arrangement, regardless of considerations of human capital. Virtually no one questioned the right of these passive owners in Smith's day. In that sense, little has changed since then.

So, where does John Bates Clark fit into this picture? Can anyone believe that what workers earn really corresponds to the contribution to the productive process? Toward the end of his book, *Created Unequal: The Crisis in American Pay*, James Galbraith called out:

> We need a rebellion against the idea that people are actually paid in proportion to the value of what they produce. We need a rebellion against the metaphor of the labor market—an entity that no one has ever seen, where no one has ever been, an entity that lacks the mechanisms of price adjustment. (Galbraith 1998, pp. 265–66)

So, in a sense, we have come full circle. Recall that Clark called for a theory of economic justice to forestall what seemed to be an immanent revolution. About a century later, Galbraith called for a revolution to overthrow Clark's theory. Unfortunately, Clark's theory has a much stronger hold on U.S. society today than the call for economic justice.

The Self-Defeating Nature of the Farm Worker Paradox

The farm worker paradox leads to a deeper paradox. Over longer periods of time, the destructive effects of inequality eventually engulf those who primarily benefit from it. In other words, when the elite class of a society decides to enrich itself at the expense of the majority, its efforts generally turn out to be self-defeating, at least in the long run. Much of the creativity of society, on the part of both rich and poor, will be consumed in conflict—the rich in protecting their wealth and the poor in protesting their lot.

The fate of the slave states in the antebellum United States is a case in point. Fear of a slave revolt made illiteracy mandatory for the majority of the population, limiting the ability of the unfree population to produce wealth. Lacking any incentive to work hard, slaves could benefit when capital goods became inoperative. By running a plow into a rock or a tree stump or by injuring a draft animal, a slave could create a few moments of leisure. To prevent such actions, the planters resorted to heavy equipment and mules, which were more resistant to abuse. Unfortunately, this technological adaptation reduced potential productivity, since horses and light plows were more suited to the sandy soils common in the South (see Perelman 2000b, chapter 5).

In addition, the elite planters developed a courtly style of life to signal their elevated position to the rest of society. In the long run, this custom meant spending well beyond their means. The admittedly enormous wealth produced in the South did more to enrich the Northerners, who lent money to the planters, handled the sale of their produce, and marketed lavish goods to them, as well as necessities for their slaves. In addition, the technologies used to produce the cotton and tobacco on the plantations were unsustainable, requiring that many planters move west once they exhausted the fertility of their land. Although the relative magnitude of the earnings from breeding slaves is a matter of debate, a number of experts on Southern economy at the time believe that this inhuman business was a major source of profit for the plantations.

At the same time, the North was developing an industrial society based on modern technologies. True, the resource requirements of the Northern states were also unsustainable, but the fact that this region of the country developed higher levels of skills meant that in the long run it would easily outstrip the slave economy.

The current manifestation of the farm worker paradox will also eventually prove to be counterproductive, even for those who currently sit comfortably atop the pyramid of unequal earnings. The potential creativity of generations of people at the bottom of the pyramid will be wasted, just as was the case with the slaves.

The Second Law of Thermodynamics

Recall that the late nineteenth-century burst of productivity depended on the utilization of abundant fossil fuels. Even though the demands for fossil fuel at the time were modest by contemporary standards, the known reserves of fossil fuel were also limited. In the United States, the Standard Oil trust dominated the petroleum market. In Europe, a similar, but somewhat less imposing, industrial structure developed.

These petrochemical behemoths added another dimension to the struggle for markets as they each competed to gain access to prized oil deposits around the world. The emergence of new, energy-intensive technologies escalated the hunt for petroleum. Just as technological advances hastened the decline of the whale stocks, new technology accelerated the depletion of the petroleum reserves faster than would otherwise be the case.

Because new technology keeps bringing new discoveries on line, the possibility of shortages seems understandably remote. The increase in proven reserves gives rise to unwarranted optimism that impedes the preparation for the necessary transition to a more sustainable energy regime. Unfortunately, opportunities for undiscovered reserves are rapidly disappearing.

Oil deposits form only under very specific geological conditions. As a result, the multinational oil companies are already aware of the location of most future oil discoveries. Within the next few years, oil experts expect that known petroleum reserves will decline rapidly (Deffeyes 2001).

Even if the world's geologists would somehow be proven wrong about declining reserves, the environmental consequences of continually burning fossil fuels will probably prove catastrophic. Fossil fuels foul the air and the soil, as well as contaminate water. To make matters worse, global warming now seems almost irreversible, yet nobody can possibly know how to prepare for it because the precise relationship between global warming and climate change is too complex.

The need for a transition to a new energy regime is pressing. Some economists would say that higher energy prices would hasten the introduction of renewable energy. Unfortunately, rationing energy resources by way of the market through higher prices will only make the lives of the unfortunate masses even more intolerable. Already, the United Nations estimates that more than one billion people survive on the equivalent of less than a dollar a day and almost three billion live on less than two dollars a day (United Nations Development Programme 2001, p. 9). Policies designed to alleviate poverty by way of the current policies of neoliberalism, inaccurately known as globalization, are not working. Higher energy prices will only make matters worse. Yet, continuing along the present course will only squander more resources, making the future for most of these people even more hopeless.

I suspect that if the governments of the world devoted a fraction of the resources that they currently budget for the military with a degree of enthusiasm only half as intense as the energies they put into warfare, we could arrive at a satisfactory solution. Given the political makeup of the contemporary world, prospects for such an outcome remain hopelessly utopian.

7

A New Direction

Calculation

I hope that I have shown how markets promote behavior that is environmentally destructive, yet no modern society has developed the appropriate means for a rational organization of society. Economists and people with a more environmental orientation first seriously debated about market efficiency in the early twentieth century (O'Neill 1996).

The two great protagonists were Austrian—Ludwig Von Mises and Otto Neurath, the first a vigorous, if not dogmatic proponent of markets, and the latter a brilliant polymath who favored a more socialist form of organization. Neurath's idea grew out of his observations of the preparations for World War I.

Neurath proposed that something like wartime planning be carried over into peacetime. Instead of mobilizing the economy to produce tanks and guns, society could just as easily produce useful goods for the population (Neurath 1919). Although his vision of a planning system was relatively crude, the actual war experience certainly validated his intuition about the capacity of nonmarket economic mobilization.

Although war is perhaps the greatest waste ever invented by human beings, wartime pressures create a premium on efficiency in production. Once the threat of all-out war becomes a reality, monetary calculations take second place to the imperative of producing the appropriate mix of armaments and sustenance for the people. Certainly during World War I all the major combatants threw aside any previous beliefs about market efficiency. In place of markets, they turned to national planning. In the words of Ralph Hawtrey, a British Treasury official who was also a very influential economist:

> The War suddenly showed up all our economic standards from a new angle. In the belligerent countries people became aware of the paramount claims of the State. They were called upon to give up former pursuits in favour of a single transcendent purpose. The economic problem presented itself in an unequivocal form; human nature had to be worked upon and induced to do what the State required it to do. Every combination of payment, persuasion and pressure was resorted to, not only to make people serve in the forces and work at the manufacture of munitions, but to regulate every part of their lives. Controls and rationing were gradually extended in all directions. Markets ceased to function. Prices lost their ordinary significance. Demand usually meant either the demand of the State or a consumers' demand limited by rationing. Cost meant a total of wages and prices determined by authority and cut off from any semblance of free competition. Wealth no longer had any useful meaning. (Hawtrey 1925, p. 384)

Hawtrey was not a radical in any sense of the word. He merely recognized that survival was the most basic need of society and when survival was at stake governments quickly abandon markets. A few years earlier, John Maurice Clark, son of John Bates Clark, went further than Hawtrey, alluding to a position similar to that of Neurath, observing: "The need of a more coherent social organization is probably not less great in times of nominal peace, merely less obvious and less immediate" (Clark 1917, p. 772).

In short, why not continue to take advantage of the coherence of a planned economy to meet social needs in peacetime? Indeed, despite the obvious waste and destruction of the war itself, wartime economies did produce with unparalleled efficiency, even with the profiteering that frequently accompanies war. For example, in the United States, a push toward standardization was an important part of the war effort during World War I. In forcing business to reduce the variation in styles and sizes, the government was "giving production problems precedence over sales problems" (Knoedler 1997, p. 1015; citing Haber 1964, p. 120).

The results of the standardization drive were impressive to say the least. The National Industrial Conference Board calculated that the War Industries Board's push toward standardization saved about 15 percent of total costs for the relevant industries (Knoedler 1997, p. 1015; citing National Industrial Conference Board 1929, p. 9; see also Knoedler and Mayhew 1994). In addition, the urgency of the war brought forth waves of innovation far in excess of what a peacetime economy could deliver.

As Clark had written, the need for a coherent social organization did not cease with the termination of war, but by 1917 Neurath's earlier suggestion of planning could not be separated from the passions enflamed by the Russian Revolution.

Von Mises and his followers were not merely targeting socialist planners, but also the early ecological economics tradition (O'Neill 2002, p. 157). Von Mises attacked Neurath by insisting that planning could not possibly be efficient. How could anybody compare alternatives without some unit of measurement, such as money? For Von Mises, in determining

> whether we shall use a waterfall to produce electricity or extend coal-mining and better utilize the energy contained in coal . . . the processes of production are so many and so long, the condition necessary to the success of the undertaking so multitudinous, that we can never be content with vague ideas. To decide whether an undertaking is sound we must calculate carefully. (Von Mises 1951, p. 114)

Von Mises admitted that in making the decision about the appropriate energy source, monetary measures leave out important considerations such as beauty or health, but he suggested: "We can value them directly; and therefore have no difficulty in taking them into account, even though they are outside the sphere of money computations" (Von Mises 1951, p. 166).

Of course, directly valuing such matters concedes a great deal to Neurath's position, especially when we consider the enormous scale and complexity involved in valuing the natural resource base. Von Mises, however, gave no indication that he sensed how making such valuations undermined his own position.

Von Mises did adopt one rhetorical strategy that served him well. He took no notice whatsoever of wartime production efficiencies. Instead, he merely assumed that markets represented the maximum efficiency that society could reach. Given this perspective, the best that planning could offer would be to match markets. Since mistakes are inevitable, planners could not hope to do as well as markets.

Most of the economists who subsequently joined the debate, whether socialist or pro-market, accepted Von Mises's framework, agreeing that markets were efficient. The only question that remained for them was whether socialist planners could match that efficiency by imitating markets. To make their case, these economists developed sophisticated mathematical techniques for creating models of a functioning socialist economy. Although these models had little to do with the way a socialist economy should work, they laid much of the groundwork for the modern, abstract, model-based economic analysis that dominates the discipline today (see Mirowski 2002).

These academic, pro-socialist economists absolutely failed in one respect. In effect, they accepted Von Mises's assumption of market efficiency without offering a coherent vision of what a nonmarket economy could accomplish. As a result, most modern economists who read about this debate remain convinced that those who supported markets were correct.

Of course, the terms of the debate were lopsided from the beginning. Even those who supposedly supported socialism virtually conceded their case before even beginning. Nobody took notice of the wartime experience. Worse yet, nobody suggested that socialism had the potential to do anything that markets could not.

War and the Reorganization of Society

Let us go back to Neurath and the idea of a war economy to obtain some idea of how a more realistic debate might have proceeded. The pressing demands of a wartime emergency tend to encourage a nation to go beyond applying capital more efficiently. Wartime society must rationalize labor, but it must also rationalize society as a whole as well. For example, in terms of rationalizing labor, the government tries to make sure that the workers and soldiers are stronger and healthier. For example, during World War I, the British *Report of the Ministry of National Service* told the country that only one man in three of nearly two-and-a-half million examined was completely fit for military service (Titmuss 1958, p. 81).

The rationalization of society creates an even greater challenge since it involves morale, which is crucial to the war effort. Toward this end, the government needs to minimize the dissipation of effort wasted in conflict between various domestic groups. For example, the government will act to minimize the disparities in the privileges that different classes enjoy. In this respect, John Maurice Clark noted that in war, leaders concern themselves with "the necessities of health, efficiency, and 'morale'" (Clark 1942, p. 3).

Similarly, during World War II, professor Cyril Falls said that in military terms, the war could not be won unless millions of ordinary people, in Britain and overseas, were convinced that Britain had something better to offer than her enemies did—not only during but after the war (Falls 1941, p. 13; cited in Titmuss 1958, p. 82). Richard Titmuss, a British professor of social administration, noted the appearance of a wide array of social legislation during the war. Family Allowances, the Beveridge Report (which formed the basis for the later British social welfare system, M.P.), National Insurance (income security), and the Education Act of 1944 were all spawned during this time (Titmuss 1958, p. 84). He concluded:

> The social measures that were developed during the war centred round the primary needs of the whole population irrespective of class, creed or military category. The distinction of privileges, accorded to those in uniform in previous wars, were greatly diminished. (Titmuss 1958, p. 82)

Immediately after the war, before the memory of the threat had fully dissipated, political leaders still took an interest in policies that could facilitate the creation of social solidarity and make the working class healthier. This legislative effort had roots in an earlier War. According to Titmuss:

> It was the South African War, not one of the notable wars in human history, to change the affairs of man, that touched off the personal health movement which led eventually to the National Health Service in 1948. (Titmuss 1958, p. 80)

In the United States, the School Lunch Program, established in 1946, was another classic case. Much of the initial support for the program was due to the persuasive testimony of Major General Lewis Hershey, Director of the Selective Service Commission. The general told congressional committees that during World War II poor nutrition accounted for many of the rejections of young men by local draft boards (U.S. House of Representatives 1989, p. 53).

Ralph Hawtrey noted that many hoped that the changes in society would go much farther:

> [culminating in] changes in human nature, which will bring new motives to bear. Mr. [Richard] Tawney looks forward to an extension through all occupations of the honorable zeal which we count on finding in the professions. This is itself a separate solution of the economic problem, a solution based like that of primitive society, upon a sense of obligation in the individual, but differing from the primitive solution in that the sense of obligation would be rational. It would take the form of a desire to render a service to society; it would not be bound up with a caste-imposed obligation to render a service of a narrowly traditional kind, but would be free to adapt itself to the changing needs of society. (Hawtrey 1925, p. 385)

Of course, those in power naturally did whatever they could to forestall such changes from going too far. In fact, even in the press of military emergencies when leaders recognize the importance of encouraging social solidarity, the powers that be still have limits to how far they are willing to go in the direction of equality. Titmuss mentioned a particularly revealing example. In May 1855 in the midst of the Crimean War, when Florence Nightingale opened a reading room for injured soldiers in Scutari, the War Office responded that soldiers "would get above themselves" if, instead of drinking, they read books and papers, and that army discipline would thereby be endangered (Titmuss 1958, p. 85; citing Woodham-Smith 1951, p. 239 although this page reference seems to be wrong).

Failure to pay adequate attention to morale can have serious consequences. For example, a recent collection of essays, comparing the respective experiences of London, Paris, and Berlin during World War I, suggests that, at least in part, Germany lost that war because the German government was less able than either France or Britain to persuade its people that it was acting fairly (see Winter and Robert 1997; especially, Bonzon 1997, p. 302; and Triebel 1997). Thierry Bonzon and Belinda Davis wrote that it was:

> ... the unequal distribution of deprivation more than the deprivation itself that annoyed people the most. In all three cities the feeling of unequal access to food, of a growing gap between the excluded majority and a privileged few set a limit on the acceptance of sacrifices endured by individuals, families, and social groups for the sake of victory . . . .
>
> Despite social tensions in London and Paris which should not be ignored (and which largely contributed to the "mobilization" of public powers on these questions), these two objectives were met. In Berlin both were unreachable . . . .
>
> The development of the black market in Berlin was no doubt the most visible symbol of the contrast between lived experience in the German capital and that on the other side of the line. Corruption existed everywhere, but only in Berlin did it emerge into a way of life, highlighting the extreme inequality of access to food in the German capital . . . .
>
> More than the blockade or the successive bad harvests, the disorganization of the market and modes of distribution (blamed perhaps unfairly on shopkeepers and middlemen), the unequal distribution of essential foods within Berlin society, the link between the access for the most fortunate to the black market and the exorbitant price paid by the majority to obtain no more than reduced rations, all these fuelled public anger and public demand for urgent action by the state. (Bonzon and Davis 1997, pp. 340–41)

Gabriel Kolko, a renowned professor of history at York University in Toronto, noted that German workers did not recover their 1913 level of wages until 1928. The Nazis realized that they could not pursue their program of military conquest, if they repeated the mistakes of World War I and undermined social solidarity by intensifying inequality. In Kolko's words: "Forced to choose, the Nazis . . . preferred to risk depriving the war effort to possibly alienating the workers and seeing them driven once again to political action in various forms, including slowdowns and sabotage." So, in World War II, Hitler protected wages. As a result, "Real weekly income in Germany grew dramatically from 1932 to 1941, and even in 1944 it was only slightly less than it had been at its peak 1941" (Kolko 1990, p. xvii).

Resolution of the Farm Worker Paradox

The wartime concern with morale is crucial to understanding how restrictive the terms of calculation debate really were. Within the narrow context of this debate, workers were, in effect, merely interchangeable parts, little different from capital goods. In contrast, within the context of actual war, planners had to realize that workers are human beings capable of making decisions about how to apply themselves. The leaders recognized that just as on the battlefield the most unlikely people sometimes prove to be the most heroic, something similar often happens on the shop floor.

Wartime conditions often give workers the opportunity to rise well beyond what might otherwise be expected of them. For example, in United States during World War II, many of the supposedly most productive workers in the country left the labor force to serve in the military. The women and rural black people who replaced them supposedly lacked the capacity to match the productivity of the young white man. In actual fact, their productivity greatly exceeded prewar levels.

Those who control the system of production, whether owners or managers, have little interest in acknowledging or even encouraging exceptional behavior on the part of employees—unless the controllers can be assured of getting credit for the accomplishments. To allow workers to excel in a more public way would lessen the rationale for the lopsided hierarchy typical of market society in which the controllers manage to extract a disproportionate share of the wealth and income.

I don't know if owners or managers actually think consciously in such terms, but if they were to consider the choice, I suspect that many, if not most, would opt to sacrifice considerable productivity in favor of more inequality—even if a more democratic form of organization would increase the standard of living for just about everybody. After all, psychologists tell us that most people regard their welfare relative to those around them. Or as H. L. Mencken once observed, a wealthy man is someone who earns $100 a year more than his wife's sister's husband.

Now let us return to the calculation debate. Rather than conceding that a market society represents maximum feasible efficiency, the economists debating socialism should have taken into account the innumerable wastes associated with markets, such as advertising and duplication, as well as the greatest waste of all—the unused potential of the people weighed down by what appears as the farm worker paradox.

The experience of war is very relevant here since it suggests that efficiency goes along with a resolution of the farm worker paradox—that efficiency and social solidarity work in unison—with one glaring exception; namely, the destructive nature of war. I explored this relationship in more detail in an earlier book (Perelman 2000b), but this idea is not unique at all. Even Adam Smith suggested as much.

Although the urgency of war forces governments to move in the direction of equality, nobody to my knowledge has given a satisfactory account of any market forces that would lead to increased equality. True, Simon Kuznets once found that capitalist development tends to first increase inequality and then decrease it back to something like where it began. Others have tried to replicate his observation using more recent data, but their work is not convincing.

Instead of pretending that markets lead to increasing equality, most economists followed the path of John Bates Clark in devoting considerable energy to showing the rationality of inequality. For such people, the farm worker paradox is hardly a paradox at all.

As we have seen, within the standard economic perspective, workers who earn little money still get what they deserve because they are not particularly productive. No thought is given to the possibility that these same ill-paid workers may very well have the potential to accomplish incredible things if they were given a supportive opportunity to do so.

The wartime economic accomplishments serve as a useful reminder of the importance of taking into account new social and economic possibilities.

Concluding Remarks About the Beginning of Sustainability

In a business-dominated society, long-term interests are kept relatively mute. Corporations focus on the next quarterly report; politicians, on the next election cycle. The current system leaves environmentalists, who are concerned with future generations, sitting on the fringe. All the while, environmental abuse spins out of control.

Wartime planning represents an alternative organizational principle that can address the question of sustainability. I do not mean to suggest that wartime planning provides a perfect model. It does not. Above all, the model of wartime planning falls short on account of its lack of democratic engagement. The planners promulgate rules and regulations or issue commands. They may take into account the need to maintain the morale of the masses, but no democratic check on their behavior exists. For example, although wartime conditions require governments to treat the masses of people better than in peacetime, those who dare to dissent are often handled roughly.

In addition, the environment does not fare well during wartime. In all-out war, society must focus as much energy as possible on immediate survival. As a result, little attention goes toward long-run consequences. Once the immediate threat of military defeat has passed, society can begin to take sustainability into account—but so far it has not.

Here too egalitarianism will pay handsome dividends. Recall that in discussing the concept of hyperbolic discounting, I mentioned that healthy individuals engage in intertemporal bargaining in which long-term interests have an effective voice in influencing choices. A more egalitarian society, especially one with a more engaged public—can create a dialogue in which intertemporal bargaining will have a large role.

The institutional specifics for such an arrangement require a wide range of inputs from virtually everybody. For a single individual to lay out a blueprint of such a society would be foolish. I will not go beyond saying that society as a whole, while engaged, presumably would not concern itself with every detail. To do otherwise would be both inefficient and boring.

Alfred North Whitehead once said "civilization advances by extending the number of important operations we can perform without thinking about them" (Whitehead 1911, p. 42; cited in Hayek 1952, p. 154). In this vein, I do not care about the particular route that the post office uses to deliver my mail unless I learn from some watchdog group that I have reason to be.

My main concern is that we should move as quickly as possible to a more democratic, more egalitarian, more sustainable society before it is too late.

References

Abowd, John M. and David S. Kaplan. 1999. "Executive Compensation: Six Questions that Need Answering." *Journal of Economic Perspectives*, Vol. 13, No. 4 (Fall): pp. 145–68.

Abrahams, Paul. 2002. "Microsoft Makes 85% Margin on Windows System: Disclosure Made in SEC Filing is Likely to Infuriate Rivals in Software Sector." *Financial Times* (November 18).

Ainslie, George. 1991. "Derivation of 'Rational' Economic Behavior from Hyperbolic Discount Curves (in Intertemporal Choice)." *American Economic Review*, Vol. 81, No. 2 (May): pp. 334–40.

———. 2001. *Breakdown of Will* (Cambridge: Cambridge University Press).

Akerlof, George A. 2002. "Behavioral Macroeconomics and Macroeconomic Behavior." *American Economic Review*, Vol. 92, No. 3 (June): pp. 411–33.

Albion, Robert Greenhalgh. 1926. *Forests and Sea Power: The Timber Problem of the Royal Navy, 1652–1862* (Cambridge: Harvard University Press).

Albrecht, William Albert. 1959. "Diagnosis or Post-Mortems?" *Natural Food and Farming* (September): p. 24.

Alchian, Armen A. and Harold Demsetz. 1972. "Production, Information Costs, and Economic Organization." *American Economic Review*, Vol. 62, No. 5 (December): pp. 777–96.

Allen, Robert C. and Ian Keay. 2001. "The First Great Whale Extinction: The End of the Bowhead Whale in the Eastern Arctic." *Explorations in Economic History*, Vol. 38, No. 4 (October): pp. 448–77.

Amsden, Alice H. 1989. *Asia's Next Giant: South Korea and Late Industrialization* (New York: Oxford University Press).

Angeletos, George-Marios, David Laibson, Andrea Repetto, Jeremy Tobacman, and Stephen Weinberg. 2001. "The Hyperbolic Consumption Model: Calibration, Simulation, and Empirical Evaluation." *Journal of Economic Perspectives*, Vol. 15, No. 3 (Summer): pp. 47–68.

Anker, Peder. 2001. *Imperial Ecology: Environmental Order in the British Empire, 1895–1945* (Cambridge, MA: Harvard University Press).

Anon. 1977. "Nitrogen Affects Corn Protein." *California Agriculture*, Vol. 31 (January): p. 20.

Anon. 1992. "Let Them Eat Pollution." *The Economist* (February 8–14): p. 66.

Anon. 1999. "Executive Pay: Up and Away." *Business Week* (April 19).

Anon. 2002. "Up Front." *Business Week* (December 30): p. 16.

Ashton, T. S. 1972. *An Economic History of England: The Eighteenth Century* (London: Methuen).

Babbage, Charles. 1835. *On the Economy of Manufactures* (London: Charles Knight; New York: Augustus M. Kelley, 1971).

Backus, Azel. 1961. *Connecticut Towns: Bethlehem, 1812 and Watertown 1801* (Hartford, CT: Case, Lockwood & Brainard).

Balmford, Andrew et al. 2002. "Economic Reasons for Conserving Wild Nature." *Science*, Vol. 297, No. 950 (August 9): pp. 950–53.

Balzac, Honoré de. 1991. *Père Goriot*, trans. A. J. Krailsheimer (New York: Oxford University Press).

Barbon, Nicholas. 1690. *A Discourse on Trade*, ed. Jacob Hollander (Baltimore: Johns Hopkins Press, 1905).

Barnett, Harold J. and Chandler Morse. 1963. *Scarcity and Growth: The Economics of Natural Resource Availability* (Baltimore: Johns Hopkins Press).

Becker, Gary S. 1988. "Family Economics and Macro Behavior." *American Economic Review*, Vol. 78, No. 1 (March): pp. 1–13.

Berle, Adolf Augustus and Gardiner C. Means. 1932. *The Modern Corporation and Private Property* (New York: Macmillan).

Biddle, Jeff E. and Daniel S. Hamermesh. 1998. "Beauty, Productivity, and Discrimination: Lawyers' Looks and Lucre." *Journal of Labor Economics*, Vol. 16, No. 1 (January): pp. 172–201.

Binmore, Ken. 1996. "Introduction." In John F. Nash. *Essays in Game Theory* (Cheltenham: Edward Elgar Publishing).

Binswanger, Mathias. 2001. "Technological Progress and Sustainable Development: What about the Rebound Effect?" *Ecological Economics*, Vol. 36, No. 1 (January): pp. 119–32.

Bishop, John H. 1991a. "Docility and Apathy: Its Cause and Cure." In Saumel Bacharach, ed. *Educational Reform: Social Change or Political Rhetoric* (New York: Allyn Bacon): pp. 234–58.

———. 1991b. "The Productivity Consequences of What is Learned in High School." *Journal of Curriculum Studies*, Vol. 22, No. 2: pp. 101–26.

Bliss, Christopher J. 1975. *Capital Theory and the Distribution of Income* (Oxford: North-Holland Publishing).

Bloom, Matt. 1999. "The Performance Effects of Pay Dispersion on Individuals and Organizations." *The Academy of Management Journal*, Vol. 42, No. 1 (February): pp. 25–40.

Blustein, Paul. 2001. *The Chastening: The Crisis that Rocked the Global Financial System and Humbled the IMF* (Cambridge: Perseus Books Group).

Boltzmann, Ludwig. 1974. *Theoretical Physics and Philosophical Problems*, ed. Brian McGuinness (Dordrecht: Reidel).

Bonzon, Thierry. 1997. "Coal and the Metropolis." In Jay Winter and Jean-Louis Robert, eds. *Capital Cities at War: London, Paris, Berlin, 1914–1919* (Cambridge and New York: Cambridge University Press), pp. 286–302.

Bonzon, Thierry and Belinda Davis. 1997. "Feeding the Cities." In Jay Winter and Jean-Louis Robert, eds. *Capital Cities at War: London, Paris, Berlin, 1914–1919* (Cambridge and New York: Cambridge University Press), pp. 305–41.

Bowle, John. 1981. *John Evelyn and His World: A Biography* (London: Routledge & Kegan Paul).

Bowles, Samuel and Herbert Gintis. 2002. "The Inheritance of Inequality." *Journal of Economic Perspectives*, Vol. 16, No. 3 (Summer): pp. 3–30.

Braudel, Fernand. 1982. *Civilization and Capitalism: 15th–18th Century*, Vol. 2. *The Wheels of Commerce* (New York: Harper and Row).

Bray, Francesca. 1984. *Agriculture*. Part 2 of *Biology and Biological Technology*, Vol. 6 of *Science and Civilization in China*, ed. Joseph Needham (Cambridge: Cambridge University Press).

Brecht, Bertolt. 1961. *The Caucasian Chalk Circle*. In *Parables for the Theater: Two Plays* (New York: Grove Press), pp. 97–189.

Brennan, Michael and Eduardo Schwartz. 1993. "A New Approach to Evaluating Natural Resource Investments." In Donald H. Chew Jr., ed. *The New Corporate Finance* (New York: McGraw-Hill), pp. 99–107.

Bridge, James Howard. 1903. *The History of the Carnegie Steel Company: The Inside History of the Carnegie Steel Company: A Romance of Millions* (New York: Arno Press, 1972).

Brown, Eleanor, Richard Spiro, and Diane Keenan. 1991. "Wage and Nonwage Discrimination in Professional Basketball: Do Fans Affect It?" *American Journal of Economics and Sociology*, Vol. 50, No. 3 (July): pp. 333–45.

Brown, Gardner M. Jr. 1990. "Valuation of Genetic Resources." In Gordon H. Orians et al., eds. *The Preservation and Valuation of Biological Resources* (Seattle: University of Washington Press), pp. 203–29.

Brown, Gardner M. Jr. and Barry C. Field. 1978. "Implications of Alternative Measures of Natural Resource Scarcity." *Journal of Political Economy*, Vol. 86, No. 2, Part 1 (April): pp. 229–43.

Carey, Henry Charles. 1851. *The Harmony of Interests: Agricultural, Manufacturing & Commercial* (New York: Kelley, 1967).

Carnegie, Andrew. 1889. "The Bugaboo of the Trusts." *North American Review*, Vol. 148, No. 387 (February): pp. 141–50.

Carswell, John. 1960. *The South Sea Bubble* (Stanford: Stanford University Press).

Carver, T. N. N.d. *Historical Sketch of American Agriculture* (Mimeo, borrowed from State University of New York at Binghamton).

Chancellor, Edward. 1999. *Devil take the Hindmost: History of Financial Speculation* (New York: Farrar Straus & Giroux).

Chang, Kenneth. 2000. "New Assignment for Satellite System." *New York Times* (December 19).

Chernow, Ron. 1990. *The House of Morgan: An American Banking Dynasty and the Rise of Modern Finance* (New York: Atlantic Monthly Press).

Churchill, Randolph S. 1967. *Winston S. Churchill*, Vol. 2. *Young Statesman 1901–1914* (Boston: Houghton Mifflin).

Cheung, Steven N. S. 1983. "The Contractual Nature of the Firm." *Journal of Law and Economics*, Vol. 26, No. 1 (April): pp. 1–22.

Clapp, Jennifer. 2001. *Toxic Exports* (Ithaca: Cornell University Press).

Clark, Colin W. 1973. "The Economics of Overexploitation." *Science*, Vol. 181, No. 4100 (August 17), pp. 630–34.

Clark, Gregory. 1994. "Factory Discipline." *Journal of Economic History*, Vol. 54, No. 1 (March): pp. 128–63.

Clark, John Bates. 1887. *The Philosophy of Wealth*, 2nd ed. (New York: Augustus M. Kelley, 1967).

———. 1888. "The Limits of Competition." *Political Science Quarterly*, Vol. 2 (March); reprinted in John B. Clark and Franklin H. Giddings. 1888. *The Modern Distributive Process: Studies of Competition and Its Limits* (Boston: Ginn & Company), pp. 1–17.

———. 1899. *The Distribution of Wealth: A Theory of Wages, Interest, and Profits* (New York: Augustus M. Kelley, 1965).

Clark, John Maurice. 1917. "The Basis of War-Time Collectivism." *American Economic Review*, Vol. 7, No. 4 (December): pp. 772–90.

———. 1942. "The Theoretical Issues." *American Economic Review*, Vol. 32, No. 1, Part 2 (Supplement) (March): pp. 1–12.

———. 1952. "J. M. Clark on J. B. Clark." In H. M. Spiegel, ed. *The Development of Economic Thought* (New York: John Wiley and Sons).

Comito, Terry. 1971. "Renaissance Gardens and the Discovery of Paradise." *Journal of the History of Ideas*, Vol. 32, No. 4 (October–December): pp. 483–506.

Costanza, Robert, Ralph d'Arge, R. de Groot, S. Farber, M. Grasso, B. Hannon, K. Limburg, S. Naeem, R. V. O'Neill, J. Paruelo, R. G. Raskin, P. Sutton, and M. van den Belt. 1997. "The Value of the World's Ecosystem Services and Natural Capital." *Nature*, Vol. 387, No. 6630 (May 15): pp. 253–60.

Coyle, Diane. 1998. *The Weightless World: Strategies for Managing the Digital Economy* (Cambridge: MIT Press).

Cranston, Maurice. 1957. *John Locke: A Biography* (New York: Macmillan).

Crystal, Graef. 1991. *In Search of Excess: The Overcompensation of American Executives* (New York: Norton).

Daily, Gretchen C. 1997a. "Introduction: What Are Ecosystem Services?" In Gretchen C. Daily, ed. *Nature's Services: Societal Dependence on Natural Ecosystems* (Washington, DC: Island Press), pp. 1–10.

———. 1997b. "Conclusion." In Gretchen C. Daily, ed. *Nature's Services: Societal Dependence on Natural Ecosystems* (Washington, DC: Island Press), pp. 365–74.

Dangerfield, George. 1961. *The Strange Death of Liberal England 1910–1914* (New York: Capricorn).

Darity, William Jr., Arthur H. Goldsmith, and Jonathan R. Veum. 1997. "The Impact of Psychological and Human Capital on Wages." *Economic Inquiry*, Vol. 35, No. 4 (October): pp. 815–29.

Dasgupta, Partha. 2001. "Valuing Objects and Evaluating Policies in Imperfect Economies." *Economic Journal*, Vol. 111, No. 471 (May): pp. 1–29.

David, Paul A. and Gavin Wright. 1997. "Increasing Returns and the Genesis of American Resource Abundance." *Industrial and Corporate Change*, Vol. 6, No. 2 (March): pp. 203–46.

Davids, Karel. 2001. "From De la Court to Vreede: Regulation and Self-regulation in Dutch Economic Discourse from ca. 1660 to the Napoleonic Era." *Journal of European Economic History*, Vol. 30, No. 2 (Fall): pp. 245–90.

Debreu, Gerard. 1959. *Theory of Value: An Axiomatic Analysis of Economic Equilibrium* (New York: Wiley).

de la Bédoyère, Guy. 1995. "Introduction." In Guy de la Bédoyère, ed. *The Writings of John Evelyn* (Woodbridge, Suffolk, UK: Boydell Press, 1995), pp. 173–332.

Deffeyes, Kenneth S. 2001. *Hubbert's Peak: The Impending World Oil Shortage* (Princeton: Princeton University Press).

Desimone, Livio D. and Frank Popoff. 1997. *Eco-Efficiency: The Business Link to Sustainable Development* (Cambridge: MIT Press).

Dobb, Maurice. 1973. *Theories of Value and Distribution Since Adam Smith: Ideology and Economic Theory* (Cambridge: Cambridge University Press).

Dorfman, Joseph. 1971. "Introduction." John Bates Clark and John Maurice Clark. 1912. *The Control of Trusts*, enlarged ed. (New York: Augustus M. Kelley), pp. 5–17.

Douglass, Elizabeth. 1994. "Light at the End of the Wind Tunnel." *San Diego Union-Tribune* (October 23): p. I 1.

Education Trust, The. 2002. *The Funding Gap: Low-Income and Minority Students Receive Fewer Dollars* (August). <http://www.edtrust.org/main/documents/investment.pdf>

Ehrenreich, Barbara. 2001. *Nickel and Dimed: On (not) getting by in America* (New York: Metropolitan Books).

Elias, David. 1999. *Dow 40,000: Strategies for Profiting from the Greatest Bull Market in History* (New York: McGraw-Hill Professional Publishing).

Evelyn, John. 1661. *Fumifugium*. In Guy de la Bédoyère, ed. *The Writings of John Evelyn* (Woodbridge, Suffolk, UK: Boydell Press, 1995), pp. 125–56.

———. 1664. *Sylva*. In Guy de la Bédoyère, ed. *The Writings of John Evelyn* (Woodbridge, Suffolk, UK: Boydell Press, 1995), pp. 173–332.

———. 1674. *Navigation and Commerce: Their Original and Progress* (London).

Fabrikant, Geraldine. 2002. "G.E. Expenses for Ex-Chief Cited in Filing." *New York Times* (September 6): p. C 1.

Falls, Cyril. 1941. *The Nature of Modern Warfare* (New York: Oxford University Press).

Farrow, Scott. 1995. "Extinction and Market Forces: Two Case Studies." *Ecological Economics*, Vol. 13, pp. 115–23.

Faulkner, Harold U. 1959. *Politics, Reform and Expansion, 1890–1900* (New York: Harper & Brothers).

Faustmann, Martin. 1849. "Calculation of the Value which Forest Land and Immature Stands Pose for Forestry." In Michael Cane, ed. *Martin Faustmann and the Evolution of Discounted Cash Flow* (Oxford: Commonwealth Forestry Institute paper No. 42, 1968), pp. 27–55.

Ferguson, Niall. 2001. *The Cash Nexus: Money and Power in the Modern World, 1700–2000* (New York: Basic Books).

Finkelstein, Andrea. 2000. "Nicholas Barbon and the Quality of Infinity." *History of Political Economy*, Vol. 32, No. 1 (Spring): pp. 83–102.

Finnegan, William. 2002. "Leasing the Rain." *The New Yorker* (April 8): p. 43.

Fisher, Irving. 1907. *The Rate of Interest* (London: Macmillan).

Flynn, Dennis and Arturo Giraldez. 2002. "Cycles of Silver: Global Economic Unity Through the Mid-18th Century." *Journal of World History*, Vol. 13, No. 2 (Fall): pp. 391–427.

Ford, Henry. 1926. *Today and Tomorrow* (Garden City, New York: Garden City Publishing Co.).

Foster, David R. 1999. *Thoreau's Country: Journey Through a Transformed Landscape* (Cambridge: Harvard University Press).

Foster, John Bellamy. 1997. "The Crisis of the Earth: Marx's Theory of Ecological Sustainability as a Nature-Imposed Necessity for Human Production." *Organization and Environment*, Vol. 10, No. 3 (September): pp. 278–95.

———. 1999. "Marx's Theory of Metabolic Rift: Classical Foundations for Environmental Sociology." *American Journal of Sociology*, Vol. 105, No. 2 (September): pp. 366–405.

Fourastie, Jean. 1960. *The Causes of Wealth* (Glencoe, IL: Free Press).

Franklin, Benjamin. 1782. "Information for those Who Would Remove to America." In Albert Henry Smyth, ed. *The Writings of Benjamin Franklin*, Vol. 8 (New York: Macmillan, 1905–07), pp. 603–14.

Frederick, Shane, George Loewenstein, and Ted O'Donoghue. 2002. "Time Discounting and Time Preference: A Critical Review." *Journal of Economic Literature*, Vol. 40, No. 2 (June): pp. 351–401.

Friedman, Milton and Anna Jacobson Schwartz. 1963. *A Monetary History of the United States, 1867–1960* (Princeton: Princeton University Press, 1971).

Furniss, Edgar. 1965. *The Position of the Laborer in a System of Nationalism* (New York: Augustus M. Kelley).

Galarza, Ernesto. 1977. *Farm Workers and Agri-Business in California, 1947–1960* (Notre Dame: University of Notre Dame Press).

Galbraith, James K. 1998. *Created Unequal: The Crisis in American Pay* (New York: Free Press).

Garber, Peter M. 1989a. "Tulipmania." *Journal of Political Economy*, Vol. 97, No. 3 (June): pp. 535–65.

———. 1989b. "Who Put the Mania in Tulipomania?" *Journal of Portfolio Management*, Vol. 16, No. 1 (Fall): pp. 53–60.

Garfield, Simon. 2001. *Mauve: How One Man Invented a Color that Changed the World* (New York: Norton).

Gates, Paul W. 1960. *The Farmer's Age: Agriculture, 1815–1860* (New York: Harper and Row).

Georgescu-Roegen, Nicholas. 1971. *The Entropy Law and the Economic Process* (Cambridge: Harvard University Press).

Gerschenkron, A. 1962. "Economic Backwardness in Historical Perspective." In *Economic Backwardness in Historical Perspective: A Book of Essays* (Cambridge: Harvard University Press), pp. 5–30.

Gilder, George. 1981. *Wealth and Poverty* (New York: Basic Books).

———. 1989. *Microcosm: The Quantum Revolution in Economics and Technology* (New York: Simon and Schuster).

Gill, Jennifer. 2001. "We're Back to Serfs and Royalty." *Business Week* (April 9).

Gladwell, Malcolm. 2002. "The Talent Myth: Are Smart People Overrated?" *The New Yorker* (July 22).

Glassman, James, K. and Kevin A. Hassett. 1999. *Dow 36,000: The New Strategy for Profiting from the Coming Rise in the Stock Market* (New York: Times Books).

Gottschalk, Peter and Sheldon Danziger. 1998. "Family Income Mobility—How Much is There, and Has it Changed?" In James A. Auerback and Richard S. Belous, eds. *The Inequality Paradox: Growth of Income Disparity* (Washington, DC: National Policy Association), pp. 92–111.

Gould, Stephen J. 1993. *Eight Little Piggies: Reflections in Natural History* (New York: Norton).

Gray, Lewis C. 1933. *History of Agriculture in the Southern United States to 1860* (Gloucester, MA: Peter Smith, 1958).

Greenspan, Alan. 1996. "Remarks at the 80th Anniversary Awards Dinner of the Conference Board." (New York, October 16).

———. 1999. "Measuring Financial Risk in the Twenty-first Century: Remarks Before a Conference Sponsored by the Office of the Comptroller of the Currency, Washington, DC (October 14).<http://www.federalreserve.gov/boarddocs/speeches/1999/19991014.htm>

Gylfason, Thorvaldur. 2001. "Nature, Power, and Growth." *Scottish Journal of Political Economy*, Vol. 48, No. 5 (November): pp. 558–88.

Habakkuk, H. J. 1962. *American and British Technology in the Nineteenth Century: The Search for Labour-Saving Inventions* (Cambridge: Cambridge University Press).

Haber, Samuel. 1964. *Efficiency and Uplift* (Chicago: The University of Chicago Press).

Hadley, Arthur Twining. 1903. *Railroad Transportation: Its History and Its Laws*, 10th ed. (New York: G. P. Putnam's and Sons, 1903) (New York: Johnson Reprint Co.).

Hamermesh, Daniel S. and Jeff E. Biddle. 1994. "Beauty and the Labor Market." *American Economic Review*, Vol. 84, No. 4 (December): pp. 1174–94.

Hardin, Garrett. 1968. "The Tragedy of the Commons." *Science*, Vol. 162, No. 3859 (December 13): pp. 1243–48.

Hawtrey, Ralph G. 1925. *The Economic Problem* (London: Longmans, Green).

Hayek, F. A. 1952. *The Counter-Revolution of Science: Studies on the Abuse of Reason*, 2nd ed. (Indianapolis: Liberty Press, 1979).

Henderson, John P. 1955. "The Retarded Acceptance of Marginal Utility: Comment." *Quarterly Journal of Economics*, Vol. 69, No. 3 (August): pp. 465–73.

Hersh, Seymour. 2003. "The Battle between Donald Rumsfeld and the Pentagon." *New Yorker* (April 7).

Hicks, John R. 1946. *Value and Capital*, 2nd ed. (Oxford: Clarendon Press).

——. 1973. *Capital and Time: A Neo-Austrian Theory* (Oxford: Clarendon Press).

Horide, Ichirou. 2000. "The House of Mitsui: Secrets of Its Longevity." *Journal of Marketing Theory and Practice*, Vol. 8, No. 2 (Spring): pp. 31–36.

Horsfall, James G. "The Fire Brigade Stops a Raging Corn Epidemic." In *That We May Eat: Yearbook of Agriculture, 1975* (Washington, DC: U.S. Department of Agriculture, 1975), pp. 105–14.

Hotelling, Harold. 1931. "The Economics of Exhaustible Resources." *Journal of Political Economy*, Vol. 39, No. 2 (April): pp. 137–75.

Hume, David. 1778. *History of England*. 5 vols. (Philadelphia: Porter and Coates).

Institute of Technology. 1935. Soy Beans. Bulletin No. 10 (Dearborn, MI, April 1935). <http://www.hbci.com/~wenonah/new/soybean.htm>

James, R. Warren. 1965. "Introduction." In R. Warren James, ed. *John Rae, Political Economist: An Account of His Life and a Compilation of His Main Writings* (Toronto: University of Toronto Press).

Jenks, Jeremiah. 1890. "The Economic Outlook." *Dial*, Vol. 10.

Jensen, Michael C. 1993. "The Modern Industrial Revolution: Exit and the Failure of Internal Control Systems." *Journal of Finance*, Vol. 48, No. 3 (July): pp. 831–80.

Jensen, Michael and William Meckling. 1976. "Theory of the Firm: Managerial Behavior, Agency Costs, and Ownership Structure." *Journal of Financial Economics*, Vol. 3, No. 4 (October): pp. 305–60.

Jevons, William Stanley. 1866. "On the Importance of Diffusing a Knowledge of Political Economy." In R. D. Collison Black, ed., *Papers and Correspondence of William Stanley Jevons*, 7 vols. (London: Macmillan), vii, pp. 37–54.

——. 1871. *The Theory of Political Economy* (Baltimore: Penguin, 1970).

——. 1906. *The Coal Question: An Inquiry Concerning the Progress of the Nation, and the Probable Exhaustion of Our Coal-Mines*, 3rd ed. (London: Macmillan).

Johnston, James F. W. 1851. *Notes on North America: Agricultural, Economical and Social*, 2 vols. (Edinburgh: William Blackwood and Sons).

Jones, Colon. 1994. *The Cambridge Illustrated History of France* (Cambridge: Cambridge University Press).

Juan, Jorge and Antonio de Ulloa. 1748. *A Voyage to South America*, trans. John Adams (Tempe: Center for Latin American Studies, Arizona State University, 1975).

Kadlec, Charles W. and Ralph J. Acampora. 1999. *Dow 100,000: Fact or Fiction* (Englewood Cliffs, NJ: Prentice Hall).

Kahn, Lawrence M. 2000. "The Sports Business as a Labor Market Laboratory." *Journal of Economic Perspectives*, Vol. 14, No. 3 (Summer): pp. 75–94.

Kahn, Lawrence M. and Peter D. Sherer. 1988. "Racial Differences in Professional Basketball Players' Compensation." *Journal of Labor Economics*, Vol. 6, No. 1 (January): pp. 40–61.

Kelley, Marjorie. 2001. *The Divine Right of Capital: Dethroning the Corporate Aristocracy* (San Francisco, CA: Berrett-Koehler Publishers).

Keymer, John. 1650. *A Clear and Evident Way for Enriching the Nations of England and Ireland* (London); Kress Goldsmith Collection, Reel 91, Item 1159.

Keynes, John Maynard. 1919. *The Economic Consequences of the Peace*, In Donald Moggridge, ed. *The Collected Works of John Maynard Keynes*, Vol. 2 (London: Macmillan, 1971).

———. 1923. *A Tract on Monetary Reform*. Vol. 4. *The Collected Writings of John Maynard Keynes* (London: Macmillan, 1971).

———. 1930a. "Economic Possibilities for Our Grandchildren." *Nation and Athenaeum* (October 11 and 18); reprinted in *Essays in Persuasion*. Vol. 9. In Donald Moggridge, ed. *Collected Works of John Maynard Keynes* (London: Macmillan, 1972): pp. 321–31.

———. 1930b. *A Treatise on Money*, Vols. v and vi. In Donald Moggridge, ed. *The Collected Writings of John Maynard Keynes* (London: Macmillan, 1971).

———. 1931. "An Economic Analysis of Unemployment." In Philip Quincy Wright, ed. *Unemployment as a World-Problem: Lectures on the Harris Foundation, 1931* (Freeport, NY: Books for Libraries Press), pp. 3–43; reprinted in *The Collected Writings of John Maynard Keynes*, ed. Donald Moggridge (London: Macmillan), pp. 343–67.

———. 1933. "National Self-Sufficiency." *Yale Review*, Vol. 22, No. 4 (June): pp. 755–69; and *The New Statesman and Nation*, July 8 and 15; reprinted in Donald Moggridge, ed. *The Collected Writings of John Maynard Keynes*, Vol. 21. *Activities, 1931–1939: World Crises and Policies in Britain and America* (London: Macmillan, 1982), pp. 233–46.

———. 1936a. "William Stanley Jevons." *Essays in Biography*. Vol. 10. In Donald Moggridge, ed. *Collected Works* (London: Macmillan, 1972), pp. 109–60.

———. 1936b. *The General Theory of Employment, Interest and Money* (New York: Macmillan).

———. 1938. "Letter to Hugh Townshend (December 7)." In Donald Moggridge, ed. *The Collected Writings of John Maynard Keynes*. Vol. 29. *The General Theory and After: A Supplement* (London: Macmillan, 1973): pp. 293–4.

———. 1940. "How to Pay for the War." In Donald Moggridge, ed. *Essays in Persuasion*. Vol. 9. *The Collected Writings of John Maynard Keynes* (London: Macmillan, 1972), pp. 367–439.

Khurana, Rakesh. 2002. *Searching for a Corporate Savior: The Irrational Quest for Charismatic C.E.O.'s* (Cambridge, MA: Harvard Business School Press).

Knoedler, Janet T. 1997. "Veblen and Technical Efficiency." *Journal of Economic Issues*, Vol. 31, No. 4 (December): pp. 1011–26.

Knoedler, Janet T. and Anne Mayhew. 1994. "The Engineers and Standardization." *Business and Economic History*, Vol. 23, No. 1 (Fall): pp. 141–51.

Kolko, Gabriel. 1965. *Railroads and Regulation, 1877–1916* (Princeton: Princeton University Press).

———. 1990. *The Politics of War: The World and United States Foreign Policy, 1943–1945* (New York: Pantheon Books).

Koopmans, Tjalling. 1979. "Economics Among the Sciences." *American Economic Review*, Vol. 69, No. 1 (March): pp. 1–12.

Kozol, Jonathan. 1991. *Savage Inequalities: Children in America's Schools* (New York: Crown).

Kremer, Michael. 1993. "The O-Ring Theory of Economic Development." *Quarterly Journal of Economics*, Vol. 58, No. 3 (August): pp. 551–76.

Krugman, Paul. 2002. "For Richer." *New York Times Magazine* (October 20).

Lancaster, Kelvin and Richard G. Lipsey. 1956. "The General Theory of the Second Best." *Review of Economic Studies*, Vol. 24, No. 1 (January): pp. 11–32.

Langewiesche, William. 1998. "The Lessons of Valujet 592." *Atlantic Monthly*, Vol. 281, No. 3 (March): pp. 81–98.

Lebergott, Stanley. 1984. *The Americans: An Economic Record* (New Year: Norton).

Levine, A. L. 1967. *Industrial Retardation in Britain, 1880–1914* (New York: Basic Books).

Lewis, David L. 1995. "Henry Ford and His Magic Beanstalk." *Michigan History Magazine* (May/June).

Livesay, Harold C. 1975. *Andrew Carnegie and the Rise of Big Business* (Boston: Little Brown).

Livingston, James. 1986. *Origins of the Federal Reserve System: Money, Class, and Corporate Capitalism, 1890–1913* (Ithaca: Cornell University Press).

Lo"fgren, K. 1983. "The Faustmann-Ohlin Theorem: A Historical Note." *History of Political Economy*, Vol. 15, No. 2 (Summer): pp. 261–64.

Lowenstein, Roger. 2000. *When Genius Failed: The Rise and Fall of Long-Term Capital Management* (New York: Random House).

Lublin, Joann S. 2002. "Some CEOs Received Big Payouts as Companies they Led Faltered." *Wall Street Journal* (February 26): p. B1.

Lucas, Robert. 1979. "The Death of Keynes: Remarks at a Panel Discussion at the 27th Annual Management Conference in 1979." Reprinted in Thomas J. Hailstones, ed. *Viewpoints on Supply-Side Economics* (Richmond, VA: Robert F. Dame Inc., 1982), pp. 3–5.

Lukacs, John. 1968. *Historical Consciousness; or, the Remembered Past* (New York: Harper & Row).

Luttwak, Edward. 1999. *Turbo-Capitalism: Winners and Losers in the Global Economy* (New York: HarperCollins).

Mackay, Charles. 1841. *Memoirs of Extraordinary Popular Delusions and the Madness of Crowds* (New York: Farrar, Straus, and Cudahy, 1932).

McCloskey, Donald N. 1978. "The Achievements of the Cliometric School." *Journal of Economic History*, Vol. 38, No. 1 (March): pp. 13–28.

McKay, Jim. 2000. "Server Farms Strain Local Grids: Jurisdictions are Facing Huge Power Demands from These Digital Warehouses." *Government Technology News* (September 29). <http://www.govtech.net/news/features/feature_sept_29.phtml>

McNeill, John Robert. 2000. *Something New Under the Sun: An Environmental History of the Twentieth-Century World* (New York: W. W. Norton).

Maloney, John. 1985. *Marshall, Orthodoxy and the Professionalisation of Economics* (Cambridge: Cambridge University Press).

Malthus, Thomas Robert. 1817a. *Essay on Population*, 5th ed. (London: Johnson).

——. 1817b. "Letter to Ricardo, 17 August." In David Ricardo, *Works and Correspondence*. Vol. 7 (Cambridge: Cambridge University Press, 1952), pp. 174–77.

——. 1820. *Principles of Political Economy, Considered with a View to Their Practical Application* (London: John Murray); reprinted in part in David Ricardo, *Notes on Malthus*. Vol. ii. In Piero Sraffa, ed. *The Works and Correspondence of David Ricardo* (Cambridge: Cambridge University Press, 1951).

——. 1826. *Essay on Population*, 6th ed., 2 vols. (London: J. M. Dent, 1914).

Mandeville, Bernard. 1723. *The Fable of the Bees or Private Vices, Publick Benefits*, 2 vols. (Oxford: Clarendon Press).

Manning, Robert. 2000. *Credit Card Nation: The Consequences of America's Addiction to Credit* (New York: Basic Books).

Manzano, Osmel and Roberto Rigobon. 2001. "Resource Curse or Debt Overhang?" National Bureau of Economic Research, Working Paper No. 8390 (July).

Marsh, George Perkins. 1864. *Man and Nature; or, Physical Geography as Modified by Human Action* (Cambridge: Belknap Press of Harvard University, 1965).

Marshall, Alfred. 1873. *Lectures to Women*. Tiziano Raffaelli, Eugenio Biagini, and Rita McWilliams Tullberg, eds. (Aldershot, UK: Edward Elgar), pp. 85–132.

——. *Principles of Economics: An Introductory Volume* (London: Macmillan & Co.).

———. 1897. "The Old Generation of Economists and the New." *Quarterly Journal of Economics* (January); reprinted in Alfred C. Pigou, ed. *Memorials of Alfred Marshall* (New York: Kelley and Millman, 1956; 1st ed., 1925), pp. 295–311.

———. 1919. *Industry and Trade* (London: MacMillan).

Marshall, Jonathan. 1995. *To Have and Have Not: Southeast Asian Raw Materials and the Origins of the Pacific War* (Berkeley: University of California Press).

Marx, Karl, 1977. *Capital*. Vol. 1 (New York: Vintage).

Marx, Karl and Friedrich Engels. 1942. *Selected Correspondence* (New York: International Publishers).

Mazumder, Bhash. 2002. "Analyzing Income Mobility Over Generations." *Chicago Fed Letter of the Federal Reserve Bank of Chicago*, No. 181 (September).

Meek, Ronald. 1967. "The Decline of Ricardian Economics in England." In *Economics and Ideology and Other Essays* (London: Chapman and Hall), pp. 51–74.

———. 1973. *Studies in the Labour Theory of Value*, 2nd ed. (London: Lawrence and Wishart).

Mercado, A. D. Jr. and R. M. Lantican. 1961. "The Susceptibility of Cytoplasm Male Sterility Lines of Corn to Helminthosporium Maydis, Nisik, and Miy." *Philippine Agriculturalist*, Vol. 45: pp. 235–43.

Mill, John Stuart. 1848. *Principles of Political Economy with Some of Their Applications to Social Philosophy*. Vols. 2–3. In J. M. Robson, eds. *Collected Works* (Toronto: University of Toronto Press, 1965).

Miller, Raymond J. and David E. Koeppe. 1971. "Southern Corn Leaf Blight: Susceptible and Resistant Mitochondria." *Science*, Vol. 173, No. 3991 (July 2): pp. 67–69.

Mills, Paul K. and Sandy Kwong. 2001. "Cancer Incidence in the United Farmworkers of America (UFW), 1987–1997." *American Journal of Industrial Medicine*, 40 (NovemFber): pp. 596–603.

———. 1989a. *More Light than Heat: Economics as Social Physics, Physics as Nature's Economics* (Cambridge: Cambridge University Press).

———. 1989b. "The Measurement Without Theory Controversy: Defeating Rival Research Programs by Accusing them of Naive Empiricism." *Economies et Societés*, Vol. 23, No. 6 (June): pp. 65–87.

———. 1990. "Smooth Operator: How Marshall's Demand and Supply Curves Made Neoclassicism Safe for Public Consumption But Unfit for Science." In Rita McWilliams Tullberg, ed. *Alfred Marshall in Retrospect* (Aldershot: Edgar Elgar): pp. 61–90.

———. 2002. *Machine Dreams: Economics Becomes a Cyborg Science* (Cambridge: Cambridge University Press).

Mitra, Tapan and Henry Y. Wan, Jr. 1985. "Some Theoretical Results on the Economics of Forestry." *Review of Economic Studies*, Vol. 52, No. 2 (April): pp. 263–82.

Morris, Kelly. 2001. "Prevention Fails to Halt South Africa's Well-Treated Cholera Epidemic: Editorial." *The Lancet*, Vol. 357, No. 9252 (January 27): p. 290.

Morris, Simon Conway. 1995. "A New Phylum from the Lobster's Lips." *Nature*, Vol. 378, No. 6558 (December 14): p. 661.

Mun, Sir Thomas. 1664. *England's Treasure by Forraign Trade*. in John R. McCulloch, ed. *Early English Tracts on Commerce* (Cambridge: Cambridge University Press, 1970): pp. 115–209.

Nardinelli, Clark. 1982. "Corporal Punishment and Children's Wages in 19th Century Britain." *Explorations in Economic History*, Vol. 19, No. 3 (July): pp. 283–95.

National Research Council. 2000. *The Impact of Selling the Federal Helium Reserve* (Washington, DC: National Academy Press). <http://www.nap.edu/books/0309070384/html/>

Nelson, Robert A. 1998. "Iridium: From Concept to Reality." *Via Satellite* (September). <http://catalog.com/hitekweb/iridium.htm>

Neurath, Otto. 1919 "Through War Economy to Economy in Kind." Reprinted in Otto Neurath. *Empiricism and Sociology*, Marie Neurath and Robert S. Cohen, eds. (Dordrecht: D. Reidel, 1973): pp. 123–57.

Norgaard, Richard B. 1975. "Resource Scarcity and New Technology in U.S. Petroleum Development." *Natural Resources Journal*, Vol. 15, No. 2 (April): pp. 265–82.

Olney, Martha L. 1991. *Buy Now, Pay Later: Advertising, Credit, and Consumer Durables in the 1920s* (Chapel Hill, University of North Carolina Press).

Olwig, Karen Fog and Kenneth Olwig. 1979. "Underdevelopment and the Development of the 'Natural' Park Ideology." *Antipode*, Vol. 11, No. 2: pp. 16–25.

O'Neill, John. 1996. Who Won The Socialist Calculation Debate? *History of Political Thought*, Vol. 17, No. 3 (Autumn): pp. 432–42.

——. 2002. "Socialist Calculation and Environmental Valuation: Money, Markets and Ecology." *Science & Society*, Vol. 55, No. 1 (Spring): pp. 137–51.

Ostrom, Elinor. 2000. "Collective Action and the Evolution of Social Norms." *Journal of Economic Perspectives*, Vol. 14, No. 3 (Summer): pp. 137–58.

Pearlstein, Steven. 2002. "In Blossoming Scandal, Culprits are Countless." *Washington Post* (June 28): p. A1.

Peart, Sandra J. 2001. "'Facts Carefully Marshalled' in the Empirical Studies of William Stanley Jevons." In Judy L. Klein and Mary S. Morgan, eds. *The Age of Economic Measurement* (Durham and London: Duke University Press), pp. 252–76.

Perelman, Michael. 1977. *Farming for Profit in a Hungry World: Capital and the Crisis in Agriculture* (Totowa, NJ: Allenhald, Osmun).

——. 1996. *The End of Economics* (London: Routledge).

——. 1999a. "Henry Carey's Political-Ecological Economics." *Organization and Environment*, Vol. 12, No. 3 (September): pp. 280–92.

——. 1999b. *The Natural Instability of Markets: Expectations, Increasing Returns and the Collapse of Markets* (New York: St. Martin's Press, 1999).

——. 2000a. *The Invention of Capitalism: The Secret History of Primitive Accumulation* (Durham: Duke University Press).

——. 2000b. *Transcending the Economy: On the Potential of Passionate Labor and the Wastes of the Market* (New York: St. Martin's Press).

——. 2001. *The Pathology of the U.S. Economy Revisited: The Intractable Contradictions of Economic Policy* (New York: Palgrave).

——. 2002. *Steal this Idea: The Corporate Confiscation of Creativity* (New York: Palgrave).

Perrow, Charles. 1984. *Normal Accidents: Living with High-Risk Technologies* (New York: Basic Books).

Peters, Tom. 1997. *The Circle of Innovation* (New York: Alfred A. Knopf).

Petty, William. 1690. *Political Arithmetick*. In C. H. Hull, ed. *The Economic Writings of Sir William Petty*, 2 vols. (New York: Kelley, 1963), i, pp. 237–312.

Phillips, Kevin P. 2002. *Wealth and Democracy: A Political History of the American Rich* (New York: Broadway Books).

Pigou, Arthur Cecil. 1920. *The Economics of Welfare* (London: Macmillan).

Pimm, Stuart L. 1997. "The Value of Everything." *Nature*, Vol. 387, No. 6630 (May 15): pp. 231–32.

Pimentel, David, Edward L. Skidmore, and Stanley W. Trimble. 1999. "Letter: Rates of Soil Erosion." *Science* (November 19): p. 1477.

Plochmann, Richard. 1968. *Forestry in the Federal Republic of Germany*, Hill Family Foundation Series (Corvallis: Oregon State University School of Forestry), pp. 24–25.

Pomeranz, Kenneth. 2000. *The Great Divergence: Europe, China, and the Making of the Modern World Economy* (Princeton: Princeton University Press).

Ponting, Clive. 1994. *Churchill* (London: Sinclair-Stevenson).

Portney, Paul R. and John P. Weyant. 1999. "Introduction." In Paul R. Portney and John P. Weyant, eds. *Discounting and Intergenerational Equity* (Washington, DC: Resources for the Future), pp. 1–11.

Posner, Eric A. 2000. *Law and Social Norms* (Cambridge: Harvard University Press).

Powell, Corey S. 1996. "No Light Matter." *Scientific American*, Vol. 274, No. 3 (March): pp. 28–30.

President of the United States. 2002. *Economic Report of the President* (Washington, DC: U.S. Government Printing Office).

Price, Jennifer. 1999. *Flight Maps: Adventures with Nature in Modern America* (New York: Basic Books).

Primack, Martin L. 1962. "Land Clearing Under Nineteenth-Century Techniques: Some Preliminary Calculations." *Journal of Economic History*, Vol. 22, No. 4 (December): pp. 484–97.

Quandt, Sara A., Thomas A. Arcury, Julie Early, Janeth Tapia, and Jessie D. Davis. 2003. "Household Food Security among Latino Migrant and Seasonal Farmworkers in North Carolina." Center for Latino Health Research, Department of Family and Community Medicine, Wake Forest University School of Medicine, Working Paper 03-01 (Spring).

Radin, Margaret Jane. 1996. *Contested Commodities* (Cambridge: Harvard University Press).

Rae, John. 1834. *Statement of Some New Principles on the Subject of Political Economy*. Vol. ii. In R. Warren James, ed. *John Rae, Political Economist: An Account of His Life and Writings*, 2 vols. (Toronto: University of Toronto Press, 1965).

Rashid, Salim. 1981. "Political Economy and Geology in the Early Nineteenth Century: Similarities and Contrasts." *History of Political Economy*, Vol. 3, No. 4 (Winter): pp. 726–45.

Repetto, Robert. 1992. "Accounting for Environmental Assets." *Scientific American*, Vol. 266, No. 2 (June): pp. 94–100.

Ricardo, David. 1817. *Principles of Political Economy*, Vol. 1. In Piero Sraffa and Maurice Dobb, eds. *The Works and Correspondence of David Ricardo*, 11 vols. (Cambridge: Cambridge University Press, 1951–73).

Robbins, Lionel Charles. 1969. *An Essay on the Nature and Significance of Economic Science*, 2nd ed. (London: Macmillan).

Roney, H. B. 1907. "Efforts to Check the Slaughter." In W. B. Mershon, ed. *The Passenger Pigeon* (New York: The Outing Publishing Company).

Ross, Michael. 2001. *Extractive Sectors and the Poor: An Oxfam America Report* (Boston: Oxfam America). <http://www.oxfamamerica.org/eireport/>

Rosser, J. Barkley. 1991. *From Catastrophe to Chaos: A General Theory of Economic Discontinuities* (Boston: Kluwer Academic Press).

Rothfeder, Jeffrey. 2001. *Every Drop for Sale: Our Desperate Battle Over Water in a World About to Run Out* (New York: Jeremy P. Tarcher/Putnam).

Sachs, Jeffrey D. and Andrew M. Warner. 2001. "Natural Resources and Economic Development: The Curse of Natural Resources." *European Economic Review*, Vol. 45: pp. 827–38.

Sacerdote, Bruce. 2002. "The Nature and Nurture of Economic Outcomes." *American Economic Review*, Vol. 92, No. 2 (May): pp. 344–48.

Saini, Sarup S. and Glen N. Davis. 1969. "Male Sterility in Allium Cepa and Some Species of Hybrids." *Economic Botany*, Vol. 23. No. 1 (January/March): pp. 37–49.

Samuelson, Paul A. 1957. "Wages and Interest—A Modern Dissection of Marxian Economic Models." *American Economic Review*, Vol. 67, No. 6 (December): pp. 884–912.

———. 1976. "Economics of Forestry in an Evolving Society." *Economic Inquiry*, Vol. 14, No. 4 (December): pp. 466–92.

———. 1989. "The Passing of the Guard in Economics." *Eastern Economic Journal*, Vol. 14, No. 4 (October–December): pp. 319–29.

Sandler, Blair. 1994. "Grow or Die: Marxist Theories of Capitalism and the Environment." *Rethinking Marxism*, Vol. 7, No. 2 (Summer): pp. 38–57.

Saunders, Beatrice. 1970. *John Evelyn and His Times* (Oxford: Pergamon Press).

Scheffer, Marten, Steve Carpenter, Jonathan A. Foley, Carl Folke, and Brian Walker. 2001. "Catastrophic Shifts in Ecosystems." *Nature*, Vol. 413: pp. 591–96.

Schmitz, Christopher. 1979. *World Non-Ferrous Metal Production and Prices, 1700–1976* (London: Frank Cass).

Schoenhof, Jacob. 1893. *The Economy of High Wages: An Inquiry into the Cause of High Wages and Their Effects on Methods and Cost of Production* (New York: G. P. Putnam's Sons).

Scholtissek, Christoph and Ernest Naylor. 1988. "Fish Farming and Influenza Pandemics." *Nature*, Vol. 331, No. 6153 (January 21): p. 215.

Schultz, Theodore. 1964. *Transforming Traditional Agriculture* (New Haven: Yale University Press).

Schurr, Sam. 1982. "Energy Efficiency and Productive Efficiency: Some Thoughts Based on American Experience." *The Energy Journal*, Vol. 3, No. 3: pp. 3–14.

Scorgie, Michael E. 1996. "Evolution of the Application of Present Value to Valuation of Non-Monetary Resources." *Accounting and Business Research* (UK), Vol. 26, No. 3: pp. 237–48.

Scott, James C. 1998. *Seeing Like a State: How Certain Schemes to Improve the Human Condition have Failed* (New Haven: Yale University Press).

Scoville, Warren C. 1953. "Did Colonial Farmers 'Waste' Our Land?" *Southern Economic Journal*, Vol. 20, No. 2 (October): pp. 178–81.

Sethi, Rajiv and E. Somanathan. 1996. "The Evolution of Social Norms in Common Property Resource Use." *American Economic Review*, Vol. 86, No. 4 (September): pp. 766–88.

Shapin, Steven. 1990. "Technicians, Skill and Value." H. M. Collins, ed. *Third Quinquennial University of Bath Conference in Science Studies (14 September): Rediscovering Skill.*

Shleifer, Andrei and Lawrence H. Summers. 1988. "Breach of Trust in Hostile Takeovers." In Alan J. Auerbach, ed. *Takeovers: Causes and Consequences* (Chicago: University of Chicago Press), pp. 33–67.

Silverman, Rachel Emma. 2002. "Here's the Retirement Welch Built: $1.4 Million a Month." *Wall Street Journal* (October 31): p. A 1.

Sinclair, Upton. 1906. *The Jungle* (New York: Modern Library, 2002).

Skaggs, Jimmy M. 1994. *The Great Guano Rush: Entrepreneurs and American Overseas Expansion* (New York: St. Martin's Press).

Skinner, John S. 1824. "Guano, A Celebrated Manure Used in South America." *American Farmer*, Vol. 6 (December 24): pp. 316–17.

Sklar, Martin J. 1954. "Rejoinder." *Southern Economic Journal*, Vol. 21, No. 1 (July): pp. 91–93.

———. 1992. "Some Political and Cultural Consequences of the Disaccumulation of Capital: Origins of Postindustrial Development in the 1920s." In *The United States as a Developing Country: Studies in U.S. History in the Progressive Era in the 1920s* (Cambridge: Cambridge University Press), pp. 143–96.

Smil, Vaclav. 2001. *Enriching the Earth: Fritz Haber, Carl Bosch, and the Transformation of World Food Production* (Cambridge: MIT Press).

Smith, Adam. 1759. *The Theory of Moral Sentiments*, ed. D. D. Raphael and A. L. Macfie (Oxford: Clarendon Press, 1976).

———. 1762–63. *Lectures on Rhetoric and Belles Lettres*, ed. John M. Lothian (London: Thomas Nelson, 1963).

———. 1776. *An Inquiry into the Nature and Causes of the Wealth of Nations*, 2 vols., ed. R. H. Campbell and A. S. Skinner (New York: Oxford University Press, 1976).

———. 1790. "Of the Nature of that Imitation Which Takes Place in What are Called the Imitative Arts." In *Essays on Philosophical Subjects*, ed. W. P. D. Wightman and J. C. Bryce (New York: Clarendon Press, 1980): pp. 176–209.

———. 1978. *Lectures on Jurisprudence*, ed. R. L. Meek, D. D. Raphael, and P. G. Stein (Oxford: Clarendon University Press).

Smith, G. C., K. E. Belk, J. A. Scanga, J. N. Sofos, and J. D. Tatum [Colorado State University]. 2000. "Traceback, Traceability and Source Verification in the U.S. Beef Industry." Presented at the XXI World Buiatrics Congress, on December 5, 2000 in Punta del Este, Uruguay.

Smith, Vernon L. 1969. "On Models of Commercial Fishing." *Journal of Political Economy*, Vol. 77, No. 2 (March–April): pp. 181–98.

Sowell, Thomas. 1993. "A Student's Eye View of George Stigler." *Journal of Political Economy*, Vol. 101, No. 5 (October): pp. 784–93.

Standage, Tom. 1998. *The Victorian Internet: The Remarkable Story of the Telegraph and the Nineteenth Century's On-Line Pioneers* (New York: Walker and Co.).

Steinberg, Theodore. 2002. *Down to Earth: Nature's Role in American History* (Oxford: Oxford University Press).

Stigler, George J. 1959. "The Politics of Political Economists." *Quarterly Journal of Economics*, Vol. 73, No. 4 (November): pp. 522–32; reprinted in his *Essays in the History of Economics* (Chicago: University of Chicago Press), pp. 51–65.

Strassman, W. P. 1959. *Risk and Technological Investment* (Ithaca: Cornell University Press).

Strotz, Robert. 1956. "Myopia and Inconsistency in Dynamic Utility Maximization." *Review of Economic Studies*, Vol. 23: pp. 165–80.

Stroup, Richard L. and Jane S. Shaw. 1985. "Helium—How Much is Enough?" *Regulation*, Vol. 9, No. 2 (March/April): pp. 17–23.

Tawney, Richard H. 1926. *The Acquisitive Society* (New York: Harcourt, Brace, and World, 1948).

Teixeira, Pedro N. 2002. "How Much is too Much? The Emergence of Modern Labour Economics 1930–60." *History of Economics Society* (Davis, July 7).

Temple, William. 1770. *Essay on Trade and Commerce* (London).

Titmuss, Richard M. 1958. "War and Social Policy." In Richard Titmuss, ed. *Essays on the Welfare State* (London: Allen and Unwin), pp. 75–87.

——. 1981. *Who Owns the Wildlife? The Political Economy of Conservation in Nineteenth-Century America* (Westport, CT: Greenwood Press).

Tobias, J. J. 1967. *Crime and Industrial Society in the Nineteenth Century* (New York: Schocken Books).

Tocqueville, Alexis de. 1835. *Democracy in America*, ed. Philip Bradley (New York: Vintage, 1945).

Townsend, Joseph. 1786. *A Dissertation on the Poor Laws by a Well Wisher to Mankind.* In John Ramsay McCulloch, ed. *A Select Collection of Scarce and Valuable Economic Tracts* (New York: Augustus M. Kelley, 1966), pp. 395–450.

Triebel, Armin. 1997. "Coal and the Metropolis." In Jay Winter and Jean-Louis Robert, eds. *Capital Cities at War: London, Paris, Berlin, 1914–1919* (Cambridge and New York: Cambridge University Press), pp. 342–73.

Trotsky, Leon. 1932. *The Russian Revolution: The Overthrow of Tzarism and the Triumph of the Soviets*, ed. F. W. Dupee (New York: Doubleday).

Tucker, Josiah. 1758. *Instructions for Travelers* (Dublin: William Watson); Kress-Goldsmith Collection, Reel 712, Item 9323; originally printed as Section IV of Part V of *The Elements of Commerce and Theory of Taxes* (1755, privately printed; Kress Goldsmith Collection, Reel 664, Item 9002).

Turgot, Anne Robert Jacques. 1766. "Reflections on the Formation and Distribution of Wealth." In Peter D. Groenewegen, ed. *The Economics of A. R. J. Turgot* (The Hague: Nijhoff, 1977), pp. 43–96.

U.S. Department of Labor. Office of the Assistant Secretary for Policy. Office of Program Economics. 2000. *Findings from the Demographic and National Agricultural Workers Survey: Employment Profile of United States Farmworkers*, Research Report No. 8 (NAWS) 1997–1998 (March) <http://www.dol.gov/asp/programs/agworker/report_8.pdf>

U.S. House of Representatives, Committee on Education and Labor, Subcommittee on Elementary, Secondary and Vocational Education. 1989. Child Nutrition Programs: Issues for the 101st Congress, One Hundredth Congress, 2nd Session (December).

U.S. President. 2001. *Economic Report of the President* (Washington, DC: US Government Printing Office).

——. 2002. *Economic Report of the President* (Washington, DC: US Government Printing Office).

United Nations Development Programme. 2001. *United Nations Human Development Report, 2001: Making New Technologies Work for Human Development* (New York: Oxford University Press).

United States Environmental Protection Agency. 1999. *Municipal Solid Waste Factbook*. <www.epa.gov/epaoswer/non-hw/muncpl/factbook/internet/mswf/gen.htm#2>

Vanderlint, Jacob. 1734. *Money Answers All Things* (London: T. Cox).

Veblen, Thorstein. 1915. *Imperial Germany and the Industrial Revolution* (New York: Macmillan & Co.).

Velupillai, Kumaraswamy. 1975. "Irving Fisher on 'Switches of Techniques': A Historical Note." *Quarterly Journal of Economics*, Vol. 89, No. 4 (November): pp. 679–80.

Verhovek, Sam Howe. 1997. "Closing of Helium Reserve Raises New Issues." *New York Times* (October 8): p. A 12.

Vickers, Marcia. 2001. "When Wealth is Blown Away." *Business Week* (March 26): pp. 39–41.

Von Mises, Ludwig. 1951. *Socialism: An Economic and Sociological Analysis* (New Haven: Yale University Press).

Wackernagel, Mathis, Niels B. Schulz, Diana Deumling, Alejandro Callejas Linares, Martin Jenkins, Valerie Kapos, Chad Monfreda, Jonathan Loh,

Norman Myers, Richard Norgaard, and Jorgen Randers. 2002. "Tracking the Ecological Overshoot of the Human Economy." *Proceedings of the National Academy of Sciences*, Vol. 99, No. 14 (July 9): pp. 9266–71.

Walras, Leon. 1874. *Elements of Pure Economics, or the Theory of Social Wealth*, trans. William Jaffe (Homewood, IL: Richard D. Irwin, 1954).

Weld, Issac. 1799. *Travels Throughout the States of North America and Provinces of Upper and Lower Canada During the Years 1793, 1796 and 1797* (London: J. Stokdale).

Wessel, David. 2002. "Bold Estimate of Web's Thirst for Electricity Seems All Wet." *Wall Street Journal* (December 5).

Whitehead, Alfred North. 1911. *An Introduction to Mathematics* (London: Oxford University Press).

———. 1929. *Process and Reality: An Essay in Cosmology* (New York: Free Press).

Whitney, Lois. 1924. "Primitivistic Theories of Epic Origins." *Modern Philology*, Vol. 21, No. 4 (May): pp. 337–78.

Wicksell, Knut. 1905. "Letter to Alfred Marshall (January 6)." In John K. Whitaker ed. *The Correspondence of Alfred Marshall*, 3 vols. (Cambridge: Cambridge University Press, 1996, vol. 3), pp. 101–03.

———. 1934. *Lectures on Political Economy* (London: Routledge and Kegan Paul).

Williams, Eric D., Robert U. Ayres, and Miriam Heller. 2002. "The 1.7 Kilogram Microchip: Energy and Material Use in the Production of Semiconductor Devices." *Environmental Science and Technology* (December 15).

Wilson, Alexander. 1832. *American Ornithology* (London: Whittaker, Treacher, and Arnot, vol. 2), pp. 201–04.

Wilson, Duff. 2001. *Fateful Harvest: The True Story of a Small Town* (New York: HarperCollins).

Winch, Donald. 1965. *Classical Political Economy and Colonies* (Cambridge: Harvard University Press).

Winter, Jay and Jean-Louis Robert, eds. 1997. *Capital Cities at War: London, Paris, Berlin, 1914–1919* (Cambridge and New York: Cambridge University Press).

Woodham-Smith, Cecil Blanche Fitz Gerald. 1951. *Florence Nightingale, 1820–1910* (New York: McGraw-Hill).

Wright, Gavin. 1990. "The Origins of American Industrial Success, 1870–1940." *American Economic Review*, Vol. 80, No. 4 (September): pp. 651–68.

Wrigley, E. A. 2000. "The Divergence of England: The Growth of the English Economy in the Seventeenth and Eighteenth Centuries." *Transactions of the Royal Historical Society*, Vol. 10 (6th series): pp. 117–41.

Wriston, Walter B. 1986. *Risk and Other Four-Letter Words* (New York: Harper & Row).

Wysong, Earl, Robert Perrucci, and David W. Wright. 2002. "Organizations, Resources, and Class Analysis: The Distributional Model and the U.S. Class Structure." Paper presented at American Sociological Association Meetings (Chicago, August 16).

Index

A

Accumulation 30, 40, 41, 42, 47,
    106, 125
Africa, as toxic dump site 67
Agricultural
    economics 14
    production 57
Agriculture
    capitalist 60
    English Game Law's interference
        with 171
    localized system of 137
    subsidized water and 133–34
    Thomas Nixon Carver and 58,
        60, 74
Ainslie, George 88, 96–97
Albion, Robert 34–36
Albrecht, William Albert 144
American Economic Association
    101, 153
American Physical Association 102
American Physical Society 101
Amsden, Alice 127
Anker, Peder 39
Aristotle 163
Assets
    paper 111
    tangible 111
Autarky 66
Axelrod, Beth 169

B

Babbage, Charles 135–37
Backstop technology 63
Balzac, Honoré de 146
Bankruptcy 28, 58, 155–56, 168
Barbon, Nicolas 37
Barnett, Harold J. 27–29
Bechtel Corp. 67–68
Becker, Gary 161
Berle, Adolf 165

Berlin 180
Bessemer process 150
Beveridge Report 178
Binmore, Ken 86
Biosphere 25
Black market 180
Bliss, Christopher 106
Bolivia, and privatization of water
    67–68, 133
Boltzmann, Ludwig 22
Bonzon, Thierry 180
Brandes, Dietrich 123
Brecht, Bertold 51
British Ecological Society 39–40
Brown, Gardner 70–71
Bureau of Mines 99
Business
    build up of military and 151
    high discount rate and 94
    John Maynard Keynes on 125
    overestimating success in 92

C

Calculation debate 181–82
California energy crisis 22, 114, 141
Capital
    human 42, 157–59, 170, 172
    immigration and 128–29
    obsolete 126
    scarcity of 41, 46
    theory of 105–06, 159
    value theory and 85
Capital accumulation 41, 47, 106
Capital goods
    railroads and 155
    technological improvements
        and 150
Capitalism, economic development
    and 44
Capitalization, process of 108
Carey, Henry 61–62

Carnegie, Andrew   128–29, 150
Cartels   128, 155–56
Carver, Thomas Nixon   58, 60,
    74–75
Challenger space shuttle   140
Chancellor, Edward   110
Change, technological   16, 130
Cheung, Steven   154
Chicago Board of Trade   115
Cholera   68
Churchill, Winston   39–40, 48, 65
Citicorp   47
Clark, Colin   69
Clark, Greg   153–54
Clark, John Bates   152–59,
    162–63, 171–72, 176, 178, 182
Class   1, 9, 12, 18–19, 33, 40, 119,
    146, 147, 159–62, 171, 172,
    179
Coal tar, Justus von Liebig and   62
Commons, tragedy of   69, 73–74,
    133–34
Compensation
    executive   160, 164, 166,
    managerial   165
Competition, among railroad
    companies   155–57
Conservation
    laws of   83–84
    rising prices and   64, 72, 101
    133, 134
Consumer credit   121
Consumption, theory of   41, 79
Corn
    hybrid   78, 142–44
    William Albert Albrecht on
    nutrition of hybridized   144
Corporate
    control of water   68, 133–34
    farming   12
    success and executives   164,
    169–70
Corporations
    identification of CEO with
    multinational   61

petrochemical   52
transnational   50, 52
Cost savings, through standardization
    during World War I   176
Costs, scale of production   150
Council for Foreign Plantations   29
Cox, Christopher   99
Credit, consumer   121
Crimean War   180

D
Daily, Gretchen   75–77
Davis, Belinda   180
Debreu, Gerard   104
Decker, Matthew   30
Decreasing returns   107–08
Deffeyes, Kenneth   23, 99, 174
Deficient demand   151
Deforestation
    John Evelyn on   35–37
    Karl Marx on   56
    loss of value and   57
Deprivation, unequal distribution of
    during war   180–81
Deregulation of energy in
    California   141
Dictatorship   50
Discount rate   88, 93–97, 101–02,
    106, 108, 119–31
    future benefits and   101, 124
    interest rate and   95, 123–24, 130
    market society and   119,
    121–22
    negative behavior and   120
    profit rate and   121
    stagnant economy and   127
Discounted utility model   96
Discounting   25, 77, 87–89, 93–98,
    100–02, 119, 124, 183
    calculating present values by   88,
    89, 95–96, 98, 102
    decision-making in real estate
    and   87–88
    hyperbolic   95–98, 100,
    102, 183

irrational behavior and 97
optimal management of resources
    and 89
relationship between scarcity and
    98, 101, 129
theory of 89, 93, 95, 98, 102
Disposable income 121
Distribution, of wealth 49, 51,
    131, 152
Diversity, genetic 144
Dot.coms 108, 111–12, 114
Duke Ferdinando of Tuscany 31

E
East India Company 53, 165
Ecological efficiency, market-driven
    62
Ecology
    industrial 62
    Peder Anker on British 39
Economic
    analysis 3, 23, 30, 102, 114
    future, John Maynard Keynes on
        41, 85, 125
    growth, and resource base 37,
        49, 84
    mobility 160–61
Economic theory
    absence of time in 87
    individual and 88
    John R. Hicks on 108
    labor markets and 158, 162
    mathematical 85
    Nicholas Georgescu-Roegen
        on 24
    present value calculations and
        96, 98, 106
    reformulation of 152
    Robert Lucas on 81
Economics
    absence of conservation laws in
        83–84
    agricultural 14
    as justification of market society
        119

conservative intellectual
    environment of 162
Ken Binmore on equilibrating
    process of 86
mathematical equations and 79
model-based 177
natural science and 83, 101, 113
neoclassical 41, 101, 156
protecting academic investment in
    80
scientific foundation of 70
Tjalling Koopmans on superiority
    over natural science 101
Economy
    Chinese 26
    distorted bell curve and 90
    extractive 21–25
    socialist 177
    weightless 112, 114, 116, 171
Ecosystem
    cumulative damage to 75–78, 122
    forest 122
    Gretchen Daily on value of 75–77
    high- and low-diversity 77
    market value of 76
    services 75–76
Education
    labor market and 2, 159–60
    of poor 2, 158, 160
Education Act of 1944, 179
Efficiency
    just-in-time production and 141
    redundancy and 139–42
Egalitarianism 163, 183
Energy
    atomic 63
    deregulation in California 141
    human 2
    inanimate 10, 68, 149
    renewable 174
Enron Corp. 99, 109, 115, 169,
    170
Entropy 22, 39, 64
    Ludwig Boltzmann on 22
    substitutability and 64

Environment, market-based
  management of   72
Environmental
  consequences of war   183
  deterioration, George Perkins
    Marsh on   56
  devastation   56–67, 93
  disasters   50, 73
  efficiency and epidemics   138
  limitations and growth   38, 45,
    74
  movement   57, 73, 122
Environmental Protection Agency
  83
Equality, social   180, 182
Evelyn, John   29, 31, 35–37, 54,
  56, 66
Executives
  compensation of   164–67, 169
  corporate success and   164
  stock prices and   114, 165, 157
Explosives   63
Externalities   24
Extraction   22, 24, 25, 28, 51, 75,
  100, 101
  imperialism and   137–40
Exxon Corp., 99

F
Falls, Cyril   178
Farming, corporate   12
Faustmann, Martin   122–23
Federal Reserve Board   91
Federal Reserve System   91, 112
Fertilizer   60, 62–63, 75, 144
Feudalism   27
Field, Barry   71
Financialization   115–16
Food, excess of   33
Forbes 400   163
Ford, Henry   139
Foreign trade, Chinese   26
Forests   27, 35, 38, 56–57, 70, 84,
  122, 134
  destruction of   56

discounting value of   122
  management of   35, 122–25
  monoculture of   123
  Paul Samuelson on management
    of   123
  production   122
Fossil fuel   10–11, 22, 38, 60, 63,
  69, 100, 114, 116, 149–51,
  173–74
  Industrial Revolution and   149
Foster, John Bellamy   60
Fourastie, Jean   163
Franklin, Benjamin   130
Frederick the Great   32
Free trade, John Maynard Keynes
  on   43, 65
French Revolution   163

G
Galarza, Ernesto   159
Galbraith, James   172
Game Laws   171
Garber, Peter   110
Garten, Jeffrey   115
General Dynamics Corp.   107
General Electric Corp.   166–67,
  170
General Motors Corp.   164, 166
Genetic diversity   144
Genetic engineering, Donald F. Jones
  on   143
Georgescu-Roegen, Nicholas
  24–25, 38–39
Germany   126, 180–81
Gerschenkron, Alexander   127
Gilder, George   113, 160
Gladstone, William   38
Globalization   174
Gold   22, 28 29–32, 37–38, 49,
  52–53, 110
  John Maynard Keynes on   53
  Latin America and   49, 53
  Spain and   29, 38, 49, 52–53
  standard   53
Golden Hinde   63–64

Gould, Stephen 71
Gray, Lewis 58
Great Depression 41–42, 163, 165
Great Fire of London 33, 37
Greenspan, Alan 91, 109, 112, 113
Gross domestic product 46, 57, 94–95, 166
  John Robert McNeill on 25
  of Philippines 57
  of world 25
Gross national product 84
Growth, and environmental limitations 45, 74
Guano 58, 60, 62–63
Guano, John Bellamy Foster on 60
Guano Island Act 60

H
Hadley, Arthur T. 155
Handfield-Jones, Helen 169
Hardin, Garrett 73–74
Hauge, Gabriel 156
Hawtrey, Ralph 175–76, 179
Hayek, Friedrich von 103, 183
Helium 72, 75, 98–102
  discounting of 98, 100–02
  federal monopoly of 98–99
  in natural gas deposits 99
  private consumption of 99
  privatization of 99, 101
  properties of 98
Helium Act 99
Helium Study Committee 101
Helminthosporium maydis 78–143
Henwood, Doug 139
Hersh, Seymour 142
Hershey, Lewis 179
Hicks, John R. 106, 108
High discount rate, and negative behavior 120–21
Holland, and tulip trade 110–11
Hotelling, Harold 27, 64, 71–72
Human capital 42, 157–59, 170, 172
  employers' evaluation of 158

  ownership of 170
  theory of 159
Human Development Index 52
Hunger, Joseph Townsend on benefits of 145
Hybridization 143–44
Hydroelectric power 114
Hyperbolic discounting 95–98, 100, 102, 183
Hyperbolic discounting, George Ainslie on 96–97

I
Immigration and cost of labor 128
Imperialism, Alfred Marshall on 47–48
Income
  disposable personal 121
  distribution of 117, 152, 158, 163, 168
Induced innovation 127
  Alexis de Tocqueville on 127–30
  Jeremiah Jenks on 128
Industrial ecology 62
Industrial Revolution 12, 25, 26, 37, 145, 149
Industrial Revolution and China 23–26
Inequality 3, 148, 163, 166, 168, 170, 172, 180–82
  land ownership and 148
  of income distribution 163, 168
  rationalization of 182
Influenza 138
Intellectual property 111, 113, 116–17
  artificial scarcity of 116
  corporate ownership and 116–17
Interest rates, relationship to discount rate 95, 123–25, 130
Intergenerational accounting 28
International trade, John Maynard Keynes on 42, 66
Internet and productive system 112

Intertemporal bargaining   97, 183
Inuit   138
Inventory, reduction of   142
Ireland   31, 34
Iridium Corp.   107

J
Jenks, Jeremiah   128
Jevons, William Stanley   37–41,
   45–48, 65, 104, 152
Jevons, William Stanley, John
   Maynard Keynes on   40–41
John Bates Clark Medal   153
Johnston, James F. W.   58, 60
Jones, Donald F.   143
Jones, William Richard   129
JSTOR   27
Just-in-time production   141

K
Keynes, John Maynard   40–45, 53,
   65–66, 85, 88, 92–93, 125
Khurana, Rakesh   169–70
Kolko, Gabriel   154, 180–81
Koopmans, Tjalling   86, 96–102
Kozlowski, Dennis   166
Kozol, Jonathan   160
Kremer, Michael   140
Kuznets, Simon   182

L
Labor
   child   153
   economic theory and   152, 158,
      162
   education and   2, 158, 160
   elimination of and managerial
      productivity   166–67
   market   2, 159–60, 168, 172
   shortages   128
Land
   public   134
   theory of equal distribution   148
   timber companies' access to
      public   134

Land ownership, Knut Wicksell on
   152–54
Landlords, hunting privileges in
   Britain and   19, 48, 171
Latin America   49, 126
Lay, Ken   170
Lebergott, Stanley   56
Legislation, social   178
Lenapes   148
Levant Co.   53
Liebig, Justus von   62–63
Living standards   11–12
Locke, John   44
London   12, 33, 36–38, 42, 66, 180
Long Term Credit Management
   91–93
Low discount rate   119, 121,
   125–27
Lucas, Robert   81
Lukacs, John   149

M
Machinery, widespread scrapping
   of   130
Mad cow disease   137–38
Malthus, Thomas Robert   32–34, 55
Mandeville, Bernard   30, 145
Manhattan Island, purchase from
   Lenapes   148
Manufacturing, Benjamin Franklin
   on   130
Market
   black   180
   economy   11, 28, 69, 74, 112, 178
   prices   15, 72, 88, 106, 110, 133
   principles   9
   rationality   14
   relations   12, 29, 109
   rules   103
   share   150
   society and discount rate   119,
      121–22
   valuation process   27
   value of ecosystems   76–78
   values   11, 22, 84

Market efficiency 81, 89, 175, 178
  mathematical models and 89
  socialist economy and 175, 178
Market forces 3, 68, 70–71, 73,
  154, 157, 182
  fairness of 154
  forces and passenger pigeon and
  70–73
Marketplace, rationing and 45
Markets
  economic justice of 154, 156, 172
  grow or die 74
  labor 2, 159, 160, 168, 172
  speculative 87–88, 112
  sustainability and 68–70, 74,
  78, 182
Marsh, George Perkins 36,
  56–57
Marshall, Alfred 1–2, 45–48, 105
Marshall, John 147
Marshall, Jonathan 40
Marx, Karl 56–57, 61, 113, 152–53
Marxian exploitation theory 152
Material goods, denigrating
  production of 171
McCloskey, Donald 104
McKinsey & Co. 169
McNeill, John Robert 25
Means, Gardiner 165
Mechoopda 147
Media, consolidation of 115
Mencken, H. L. 182
Menger, Carl 152
Merchant-economists 31–33
Merton, Robert 91
Michaels, Ed 169
Micro Craft Corp. 107
Microsoft Corp. 111
Mill, John Stuart 82
Minuet, Peter 148
Mirowski, Philip 22, 46, 83,
  100–01, 177
Mises, Ludwig von 175, 177–78
Mitochondria 143–44
Mitsui Corp. 120

Modern Corporation and Private
  Property, The 164
Monoculture 123
Monopolies 29, 128, 155–58
  informational 29
  John Bates Clark on benefits of
  155–56
Moral philosophy 11, 30
Morale and social organization
  178, 180
Morganize 165
Morse, Chandler 27–28
Mun, Thomas 30–31

N
Nardinelli, Clark 153–54
NASDAQ stock exchange 91, 108,
  111–13
Nash, John 86
National Basketball Association
  157
National Health Service 179
National Helium Reserve 99
National Industrial Conference
  Board 176
National planning 175
National Research Council
  99–102
Natural gas, helium deposits in
  99–100
Natural resources 21, 23–24,
  27–32, 34, 42, 48, 49, 78, 93,
  97, 116, 130, 134
  depletion of 130
  economic growth and 24, 27, 49
  standard of living and 48–49
  Warren Scoville on 60, 89
Natural sciences 4, 93, 104
Neoclassical economics 41, 156
Neurath, Otto 175–78
New economy, Alan Greenspan on
  109, 112–13
Newton, Isaac 82
Nightingale, Florence 180
Nitrogen fertilizer 60, 62–63

Nonmarket economic
    mobilization   175
Norgaard, Richard   25, 28
North Sea   52, 66
Norway   62
Nuclear power   64
Nutrition, government concern
    about during war   179

O
Office of Management and Budget,
    United States   94
Oil
    declining reserves of   174
    depletion of   39, 68, 69, 125, 174
    discoveries in North Sea   62, 66
    imports of   40
    Kenneth Deffeyes on   23, 99, 174
    use in Norway   52
    whale   47, 68
Ojibwas   12
Opium   25
Optimal equilibrium values   103
O-ring production function   140
Ostrum, Elinor   73
Outsource work   140
Overpopulation, Ricardo David
    on   34
Ownership
    of human capital   157, 180
    of intellectual property   111, 117
    passive   170–71

P
Panhandle Eastern Corp.   9
Paris   149, 180
    slaughterhouses in 19th-century
        135
    takeover by workers in 1871   152
Passenger pigeon   28, 70–73, 76, 77
    Gardner Brown on market price
        of   70–72
    Jennifer Price on   70
    James Tober on marketing of   71
    Stephen Gould on slaughter of   71

Perfect competition   103
Peters, Tom   112
Petty, William   31, 36
Philippines   57, 143
Physiocrats   24
Pigou, Arthur Cecil   97–98
Pin makers   10
Pinchot, Gifford   123
Pinkerton Detective Agency   151
Pinto, Isaac de   30
Planners, socialist   177
Planning
    in wartime   175, 183
    Ludwig von Mises on   175, 177
    national   175
Plato   163
Political economy   33, 44, 46,
    83, 145
Pollution   36, 61, 63, 67, 109
Polychlorinated biphenyls   114
Pomeranz, Kenneth   26
Poor, education of   2, 120, 158, 160
Posner, Eric   120
Poverty   2, 26, 41, 43, 49, 52, 119,
    130, 145–60, 174
    discounting and   119–30
    John Rae on   119
    of farm workers   2, 146, 160
Present value calculations   89, 92
Present value, discounting and   96,
    98, 106
Price system   63–64, 67, 70, 72,
    96, 98, 102–03, 134, 162
    discounted commercial values and
        efficiency of   103
    lack of environmental
        considerations and   103
    range of influences and   103
    to ration resources   102
Price, Jennifer   70
Price-Anderson Act   64
Prion   137
Production
    agricultural   57, 65, 115
    efficiency during war   175–76

excess 150–51
nonmaterial 171
Profit 19, 24, 30, 56, 69, 74, 79,
    88, 91, 97, 100, 102, 108, 111,
    116, 121–25, 136, 147, 173
    maximizing over time 122
    rate and discount rate 121
    system 100
Property, private 73, 148, 165
Property rights 73, 111, 116–17,
    147–48, 157
    intellectual 111, 116–17
    John Marshall on justification
        of 147
Protectionism, Henry Carey on 62
Public lands, timber companies'
    access to 134

Q
Quantum theory 82

R
Rae, John 119–20, 126
Railroads 85–86, 127, 154–57
    Arthur T. Hadley on economics
        of 155
    gauges hampering national rail
        network 116, 125
    investment in capital goods and
        65, 127, 155
    speculation and 85, 111
Rainforests 57
Recycling 61–62, 135–36
    of coal tar 62
    of soil nutrients 61, 135
Redundancy 139–42
    hazards from lack of 139–41
Repetto, Robert 57
Resilience 76–78, 140
Resource base 3, 19, 36–37, 43,
    47–50, 84, 92, 131, 177
Resource extraction 25
Resources
    abundance of 26, 28, 47, 49,
        52, 131, 173

Adam Smith on waste of
    134–35
Alfred Marshall on 45–57
cockroach's adaptability to
    scarcity of 138
Colin Clark on overexploitation
    of 69
control over 147
JSTOR and 27
Winston Churchill on imported
    39–40, 48, 65
Restorer gene 143
Ricardo, David 34, 65
Richards, John 68, 123
Robbins, Lionel 41, 101
Roche, James M. 164
Rockefeller, David 160
Rosser, Barkley 105
Russian Revolution 177

S
Samuelson, Paul 96, 100, 123,
    153–54
Sandler, Blair 74
Saudi Arabia 66
Scholes, Myron 91
School Lunch Program 179
Schultz, Theodore 25
Schwab, Charles 128
Scoville, Warren 60, 89
Second Dutch War 34
Second Law of Thermodynamics
    22–23, 27, 48, 64, 173
Selective Service Commission
    179
Self-sufficiency, John Maynard
    Keynes on 43, 65
Shapin, Steven 159
Shleifer, Andrei 167–68
Silver 26, 29, 30, 32, 38, 47, 49
Sinclair, Upton 136–37
Slaughterhouses
    labor-intensive 19th-century
        135–37
    waste in modern 137

Smith, Adam 7, 13, 18–19, 21, 26,
   30, 33–34, 54–56, 69, 81, 85,
   92, 135, 145–46, 165, 171–72
Smith, Vernon 69
Social organization, Richard
   Titmuss on equality of 180
Social relations 9–11, 13, 27
Social Security 28
Social solidarity during war 179–82
Socialist economy, and market
   efficiency 177
Society, rationalization of 178
Soil erosion 60–61
Soil fertility 56–58, 60, 74
   James F. W. Johnston on 60
   Karl Marx on 56–67
South Sea Bubble 82
Sowell, Thomas 162
Soybeans 139, 144
Spain 25, 29, 38, 49, 53, 134–35
Specialization 25, 29, 38, 49, 53,
   134–35
Speculation 82, 85, 90, 110, 112
   paper assets and 111
   past history of increasing stock
      price and 90
   railroads and 84
   stock market crash of 1987 and
      110
Speculative markets 87–88, 112
Speculators and present value 88,
   106
Standard Oil Corp. 173
Standardization 176
Stationary state 54
Stigler, George 162
Subjective value 108–09
Substitutability 63–65
Sumitomo Corp. 17, 66, 139
Summers, Lawrence 66, 167–69
Sustainability 68–70, 74, 78, 102,
   123, 182–83
   common lands and 69, 74, 78
   forests and 69, 123

markets and 68–70, 74, 78
nonmarket societies and 74
System vulnerability 139, 141

T
Tacit knowledge 149
Tawney, Richard 171, 179
Technology
   backstop 63
   fossil fuels and 10, 63, 69, 100,
      150, 174
   increased production scale and
      16, 129, 150
   John Lukacs on early
      improvements in 149
   obsolete capital goods and 86,
      126–27
Telegraph 71–72, 149–50
Temple, William 44
Terminator gene 78
Texas Male Sterile gene 78, 143
The Distribution of Wealth 152
Theory of capital 105–06
   Barkley Rosser on 105
   Christopher Bliss on 105–06
   Knut Wicksell on 105
Theory of consumption 41
Theory of discounting 87, 89, 93,
   95, 98, 102
Theory of human capital 42,
   158–59
Theory of substitutability 65
Theory of value, Gerard Debreu on
   104
Theory of wages 14
Thoreau, Henry David 70
Timken Corp. 139
Titmuss, Richard 178–80
Tober, James 71
Tocqueville, Alexis de 127–30
Townsend, Joseph 44, 145
Toxic waste 62, 66–67, 139
   Lawrence Summers on disposal of
      66–67

Microchip processing and 114
Weightless economy and 114
Trade
  free 43, 85
  international 30, 42, 66–67
  Thomas Mun on 30–31
  tulip 110
Trade routes, control of 32
Trans World Airlines 167
Transnational corporations 50
Trotsky, Leon 126
Trusts 128, 155–56
Tucker, Josiah 54, 61, 135
tulipomania 109–10
Tyco Corp. 166

U
Unemployment 43–44, 74
Unions 82, 151, 159, 165
United Nations 52, 174
United States Department of
  Agriculture 60, 78
Utility 79, 96, 108, 126

V
Value
  fictitious 110–12
  self-expanding 82–84, 109
Value theory 37, 40, 80–87, 93,
  104, 106–09, 152, 162
  John Stuart Mill on 82–83
  new economy and 109
Valujet Corp., 140
Vanderlint, Jacob 30
Veblen, Thorstein 126–27

W
Wage workers 10
Walras, Léon 86, 152
War 34, 40, 42–43, 47, 51, 54,
  113, 121, 151, 158, 163, 169,
  175–83

lack of democratic engagement
  during 183
planning during 175, 183
productivity and 181
social solidarity and 179–82
War for Talent 169
War Industries Board 176
Waste
  daily in New York City 139
  Henry Ford and recycling
    of 139
  military and 67
  toxic 62, 67, 139
Watt, James 10–11
Wealth of Nations 7, 9, 18
Weightless economy
  Alan Greenspan on 112
  as refutation of Karl Marx 113
  George Gilder on 113
  intellectual property and 113,
    116
  toxic waste and 114
Welch, Jack 166–67, 170
Whale oil, production of 47, 68
Whales, economic exploitation of
  47, 63, 69
Whitehead, Alfred North
  22, 183
Wicksell, Knut 105, 152–54
Wilson, Alexander 70
Wilson, Charles E. 166
Work force, William Temple on 44
World Resources Institute 67
World War I, 42, 113, 121,
  151, 158, 163, 175–76,
  178–81
  Ralph Hawtrey on economic
    standards during 176
  standardization during 176
World War II 42, 113, 121, 158,
  178, 191
Wriston, Walter 47

CPSIA information can be obtained at www.ICGtesting.com
Printed in the USA
LVOW11*1803150115

422994LV00005B/17/P